RECORDS MANAGEMENT HANDBOOK

Records Management Handbook

Ira A. Penn   Anne Morddel
Gail Pennix   Kelvin Smith

Gower

Published by
Gower Publishing Company Limited,
Gower House,
Croft Road,
Aldershot
Hants. GU11 3HR,
England.

Gower Publishing Company
Old Post Road
Brookfield
Vermont 05036
USA

British Library Cataloguing in Publication Data

Penn, Ira A.
  Records management handbook.
  1. Records management
  I. Title   II. Morddel, Anne
  651.5

ISBN 0-566-05666-6

Reprinted 1989

Printed and bound in Great Britain by
BPCC Wheatons Ltd, Exeter

Contents

Illustrations

Tables

Foreword

Donald S. Skupsky, JD, CRM, President and General Counsel,
Information Requirements Clearinghouse, Denver, Colorado

Analysts have identified three vital resources of an organization – people, capital and property. These components contribute to the success, unique quality and competitive advantage of each organization. When any vital resource is diminished, an organization can expect diminished returns, lower acceptance in the marketplace, and a long-term, uphill battle to achieve respectability again. Vital resources have also been considered either irreplaceable or replaceable only after a substantial investment of time and effort.

Today, we operate in the information age. Where previously people, capital, and property provided the competitive advantage, today information has moved to the forefront as the fourth vital resource – perhaps the most important one. People can be replaced, as evidenced by the high mobility of people from job to job. Capital previously accumulated inside an organization is now also available from a variety of sources such as loans, stock sales, and acquisitions or mergers. Property, including manufacturing facilities, buildings and equipment, is replaced on a regular basis as a result of wear-and-tear, obsolescence or upgrading.

Information, on the other hand, cannot readily be created, replaced or reconstructed – except through years of effort. Statistics show that approximately 30 per cent of all organizations that suffer a catastrophic fire will cease to operate in one year. While insurance proceeds may fully replace the equipment and facilities, staff may be retained or added to do the job, and money safely protected outside the building in banks or other financial institutions, these organizations cannot continue to operate. Why? Often because their vital information has been lost forever.

Records management is the professional discipline to control the creation, maintenance, and disposition of information in the form of records. It includes the management of forms, reports, directives, active filing, inactive storage, records retention and a variety of other components. While some view records only as paper produced or received by an organization, records include any reproducible form of information including microfilm, computer data, video tapes, photographs, etc. The records management function protects this vital resource of an organization.

Unfortunately, most organizations have not yet realized the relationship between their vital information and the management of this information through a records management programme. Some have simply not yet directed their attention toward this important area. Others consider the 'bottom line' or another goal as a higher priority, if not the only priority. Too often, it takes a major disaster such as flood or fire or a frustrating incident such as losing an important file to awaken the right people to the importance of records management.

But the consequences of these disasters or frustrating incidents can be averted by getting the right information and developing the right programme. *Records Management Handbook* is the right place to start.

Records Management Handbook represents a departure from other books on the topic of records management. Rather than attempting to identify and classify the different systems which one could develop, *Records Management Handbook* focuses the reader on the approach to be taken to develop systems which best meet the needs of the organization. The book is packed with questions to ask and issues to examine before developing any type of records management programme.

With a vital resource like information, an organization cannot afford merely to purchase the first system offered by salesmen or develop a sophisticated technology because it's the 'latest trend.' The needs of the organization must dictate which of many alternative records management approaches should be selected.

As *Records Management Handbook* advocates, records management systems should be developed primarily to manage information – provide the right information to the right people at the right time – rather than just to save money. Often, however, cost saving and improved efficiency will be an added bonus.

Whether the reader is new to the field of records management or an experienced practitioner, this book will provide valuable guidance to manage records. Newcomers to the field will learn the right questions to ask; experienced practitioners will be reminded of the questions they may have forgotten to ask.

With so much at stake, an organization can no longer close its eyes and allow its valuable records to remain unmanaged and unavailable to help the organization. While the initial cost of developing a records management programme will probably be recouped in a short time, the failure properly to manage information, the fourth vital resource, could cost an organization plenty.

Preface

This book is written for the practitioner. Although suitable for use as a college text, the intention of the authors was to provide a practical reference for records managers, analysts, and other information management professionals.

Four people developed this book. Two reside in the United States and two in Great Britain. There are very different approaches to doing things in the two countries, and therefore this effort represents an amalgamation. For example, the Registry System, which is all but unknown in the US, is actively used in Great Britain and throughout much of the Third World as well. Therefore, a section on the Registry System is included. In like manner, Directives Management is relatively unknown in England, yet is the basis for the majority of policy and procedure issuances in the US, so it has been included in this publication.

This book does not contain answers to every question one might have about information and records management. Decisions had to be made as to what to put in and what to leave out, and those decisions were based on what was already available in the literature and also on what was considered to be most important.

Because the majority of records management publications have dealt extensively with filing systems and correspondence control, those subjects have not been included here. Because the specifics of forms design and micrographics have been covered in several books devoted exclusively to those specialities, they, too, have been omitted. Copy management and mail management have likewise not been included. They are considered to be a peripheral aspect to the operation of a successful records management programme.

What is left is a book on records management basics. It is hoped that the material included will prove useful and helpful to the readers as they pursue the challenge of managing records and the information that they contain.

Acknowledgements

Many persons, too numerous to mention, have provided the inspiration to write this book. They come from England, the United States, and Canada, and are involved in records management in governments, private corporations, and through professional associations.

A few people, however, must be singled out for special thanks. The British authors wish to thank Dr Anne Thurston of the Institute of Commonwealth Studies and University College London, whose unstinting support and encouragement have enabled them to experience a large number of records management operations in various parts of the world. The American authors wish to thank Susan Penn and Brian Pennix, whose patience and understanding regarding the effort were a major factor in its accomplishment.

Special thanks are also due to Beryl Saddington, who so expertly and efficiently typed the manuscript, and to Veronica Davies, Dee Dee O'Connor and Donald S. Skupsky, JD, CRM, all of whom were kind enough to review many of the chapters of this book.

Part I
Introduction

INTRODUCTION

Records management is concerned with the management of *information*. Both the public and private sectors need information to function properly; if that information is mismanaged or is not available, organizations might cease to exist. As government and business have expanded during the 20th century, so has the need for information and records management.

In examining the records management function in Chapter 1, as much importance has been placed on management as on records, and this is studied further in succeeding chapters. We have considered that management is a *practical* function and that records management, the concern of the whole organization and not just an individual, is a *staff* function.

Chapter 2 examines the concept of the life cycle of information — its creation, maintenance and use; and its disposition. These three phases form the basis of records management programmes and it is on this concept that the effective, efficient and economic use of information is founded.

1 The Records Management Function

We live in an information society. This is not something that will happen or is happening; it has already happened. Information is our basic resource, and information is our product.

Although we consume more food than ever before, only 3 per cent of the workforce is engaged in agriculture. Although we consume 'hard goods' at an ever increasing rate, only 14 per cent of the workforce is involved in manufacturing. By contrast, over 50 per cent of the workforce is employed in offices and 80 per cent of the office employees are considered to be 'information handlers'.

What is this *information* that has taken over the economy so completely in only a few short decades? There is probably no single answer to that question. Depending on the philosophic approach one might take, information could be considered to be raw facts, commonly referred to as data, or it could be knowledge, which would be the same facts evaluated, organized and synthesized into meaningful intelligence.

Regardless of the definition one wishes to ascribe to information, there is little doubt that it all has to be managed. Information must be managed so that it can be used. Unmanaged, data are relatively useless, merely a conglomeration of unrelated details. Unmanaged, knowledge is not worth much more than the original data from which it was derived — not updatable and, possibly, not even retrievable.

If we accept that information must be managed to be usable, where do records fit into the picture? The answer is quite simple — records *are* recorded information. Indeed, a record may be defined as *any information captured in reproducible form that is required for conducting business*.

Obviously, within this broad definition there are limitations. A standard dictionary, for example, would meet the criteria just described, yet is most certainly not a record. The determination as to what constitutes a record is based on the context in which the information is created. The standard dictionary may well be required for conducting business, but it was not specifically created by or for the particular organization using it. The only organization that would have a record copy of a dictionary would be the publishing company that produced it.

Records require a specific type of management. It is not sufficient to manage records like other forms of information because they are a distinct category of information and must be treated accordingly. Distinguishing between library material and records may serve to illustrate this point.

Library material must be managed. The information in various books, periodicals, and published monographs would not be a usable resource if it were all just thrown in a big pile in the middle of the library floor. But library material is received in a historical manner. Library material is not specifically created by or for the library. The library obtains information after the fact, places it in logical order so that it is readily available to the users, and disposes of it when it is obsolete. The library's concern, therefore, is information maintenance and disposition.

Records, on the other hand, must be managed by the organization that originates them from the moment they are created. How records are created and what information they contain is as much a records management consideration as is the maintenance of that information while it is being used, and its ultimate disposal when it is no longer needed.

An author would not ask a librarian for advice about the content or format of a book prior to its publication. A creator of records, however, might well pose that question regarding information to a professional records manager.

RECORDS MANAGEMENT IN HISTORICAL PERSPECTIVE

Records management, as a profession, is a relatively new concept. Even the term records management was unheard of until the mid 20th-century. But records management as a *function* has existed for some 7000 years.

Around 5000 BC, the people of the Sumerian civilization produced the first records. These written documents are not just considered to be 'records' today because they are a record of a bygone era. They were created to be records by those originating them. The Sumerian records dealt with business matters such as taxes, loans, and inventories, and they were managed by the temple priests who controlled the Sumerian economy.

Obviously, the management of these clay tablet records was somewhat primitive. But the fact that they were created and kept at all was a major advance for civilized society.

During the New Empire period in Egypt (1530-1050 BC), creating and managing records was a significant government operation. Likewise, in Babylonia, records management was an important function during the reigns of both Hammurabi (1792-1750 BC) and Nebuchadnezzar II (630-562 BC).

The records of ancient civilizations were housed in the libraries of the rulers. Such repositories would today be considered archives, but that distinction was not made at the time. Early 'libraries' contained business records and later evolved to contain collections of literature and information on science, medicine, and religion.

As the centuries passed, the record media changed. Clay gave way to papyrus and parchment, and these, in turn, slowly gave way to paper. Except for this media transition, improvements in recordkeeping techniques were slow to develop. Why this was so is a matter for conjecture, but, at the risk of over-simplifying, it could be said that improvement had not yet become a necessity. Information was recorded by that portion of the population that was literate — priests, teacher/philosophers, scribes, rulers, nobles, and landed gentry — and the recorded information was referenced by that same literate segment of society. Proportionately, there were few people creating documents and few people using them.

There is evidence that a case file system was established in Rome around AD 1200, and that statutes regarding records retention and disposition existed in the city-states of Northern Italy during the same period. These records management principles, however, like many other managerial principles developed over the centuries, seem to have had little application and were relatively short-lived. They came and went until rediscovered at a later date.

It was not until the 15th century that any lasting records management innovation was developed. At that time the registry system (in which all incoming and outgoing documents are numbered and entered into logs or registers) was established. Although the registry system is cumbersome, it was an improvement on the previous non-existence of a system. And although archaic by today's standards, it is still in use over much of the world.

In 1789 the Archives Nationales was established in France. This institution provided for unified administration of archives, including the records of public agencies, and developed many of the archival theories subscribed to today. In 1838 the British Public Record Office Act was passed, establishing the principle of a centralized public record office under the direction of a records administrator. In 1877 a British Order in Council authorized destruction of valueless material, and in 1889 the first General Records Disposal Act was passed by the United States Congress. Except for the previously mentioned brief efforts in Rome in the 13th century, no routine and systematic disposal of unneeded records had ever been done before. In 1913 the US Bureau of Efficiency was created. For the first time the use of labour-saving office equipment was studied and promoted. In 1934, the National Archives of the United States was established and, within that Federal agency, the life cycle concept of records management was developed.

With the development of the life-cycle concept, records management went from being a series of sporadic and unrelated efforts to an organized, structured, and logically-based approach to creating, maintaining, and disposing of recorded information. Because it is the foundation of all records management principles, practices, methods, and techniques used today, the life-cycle concept is discussed in detail in Chapter 2.

WHAT IS RECORDS MANAGEMENT?

Having defined a record as any information captured in reproducible form that is required for conducting business, it is not too difficult to go one step further and define records management as well. We simply say that records management is the *management* of any information captured in reproducible form that is required for conducting business. But while this is certainly a definition in the classicial sense, it is similar to the original record definition in that it requires additional explanation. This explanation is necessary, not so that we will have a further understanding of the terms 'information' or 'record', but so that we will have some understanding of the functions of 'management'.

Management

Numerous words have been written about management. Advanced degrees in management are offered at the most prestigious universities throughout the world. Yet an individual can become a manager with no prior training or knowledge of the subject. This is not meant to be derogatory to managers but it shows that it is necessary to look at the subject of management from an objective viewpoint, not from the perspective of one who is awestruck.

First, management is not a science. Although management literature abounds with various theories and principles, they are not applicable in the same manner as scientific knowledge is applied. Secondly, management is not an art. Although that word has been used to describe the discipline, such description is totally erroneous and is usually only proposed by those persons who are desperately arguing against the idea of management being a science.

Management is a practice. It is performance based on knowledge, skill and responsibility. If managers are to be effective they must practice management using all three of these attributes. Through this practice the purpose and scope of the organizational mission should be defined; work should be organized logically so that employees achieve a high level of productivity; and a relationship between the organization and the society in which it operates should be maintained.

If the manager as *practitioner* seems somewhat ethereal, consider the manager as administrator. A manager must carefully adminster the organizational resources available so as to obtain the maximum possible productivity from them. While this may not, on the surface, seem like an inordinately difficult task, the magnitude of the problem comes more clearly into focus when one considers that the primary resource in most organizations is people. As an administrator of people, a manager is responsible for creating and maintaining a working environment where groups of individuals can perform efficiently and effectively toward the attainment of the organization's goals.

The organization's goals referred to here are those of the organization as a whole, for example, the corporation, academic institution, law partnership or government agency. The goals of any entity within an organization, such as a division, department or branch, must be consistent with the overall organizational goals or they become, by definition, antithetical to them and the organization will be destroyed from within.

Although this seems obvious when stated in a theoretical manner, the concept, when implemented, often becomes distorted. It is not uncommon to find entities within an organization that seem to have lost sight of the reason for the organization's existence. One of the main reasons for this problem is the misunderstanding of the functions of line and staff.

Within all organizations there are two types of functional entities: line entities which have *direct* responsibility for accomplishing the objectives of the organization (production, marketing, sales); and staff entities which support the line in their efforts (personnel, accounting, purchasing). In general, the characteristic that distinguishes line from staff is that staff operate in an advisory capacity unless specifically delegated functional authority. Using the personnel function as an example, unless the managing director of a corporation specifically delegates functional authority to the director of personnel, the personnel department would only be able to advise in matters of hiring, firing, employee relations, etc., and all actions/decisions would have to be made by the managing director. To avoid the bottleneck that would inevitably occur from such an arrangement, functional authority for personnel activity is delegated from the managing director to the director of personnel. For that particular functional area, the staff entity has authority over the other line areas within the organization.

How the delegated functional authority is handled by the staff entities is the key to a successful operation. Far too often, staff managers and staff personnel forget that regardless of the functional authority delegated, their one and only purpose is support of the line entities. No organization 'exists' to perform staff functions. An automobile manufacturer exists to produce cars, not to prepare budgets. A transportation authority exists to operate buses and trains, not to prepare press releases. A department store exists to sell merchandise, not to perform employee appraisals. Whenever the staff entities exercise their delegated authority in such a manner as to become nuisances, or become so large and powerful that the line entities appear to be working for them, instead of vice versa, then the organization has reached a critical stage of bureaucratization and is, for all practical purposes, internally haemorrhaging.

It should not be inferred from this discussion that a line manager should have no interest in, or responsibility for staff activities. That is the exact opposite of the situation. A line manager is inherently responsible for dealing with functions such as personnel, budget, and public relations as part of the practice of management. To ignore responsibility for these areas is to be guilty of mismanagement. It is the prioritization of activities and the overall balance that is important, and in this respect the records management activity may be viewed in perspective. Records management is a *staff* function.

The records management function

Records management is a logical and practical approach to the creation, maintenance, use and disposition of records and, therefore, of the information that those records contain. With a viable records management programme in operation, an organization can control both the quality and quantity of the information that it creates; it can maintain that information in a manner that effectively serves its needs; and it can efficiently dispose of the information when it is no longer valuable.

A complete records management programme encompasses a multitude of disciplines including forms, reports, correspondence, directives, mail, files, copying, retention scheduling, vital records protection, archival preservation, and ultimate disposal. Each discipline has its own particular principles, practices, methods, and techniques for accomplishing the necessary end results, and certain technological tools that may be employed to help in achieving the results more efficiently, effectively, and economically.

Because a records management programme consists of so many diverse elements, a professional records manager must be a combination generalist/specialist. Essentially, the function requires specialized subject matter expertise in several interrelated disciplines. Although it might, on the surface, appear that the design of a form and the determination as to the long-term value of the information it contains are two entirely unrelated activities, we will see, when the life-cycle concept is discussed in Chapter 2, that one is very much dependent on the other. The records manager, therefore, must be able to relate all the various elements together and to explain the relationships to persons at all levels within the organization.

The explanation aspect of the records management function cannot be overemphasized. For while the records manager will have delegated functional authority to plan, organize, and direct the records management programme, the successful operation of that programme will require the co-operation of the line (and other staff) entities that the programme is designed to support. Co-operation from within these entities will be more readily forthcoming if the people understand *why* they are being asked to perform a certain activity and are not just told to do it.

The records management function is unique in an organization because although it is a staff operation, and therefore basically an overhead, it could be considered as an 'invested overhead' in that unlike most staff areas it has the potential for saving more than it costs. Figures from both the UK and US governments have shown that a return on investment of 20 to 1 on records management system improvements is not unusual. In developing countries, the return would be even higher.

But while the savings which can accrue from a records management programme are substantial, they must be placed in proper context. The savings are not the rationale or justification for the programme and should never be considered as such. The records management programme must exist because the function of managing recorded information is a necessity. The savings are merely a bonus that may be obtained from managing the information efficiently.

One of the major areas of contention in organizations that have established records management programmes is the integration of the information handling technologies into the programme operation. Although not always considered to be a part of records management, these associated technologies (such as word processing, micrographics, optical character recognition, etc.) are a legitimate records management concern in so far as they are used for creating, maintaining, using, or disposing of recorded information. While records management is often thought of as being synonymous with the term 'paperwork management', nothing could be further from the truth. There is nothing in the records management definition that is media specific. 'Reproducible form' is not limited to paper. Information captured on a microform, a magnetic tape, or an optical disc is just as much a record as that captured on an A4 or $8\frac{1}{2} \times 11$ inch piece of paper. As such, it must be managed and the equipment that is used in conjunction with it must be managed concurrently.

Whether or not records managers should have the delegated functional authority to manage and control the associated information technologies is not the issue. The point is that records managers, as a part of their basic records management authority, must at least be involved in matters such as equipment selection, placement, and utilization procedures to ensure that all recorded information receives proper treatment.

RECORDS MANAGEMENT TODAY

In the historical section of this chapter, it was suggested that advanced records management concepts were not developed earlier in time because they were not yet necessary. Carrying that line of thinking to the present, we now see that not only are sophisticated records management principles and practices necessary in today's information-oriented society, but that they are absolutely critical to its continued survival.

Governments at all levels establish requirements for maintaining records. Almost all business transactions depend on the proper creation and maintenance of recorded information. Decisions in court cases have resulted in proper records disposal becoming an important factor in day-to-day business operations. Quite simply, an organization today cannot ignore its records any more than it can ignore the working conditions of its employees or the environmental concerns of the community in which it is located.

As important as these factors are, however, there is another one which is even more necessary to consider. That is, the changing record media and the advent of electronic recordkeeping. Traditionally, records have been kept on paper. As long as information is on paper it can be seen. As long as the paper exists it can be found. A paper document that is misplaced or misfiled may cause inconvenience and the expenditure of excessive funds to locate, but it is retrievable given enough time and effort. With electronic recordkeeping this may not be the case.

When information in electronic form is updated, the previously existing information is lost. Electronic data-base operations may not provide for back copies or chronological files which can be referenced to obtain the original data. Information stored on electronic media can be adversely affected by dirt, heat, smoke, abrasion, and even the magnetic impulses of an ordinary telephone. Information being entered into electronic storage can be totally wiped out by a power surge or a power loss. Information filed electronically is not retrievable by anyone who does not know the type of system used to file it, and is retrievable by virtually anyone who does.

The issues just described are not automated data processing issues; they are not management information system issues; they are records management issues because they directly relate to how recorded information is created, maintained, used and disposed of. Their resolution, therefore, is dependent on how recorded information is managed.

Records management in the information society is a necessary part of the societal foundation. Without management of the basic societal resource and of the principal societal product, chaos would very likely result. How much managing an organization does is dependent on the attitudes and perceptions of its various managers. Those who appreciate the necessity for establishing a comprehensive records management programme will find guidance for its implementation in the pages of the following chapters.

2 The Information Life-cycle

Records do not just materialize on desks, in file cabinets, or in computer memories; people create them and put them there. While this may seem obvious to anyone reading this book today, it was not so obvious prior to the mid 20th-century. The approach to records management from about 5000 BC to about AD 1945 was basically one of attempting to 'keep track of it all'. The fact that 'it' (records) existed because someone had made a conscious effort to capture information in reproducible form had never really been considered.

A NEW THEORY

When the life-cycle concept was developed in the United States, people began to realize that there was something that could be done to control the creation of records. If that something was done properly, maintenance, use and disposition of the recorded information would be much less of a problem. The life-cycle concept may be easily understood. The theory is that recorded information has a 'life' similar to that of a biological organism in that it is born (creation phase), it lives (maintenance and use phase), and it dies (disposition phase). Each of the phases has various elements associated with it and functional activities are performed within each element.

Within the creation phase, there are elements such as forms, reports, directives, and correspondence; during maintenance and use there are elements such as files, mail, communications, active storage, security, and vital records. Within the disposition phase there are elements such as scheduling, appraisal, storage in records centres, archives and ultimate disposal.

Creation

There are various ways in which a record is created. An individual writes a letter or memorandum to a business associate; a form is sent to a job applicant who must complete it and return it to the organization that has the vacant position; an existing record is placed on a copying machine and, in a matter of seconds, one becomes two; and so on. There are, of course, different levels of effort involved in creating these records. It does not take a whole lot of time or intelligence to duplicate a record on a quick copy machine. To write a letter or

9

complete a form, however, might involve considerable research. A report might have to be reviewed and edited by a number of people. So before a record is created some thought should be given to the necessity for its existence. If it is unnecessary, it should not be created.

Seventy per cent of the cost of information is in records creation, and yet superfluous records are created unnecessarily in almost all organizations on a daily basis. A letter is written when a phone call would have been perfectly adequate. A form is completed in triplicate and only two copies are used. Reports are required even when the response is negative. Little consideration is given to the most fundamental question: '*Is it necessary to capture the information in reproducible form*?'

Obviously there are instances where the capture is not only desirable, but absolutely imperative. One does not conclude treaties, contracts, and multinational mergers without adequate documentation. But assuming that a record should be created, there are still the additional questions regarding how it is to be created. What exactly is it that constitutes 'adequate' documentation? Is a 400-page report necessary, or will a two-page memorandum do the job? Do we want the information to be in a consistent format, necessitating use of a form, or can it just be obtained in a random manner? What type of directive will be needed to ensure that those who are involved in the creation process are aware of the various requirements?

These are the types of issues that must be dealt with when considering records creation. When they are not dealt with, creation quickly becomes proliferation, and the successive phases of life become increasingly more difficult. Because situations differ, the answers to the questions will necessarily differ as well. The goal of a records management programme is not to develop a set way for handling all of the various problems and conditions, but to establish a sound methodology for evaluating the situations so that the most appropriate course of action can be taken in each instance.

Additionally, questions regarding the future life of the information must be asked prior to the creation process. Although the maintenance and use activities can obviously not take place until the information has been created, the maintenance and use systems must be developed at this early stage so that when the information does come into being it can be stored and retrieved in an orderly and efficient manner. Thus we begin to see the interrelationships of the various phases.

Maintenance and use

For proper maintenance, all questions regarding information storage and retrieval systems must be answered. As already stated, they should be answered *before* the records are created because the answers will determine the way in which information is captured.

Just because a record ceases to be fully active, that does not mean that it should cease to exist. Its existence may be required by statute or regulation, or it may be desirable for historical reference purposes. Nor does it mean that it should be archived immediately, for it may, after a given period of time, lose all value.

Disposition

The disposition that is made of an inactive record will depend on the value of the information that it contains. The value of information is measured sometimes in minutes and sometimes in centuries. The information in a memorandum from the company managing director regarding the annual staff party, for example, may be needed only until the party is over. The information in a letter from the same individual discussing the corporate strategy for avoiding a takeover may be deemed historically significant and kept permanently.

If information is considered to be of a permanent nature, it must be captured in reproducible form in a manner that ensures permanence. Thus, disposition should be considered during both the active and semi-active phases. For example, if information is known to be archival at the time it is originated, it can be captured on 100 per cent rag bond paper, maintained and used appropriately, and archived at a predetermined time. However, if information is not considered to be archival at the time of origination, but is determined to be archival at a later date, it could be recaptured at that later time in a different form such as microfilm, and the film could be processed to archival standards to ensure permanence. Again, we see the interrelationships of the various life-cycle phases.

INTERRELATIONSHIPS

We have referred to the interrelationships of the phases. There are interrelationships between the various elements as well. For example, the files element is interrelated with the records centre element inasmuch as the amount of space needed for remote storage is dependent on the volume of records in the active files and the frequency with which they become inactive. Similarly, the vital records element is related to the security element because, by its very nature, a vital record must be protected and stored securely. Or again, scheduling relates to appraisal. In fact, the purpose of appraising records is to determine the value of the information they contain during the various life stages so that a schedule may be developed to provide guidance on proper record handling, transfer, media conversion, storage, etc. Likewise, scheduling relates to archiving and to final disposition, both of which are possible last steps in the information life-cycle.

TECHNOLOGY

In addition to the phases and elements, we must also consider the technologies of records management and their relationship to the information life-cycle. Technologies are tools. Their purpose is to make information handling easier, more efficient, and less costly. They can do these things if they are properly used. But technologies are merely the means to an end — not the end themselves. As such, they must be fitted to the function, not *vice versa*. High-technology devices such as computers, optical character readers, facsimile transceivers, and laser printers should be looked at no differently than filing equipment, and should, therefore, be obtained only to fill a specified need.

Care must be taken to ensure that the implementation of technological improvements does not get out of hand. Life-cycle management efficiencies can be completely eliminated when technology is misapplied. Word processing in certain situations can actually slow down keyboard productivity rather than increase it. Electronic mail can be disastrous if documentary evidence is needed for litigation. A microfilm conversion can cost much more than storing hard copy documents in a record centre.

With the advent of electronic recordkeeping, the technological issue becomes even more involved. One must be concerned not only about the medium on which the information is captured (magnetic tape, floppy disc, optical disc), but about the equipment on which the medium depends in order to be read. With paper this is not a problem. Assuming that the document has not been destroyed, the information it contains is easily readable. Even with a microform (other than ultrafiche) the recorded information can be read in an emergency with very unsophisticated magnifying lenses. But with electronically-encoded media, there is only one way to get the information out. The electronic equipment that reads the codes must be available — and operable.

Given the rapid changes in technology, the machine availability issue is a major records management consideration. Organizations which make a wholesale commitment to electronic media may find themselves archiving machines and spare parts as well as records, or investing in massive media conversion efforts in order to eliminate the equipment dependency.

THEORY TO PRACTICE

The life-cycle concept of records management is, like most theories, relatively valueless unless it is put to use. The idea is to implement the theory and turn it into practice. If we consider the life-cycle as the basis for a total records management programme, we can see that it affords great potential for the effective management of recorded information. However, as far as interrelationships and interdependencies are concerned, it can be seen that all of the phases and all of the elements must be managed in a unified and co-ordinated manner if significant programme effectiveness is to result. This is where the management aspect comes into play. The various records management elements all require planning, organizing, directing, and co-ordinating, and, obviously, the overall records management programme requires that those managerial functions be performed as well. Establishing, organizing, and managing an effective records management programme is the subject of Chapter 3.

Part II
Programme Structure and Operation

INTRODUCTION

Without a structured programme or adequate organization, the effective management of records and information could not be carried out.

Under the overall charge of a records manager, who must have top management support, an organization will include all the functions mentioned in Chapter 1 and examined in detail in later chapters. The organization must be flexible and provide sufficient expertise to cover not only programme operations but also policy development and evaluation. Chapter 3 examines a traditional pyramid organization but considers that records management is more suited to a matrix management structure. It also discusses the importance of people in the organization and examines three different staffing arrangements.

In order to maintain the effectiveness and efficiency of an organization, it is necessary to monitor management operations closely. Chapter 4 discusses how this might best be done and examines in detail the techniques of management analysis, including project management, problem solving, costing, and drawing conclusions.

The first and most important step to the proper control of records is the information survey. This comprehensive gathering of information about records created or processed by an organization is examined in detail in Chapter 5. Without such an objective overview of records collections and their uses, no amount of management analysis will enable a true assessment of the problems that have to be overcome.

3 Organizing an Integrated Programme

The major prerequisite for establishing a records management programme is a top level manager who is convinced that such a programme is needed. Top management support is the key to success for every type of line or staff operation and records management is no exception.

A top manager who realizes the importance of records management will delegate the functional authority for such management to a competent, professional records manager and issue an authorizing directive establishing a comprehensive records management programme at a level commensurate with other staff functions such as budgeting, personnel, or data processing. While the size of the programme will depend on the size of the overall organization, the records manager must be an individual who will develop and expand it to match the organization's growth and who will foster that growth through the effective management of its recorded information. Such an individual should possess a variety of managerial skills and abilities, among which are communicating, goal setting, motivating, decision making, problem identifying and solving, and change facilitation.

The records management programme directive, or policy statement, is the official charter for performing all records management functions and should, therefore, be written in terms as broad as possible. Included should be a reference to a total, comprehensive records management programme which provides for the management of recorded information throughout its life cycle. By establishing the programme on this basis, all records management elements are included and all functional activities are able to be performed. Depending on the way organizational directives are to be written, the records management charter might also incorporate a statement of programme objectives and the outline of specific programme responsibilities.

Once the directive is officially approved and issued, no further authorization should be necessary for any programme activity as long as such activity falls within the range of the authority which has been delegated and stays within budgetary constraints. This is not to say, however, that the records management staff can operate in a totally independent manner and receive no guidance from higher authority. In fact, for some functions, the input of senior level managers is not only desirable, it is an absolute requirement. But most records management programme activities such as conducting inventories, developing referencing systems or reviewing the operation of information storage and retrieval systems, can be routinely performed without receiving specific top management approval because such approval was inherent in the issue of the programme charter.

Those issues which require decisions at a level of authority higher than that delegated to

15

the records manager should be discussed by a senior level records management committee. The committee, which should be a formally established body chaired by the records manager and consisting of members including legal counsel, accounting or tax personnel, internal auditing manager, data processing manager, director of administration, and other key figures in the hierarchy as appropriate, should deal with overall policy issues and should provide input for decisions of critical import such as vital records determination and retention scheduling.

The committee serves two extremely important purposes. Firstly, it provides high-level managerial expertise to assist the records manager in problem solving and decision making, and, secondly, it serves as a communications forum to ensure that senior managers are appraised of records management issues and have the opportunity to offer suggestions for future programme initiatives. This second factor is extremely important from a 'political' standpoint. If senior management officials are a part of the records management development process, full co-operation is much more likely at the time initiatives are undertaken.

WHY ORGANIZE?

Organizations do not have to have a formal structure in order to function. Indeed, it has even been suggested that a certain organizational ambiguity is preferable because such an arrangement forces people to truly work together to get things done. Whether the structure is formal or informal, however, some organizing is necessary. All things being equal, people generally work more effectively if they know the who, what, where, why, and how regarding the organization in which they are employed.

Organizing is a managerial concept second only to recordkeeping in age. It is basically the logical grouping of activities necessary to obtain objectives, the assignment of each grouping to a manager who has the responsibility to supervise it, and the provision for co-ordination and communication between all of the organizational entities.

Traditional organization

Records management functional activities appear to lend themselves quite well to being organized in the traditional manner, that is, into a functionally divided hierarchical pyramid. A traditionally structured records management programme might be organized as shown in Figure 3.1. (Note: No attempt is being made to try and include every possible functional activity or element in these illustrations.) This structure seems to be logical. The correspondence and policy elements, for example, are shown grouped together under one programme manager (this would depend, of course, on the organization's size and the workload involved); management of the technologies of word processing and copy management are placed in this unit (the majority of the work produced using these technologies is either correspondence or policy related); and there are analysts to do the necessary professional work and clerical personnel to provide support.

The files element also shows a programme manager, with clerical and professional personnel, correspondence and security, and the technology of micrographics (appropriately placed since micrographics is merely an alternative medium for information storage and retrieval).

All in all, it might be thought that the structure in Figure 3.1 represented a model records management programme. Indeed, it is the type of structure found in many organizations. But consider the nature of the records management effort. Why does an organization establish a records management programme? As discussed in Chapter 1, the records management programme should be established to *manage* the information captured in reproducible form that is required for conducting business. As discussed in Chapter 2, the

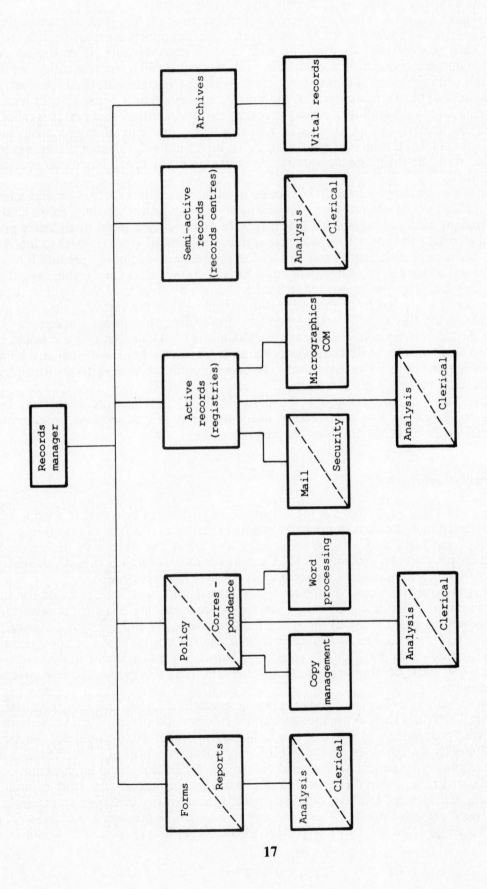

Figure 3.1   A traditionally structured records management programme

17

programme should be based on the life-cycle concept which necessitates a 'multifunctional' approach because of the interrelationships and interdependencies.

Even though Figure 3.1 shows no programme fragmentation (the records management functions are placed under the records manager), there is complete compartmentalization wherein each element is in its own box with its own separate staff. Even though co-ordination and communication are possible, each element is still a separate entity and the individuals within those entities may have a somewhat restricted or parochial approach to things because of this separateness. For example, an individual may be capable, by nature and training, of being a multidisciplinary management analyst. But if that person is called a micrographic analyst, and is working in a micrographic operational environment, and reports to the chief of the micrographic branch, it is highly unlikely that that person is going to be able to sustain the global perspective necessary for doing broad-based management analysis work.

In that same vein, consider the difference between the functions of records management systems, procedures development and implementation (retention scheduling, forms analysis and design, media conversions), which require highly-skilled multi-disciplinary professional efforts, and those of records management operations (files transfer to inactive storage, forms replenishment, word processing production, document preparation for microfilming) which can be routinely handled by well-trained clerks and technicians. The probabilities are, given the segmented structure, that at any given time there will be either too much or too little work for the professional employees in the various units. It is not reasonable within this type of arrangement to think that professional workers can be laterally shifted between units to achieve workload/staff balance. Although it would be possible to detail a forms analyst to the policy branch for two weeks or two months, it is bad management practice to do so. Even under the best of conditions such shifts are disruptive and often result in morale deterioration.

The pyramidal organization, like the pyramid itself, provides great stability, but virtually no flexibility. For an effective and viable records management programme, managerial flexibility is of paramount importance.

An alternative approach

In contrast to Figure 3.1, there is the organization structure illustrated in Figure 3.2, usually referred to as a matrix or grid management structure. This type of arrangement is reflective of the tasks and activities necessary to achieve the objectives of a records management programme, provides for their accomplishment, and gives virtually unlimited flexibility to a records manager to place resources where they are needed.

The matrix structure works as follows. One records manager is responsible for the overall programme. Reporting directly to the records manager are two distinct categories of professional. Across the top of the grid are shown the policy and operations managers responsible for the direction and maintenance of the records management programme elements, and down the left side of the grid are shown the management analysts whose function is the study, development, and implementation of records management systems and procedures.

In terms of policy development and programme operations (operations being essentially the 'control' activities such as maintenance of inventories and the 'production' activities such as word processing and microfilming), the matrix organization would not function much differently than the hierarchical pyramid organization previously described. But in terms of records management systems and procedures development and implementation, the matrix structure is very different indeed. By having an independent staff of multi-disciplinary management analysts, each system and procedure can be viewed from a global perspective. A request for a new form, for example, might be processed as follows: The request would go from the form originator to the forms branch just as it would in a

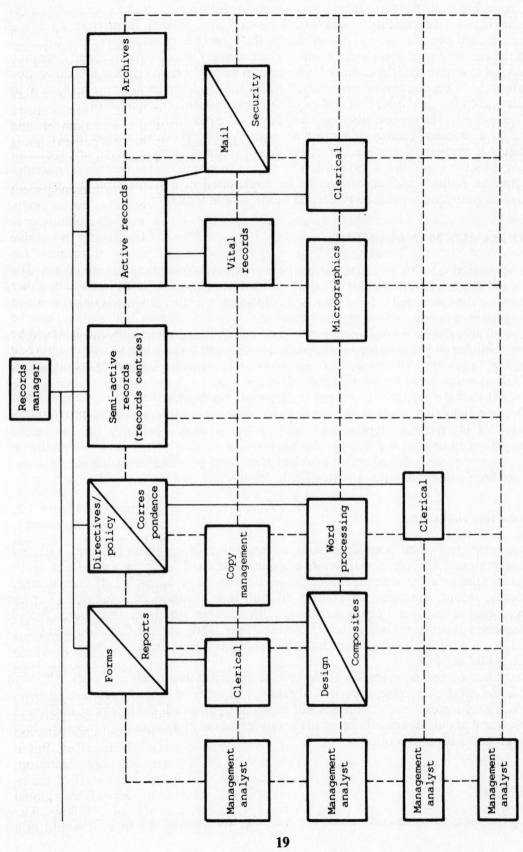

Figure 3.2 A matrix management structure

pyramidal organization. Then, however, the request would be forwarded to the records manager who would assign the review project to an independent management analyst. The analyst would study the form from the viewpoint of how it related to a system of records, considering the information which would be captured on that form from an overall organizational perspective, and co-ordinating the forms design and procedures for its use with the various forms users and with all of the necessary records management operations personnel to ensure that the captured information would be correctly handled throughout its life cycle. When the review and analysis was completed, the form would go back to the forms branch for final adoption and incorporation into the forms inventory.

Theoretically, the process just described could take place within a pyramidal organization. As a practical matter, it almost never does. The great advantage of the matrix structure is the virtual elimination of the organizational barriers which are artificially imposed by the hierarchical pyramid. The matrix structure allows records management programme policies and operations to be maintained in a stable structure while the analytical functions are able to be carried out in a fluid structure.

PROGRAMME MANAGEMENT

The purpose of creating an organizational structure is to facilitate the accomplishment of goals and objectives. The primary goal of a records management programme — life-cycle management of recorded information — is obtained by efficiently managing the records management elements in an integrated manner.

Overall programme management is needed to ensure that the necessary integration takes place. Included in programme management are the well-known managerial functions of planning, organizing, directing, staffing, controlling, communicating, decision making, etc., all of which have been written about in great detail in the myriad of management textbooks that are available in various libraries and bookstores.

Organizing has been dealt with here because, although matrix management is not a new concept, it is certainly atypical and because the structure uniquely fits the records management functions. We will also discuss staffing because it has been traditionally one of the biggest records management problem areas, and programme evaluation because it has not been written about in any significant form.

The staffing challenge

Management has often been defined as getting things done through people. Records managers should, therefore, make every attempt to get a sufficient number of high calibre people for their staff so that the things can get done in an expedient yet effective manner. Typically, records managers have had a difficult time accomplishing this feat. For one thing, being a relatively young profession, there have not been that many records management professionals around to choose from, and, for another, the number of positions on a records management manning table has usually been somewhat under that which would be ideal.

Records managers however, do not have to be limited to using their own staff. Although that is the most preferable situation, alternative sources of labour must sometimes be found. The two most common methods of augmenting a records management staff are the employment of outside consultants, and the establishment of an organization-wide records management liaison network.

Consultants

The advantages of using consultants are basically the same as the advantages of having independent management analysts on the staff — specialized experience and expertise, an unbiased viewpoint, ability to concentrate on one job at a time, and a global perspective. (For more on this subject see Chapter 4.) Additionally, however, because consultants are not on the staff and are completely unaffiliated with the organization, there is an aura of credibility surrounding them which is often quite significant in terms of the way their work is accepted by upper-level management. Although this 'credibility factor' is based more on emotion than on logic, it is a reality and must be considered when staffing a records management programme.

A consultant can do all the types of work that a management analyst would do, but usually does not. Consultants' efforts are mostly confined to studying problems rather than implementing solutions, implementation being a time-consuming and therefore expensive process. This latter factor is an extremely important one. A study which results in a report that sits on a shelf gathering dust is not much more valuable than a study which was not done at all. When the staffing-by-consultant alternative is being considered, therefore, thought must be given to the *total* amount of funding that will be necessary to see the project through to completion, not just to the amount that is necessary to get the project started.

It is useful to have someone from the records management staff involved with the consultant on a continuous basis. If an entire consulting team is being brought in, one member of the records management staff could be assigned to be a team member. If the effort is a smaller one, then, at a minimum, regular meetings with the consultant should be held. Without continuous, open communication regarding the consultant's activities, the records manager may be placed in the position of losing some control over that aspect of the programme in which the consultant is involved.

Liaison network

The second alternative source of staffing is the records management liaison network, established by having the manager of each organizational entity designate an individual to act as a liaison with the records management staff. Indeed, it is valuable to establish a liaison network even if the records management programme is sufficiently staffed. Having a 'friend on the inside' is always a good idea, and the liaison network can provide friends organization-wide.

The key to liaison effectiveness is in developing reasonable expectations. Liaisons, or 'nominated officers', are not substitute staff professionals as are consultants. They are not expected to perform studies, or write reports. What they can do is to provide information about their own organizational entities to the records management staff and foster the idea of using sound records management techniques among their co-workers.

Persons who are selected to serve as liaisons should receive training in basic records management principles and more advanced training should be provided if interest and receptivity are shown. Since it is difficult to conceive of a records management programme suffering from having too much help, the liaisons should be encouraged to become as involved in the various projects as they want to be. The psychological implications for individuals at the working level are just as significant as they are for the persons on the records management committee. If people think about a project or system as their own, the job of convincing them of its worth is usually not necessary.

Even when liaison personnel are not involved in any particular records management project within their own organizational entity, they should attend periodic meetings so that they might keep abreast of what is happening throughout other parts of the organization. These periodic meetings are opportune times to present short workshop sessions to reinforce the training already received, and to elicit people's ideas and suggestions.

In addition to the obvious support and assistance that liaison personnel can provide, they may also prove to be a source of talent should records management staff vacancies occur.

Internal organizational transfers are sometimes easier to effect than external hires, especially during periods of austerity. If a records manager can cultivate an in-house resource pool to draw from, the staffing job will be significantly lessened.

Programme evaluation

The ultimate test of records management programme effectiveness is whether the recorded information is available to those who need it when and where it is needed. Add to those criteria the manner in which it is made available (efficiency), and at what cost (economy), and a complete programme evaluation can be made.

A programme evaluation is essentially a type of internal audit. Whether the evaluation is conducted by an organization's internal auditor or (staff) inspector, however, is not terribly significant. What is important is that the evaluation be done.

A records management programme evaluation should be conducted at least bi-annually. If the internal auditors are unavailable to perform audits of a single programme on such a regular basis, the records management staff analysts should conduct a 'self-inspection' instead. Because of the nature of the management analysis position, such individuals are easily able to perform self-inspections. In this respect, it should be pointed out that the prime purpose of a programme evaluation is not inspection to uncover waste, fraud, and abuse, but review to determine the extent of effectiveness, economy, and efficiency.

Evaluation should encompass all elements of a records management programme and should consist of a two-part review. Part one can be a checklist type of examination wherein a comparison is made between textbook theory and operating realities. The greater the similarity between the two, the better the programme. Part two of the review should include a study of an existing system which is considered to be operating smoothly. By examining the storage files, retention schedules, etc. relating to a system which is perceived to have no (or few) problems, one can assess the effectiveness of the records management programme fairly accurately. If, upon review, serious problems are found with any aspect of the information flow, whether in the phases of creation, maintenance and use, or disposition, there is a good possibility that some defect exists in the related records management programme area. If, on the other hand, the system is found to be operating smoothly, it can be reasonably construed that the records management functions are being effectively performed.

4 Management Analysis Techniques

Management analysis is a term used to describe the activities of individuals in organizations who study organizational structure and operations. On the basis of the studies performed, the management analysts advise managers on ways of increasing efficiency by doing work better, faster, or cheaper.

Management analysis is not a new concept. Over the years those performing the analytical functions have been given a variety of titles. In the early part of the 20th century such persons were known as 'efficiency experts'; in mid-century the title was 'organization and methods examiner'; and, today, an alternative name for management analyst is 'internal consultant'. Although we will refer to management analysis in this book, the title is not the important factor. Regardless of which label has been applied in the past, there has been little question as to the necessity for the work that is performed.

Part of a manager's responsibility is the concern for an organization's methods and procedures. But managers have to divide their attention between several areas relating to their particular programmes, many of which tend to seem more urgent than the methods and procedures by which those programmes operate. Put another way, getting the job done takes priority over how it gets done, and not until it stops getting done does the way in which it gets done become an issue.

So just as personnel specialists might be available to assist busy managers with employee recruitment, management analysts are available to help managers improve methods and procedures. Management analysts can provide valuable help to managers because they:

- have an unbiased and independent viewpoint;
- study the organization from a global perspective;
- concentrate on one job at a time;
- have specialized experience and expertise.

This latter factor, specialized experience and expertise, is especially important in records management analysis work. The entire information life-cycle must be considered when designing a records system. It is possible that to create even a simple system an analyst would have to understand forms analysis and design, printing, word processing, mail, filing, micrographics, inactive storage, vital records, and archival preservation.

Management analysis assignments vary widely in scope: they may include examinations of office procedures, reviews of the organization of entire departments, and specific studies in areas such as office automation. Management analysts look not only at the work which is being done, but also at the *purpose* of it, and at the overall organizational requirements. With a records system especially, the analysis cannot be done in a vacuum. The manager who perceives the problem may not have the problem at all. What may initially appear to be a registry deficiency may ultimately prove to be a mail operations deficiency — or vice versa.

Management analysis is a 'requested' service. Management analysts are not internal auditors or investigators who unexpectedly arrive on the scene. While the service is most often requested by the manager who wants to repair something, analysts can often do their best work when used as original system designers. It is far more cost effective to design a system correctly at the outset than it is to redesign one after it is malfunctioning.

Management analysis is a *staff* function. Because of this, analysts recommend actions to managers, they do not direct them. It is unrealistic to think that all recommendations will always be accepted and implemented. Acceptance is based on four factors: the value of the recommendations; the manner in which the recommendations are presented; the credibility of the analyst; and organizational politics which, unfortunately, sometimes overshadows and negates the first three factors.

The timing of the management analyst's involvement very often determines the term used to describe the effort. For example, a review of an existing system is usually referred to as a survey or study. Development of a new system, on the other hand, is usually referred to as a project. Frequently, the recommendations of a study lead to initiation of a project. Semantically, however, surveys and studies are merely types of projects. This terminology issue is mentioned merely to head-off any confusion that might result from encountering both terms in this chapter. The key idea to keep in mind is that the principles and techniques are the same regardless of what the effort is called.

THE MANAGEMENT ANALYSIS APPROACH

A management analyst should be familiar with organizational theory and practice and should have knowledge of the various subjects with which managers are concerned. While management analysis assistance is requested because of the management analyst's expertise, an individual analyst should avoid posing as a subject matter specialist. This seeming contradiction is explained when one realizes that when dealing with a managerial problem there is usually not 'one best way' to solve it, and specialists may have an inherent bias towards their own area of specialization.

Management analysts need to know how to organize tasks; deal with people; collect, record, and verify information; draw and test conclusions; and prepare recommendations. They must operate in an independent and unbiased manner, and be able to systematically collect and analyse data. Their recommendations must always be constructive, and based on reason and logic.

The individual who is likely to be successful in management analysis enjoys working with people and systems, is not easily frustrated and displays energy, initiative, and self-confidence. Above all, however, a management analyst must possess an uncommon amount of common sense.

PRELIMINARY STUDY ACTIVITY

The initial meetings with management when starting an assignment are most important. These meetings give the management analyst an opportunity to meet the organization's senior staff members in order to explain the reason for the study, and they also give managers the opportunity of supplying the analysts with information such as:

- organization charts
- functional statements
- position descriptions

- relevant statistics
- information about perceived shortcomings such as backlogs, customer complaints, high staff turnover, etc.

If possible, the management analyst should do some advance preparation by reviewing previous studies or reports and documentation related to the activity to be evaluated.

The ways in which managers can help the study effort should also be discussed. Managers can, for example:

- Ensure that the staff members of the organization to be studied understand the purpose of the study and realize that it is not designed to review the performance of individuals, but to review methods and procedures.
- Formally request the staff members whose work is to be examined to do all they can to assist the analyst in obtaining the information needed.
- Appoint a liaison person to help the analyst obtain materials or explain existing procedures.
- Recognize that the scope of the study may need to be modified as the assignment develops and understanding of the problems increases.
- Consider the possibility of accepting a less formal final report so that it can be prepared more quickly.

Preliminary review

If, for some reason, the activities to be examined are well known to the analyst, it may be possible to draw up a work plan without a preliminary review. But if the activities are not known (which is usually the case) some preliminary review should be made so as to get a better understanding of the problems, and to decide how best to carry out the study to obtain the most beneficial results.

The amount of information to be obtained in a preliminary review depends on the circumstances and on the individual analyst. Normally, only a general understanding of the work and the organization is necessary. But it may be that an unusual situation requires that more information about the organization structure or some specific procedures be obtained. Some areas for possible review include:

- The basic requirements of the work process; the amount of change to established procedures; relevant statistics for recent years; and trends related to workload.
- Estimated costs of activities for the operation as a whole and by sub-function when such figures are available.
- The extent of delays and the nature of criticisms or complaints.
- Suggestions for systems improvement previously submitted by staff personnel.
- The planning, controlling, and supervising methods of managers.
- The characteristics of the individual work tasks.
- The characteristics of the documents used in the process.
- Staff morale (comments or complaints about the process, the environment, the management style, etc.).

When the preliminary review is completed, a study cost/benefit assessment should be made as an adjunct activity to drawing-up a detailed project plan. Management analysts are more appropriately utilized to correct serious systems defects than to merely making minor improvements to relatively smooth-running operations. Although there is hardly any system that cannot be improved in some measure, the aim should be to make the best use of the usually limited resources. If an early cost/benefit assessment indicates that the study is likely to result in improvements which will be negligible in comparison to the time which will be involved, the entire effort should be re-evaluated and possibly discontinued in favour of a more lucrative endeavour.

PROJECT MANAGEMENT

Project management is a term frequently associated with the design and implementation of automated systems. It would be unfortunate to consider project management as limited to automated systems since its principles are clearly applicable to any type of project, automated or otherwise, and, in fact, were known long before automation was invented. Project management techniques are useful whether the project is conducting a micrographics feasibility study, designing a records storage facility, or developing a computerized information retrieval system.

It should be obvious that various types of projects require various levels of managerial effort. The level of project management should be proportional to the length, difficulty, and importance of the project. This is not to suggest that any projects that are undertaken are unimportant, but, in the real world, some things are just 'more equal' than others.

Any project requires resources — people, time, money, and sometimes equipment or other materials. Resources are characteristically dynamic in nature. Personnel changes, budget cuts, equipment availability, and the like, can alter the direction of a project at any given moment or even cause its demise. In this regard, the project manager, who in essence manages the project by directing and monitoring its progress in terms of a specific plan, must be constantly aware of the overall organizational situation.

The success of a project depends on various factors:

- Clearly defined scope and objectives.
- Clearly defined roles and responsibilities.
- Management commitment and support.
- User/customer commitment and involvement.
- Clearly defined tasks and dependencies.
- Realistic scheduling of tasks.
- Co-operation among the participants.
- Realistic estimates of cost and effort.
- Periodic review and adjustment as necessary.

Project Management Philosophy

All projects must have a project manager or leader. This could be the records manager, supervisor, or analyst, depending on the size and scope of the effort. The project manager should be an individual who can organize, lead, communicate, and negotiate.

Having a clear understanding of the philosophy of project management at the outset can help to avoid problems once the project is underway. The following are some basic project management guidelines:

- There should be just one overall plan and schedule for the project.
- The plan must be comprehensive and detailed.
- Progress reports should specifically relate to the tasks on the plan and should be prepared on a regular basis.
- Time estimates should be regarded as commitments.
- Critical activities should be identified and closely monitored.
- Project review meetings should be held regularly, as the project demands.
- Project participants should be represented at review meetings and the representatives should have the authority to make decisions.

The Plan

It is said about Christopher Columbus that he started out on his voyage not knowing where he was going, did not realize where he was when he got there, did not know where he had been when he got back, and did it all on borrowed money. The end result, of course, was that Christopher Columbus discovered America. Few management analysts will be able to use Columbus's method and achieve the same degree of success. A plan is necessary before a study can be conducted.

A plan is, in some respects, a map for the voyage. While the analogy is not perfect, inasmuch as one will not know at the outset what the end result will be, still the plan does help to guide the effort from point to point towards the ultimate goal of system improvement. A plan is any detailed method, formulated beforehand, for doing or making something. It is during the planning stage that the specifics of the study (scope, objectives, tasks, costs, etc.) are identified.

The scope is the extent or range of the study. It identifies the area within which action can take place and the limits between which variation is possible. Answering the following questions will help to define the study scope:

- What will the study cover?
- What will the study *not* cover?
- Who is affected by the study?
- What are the overriding constraints (budget, time, staff, etc.)?

There is much debate over which comes first: goals or objectives. Since both are similarly defined as ends toward which efforts are directed, the term 'objectives' is used here to include both. Stating the objectives should be one of the first steps in the planning process. What happens more often than not, though, is that the objectives are either poorly stated or not stated at all. In larger studies, the scope and objectives should be distinct; in smaller studies there may be some overlap. Objectives describe the schedule, budget, and quality of the operation, and may relate to many different areas. A good objective is one that is clearly stated, reasonable (obtainable), and quantifiable. Objectives should be listed in order of priority. Failing to have written objectives or stating them in such a way that they conflict with one another will delay or misdirect the study.

Once the scope and objectives are determined, task lists should be developed for each phase of the study. For each task, five specifications may be defined: purpose, functional description, resources/documents used, results, and completion criteria. The name of the individual to be assigned to the task should be included, as should the beginning and end dates and the time estimated for completion.

Estimating

Another key element in the planning process is estimating the cost and effort required to complete the study. This is no easy undertaking, however, because there are several barriers which impede estimating and which can lead to inconsistent results. Erratic work methods, insufficient data, oversimplified analysis, lack of time to estimate or train in the estimating process, premature commitment, unrealistic administrative limitations, cost and scheduling edicts, ineffective communication, and lack of scope control all serve to inhibit accurate estimation.

Estimating cost and effort should not be confused with scheduling, which comes afterwards. The estimating process begins with an inventory of staff skills and experience. All members of the study team can be rated on a scale from 0 (low proficiency) to 10 (high proficiency) on their applications knowledge, technical skills, and productivity. From these ratings, variance factors can be established, preferably by individual, or alternatively, by job title.

- *Knowledge factor* This is two-fold. The *required* level of knowledge (that which is needed to perform the job) may change from task to task depending upon the complexity of the topic. Required knowledge may be expressed in terms such as 'much' (detailed knowledge of the topic is required; the topic is complex), 'some' (proficient knowledge of the topic is helpful; the topic is not complex), and 'none' (background understanding of the topic is not necessary; the topic is easy).

The *staff* level of knowledge refers to the experience (or lack of experience) brought to the task. This may be represented as 'expert' (extensive experience with the topic), 'proficient' (previous experience with and good knowledge of the topic), 'familiar' (acquaintance with and understanding of the topic; possibly without prior experience), 'related' (unfamiliarity with the topic, but good knowledge of related topics), and 'none' (no experience with this or related topics).

- *Technical skill factor*   The technical skill factor of the person assigned to the task will vary based on the required skills for that particular task. An individual with multiple skills may have multiple skill levels, and a task may require one or more of the skills at any one level. Technical skills may be described as 'senior level' (expert with many successful assignments), 'middle level' (proficient with successful responsible assignments), 'junior level' (gaining proficiency with some assignments completed), and 'trainee' (novice with only classroom-type exercises or assignment experience).
- *Productivity factor*   Variance in the productivity factor can have a considerable effect on both the cost and schedule of the study, and must, therefore, be carefully considered in the estimating process. The productivity factor represents the portion of an individual's day that is actually productive. It takes into account the usually ignored time consumers such as computer downtime, unavailability of resources, coffee breaks, travel, and unscheduled meetings. Studies conducted on the amount of time spent productively during an average eight-hour day have shown that 5.6 hours may be considered the norm. Since that is only 70 per cent of the time that is usually considered to be available (that is, eight hours), any plan based on the 100 per cent figure is doomed to failure at the outset.

The number of work days and the cost of labour are easier to calculate than the individual variance factors. Most organizations have a breakdown of the charge rate for each job classification which includes annual salary, benefits, and overheads.

Once an inventory of the skills and experience of the staff has been made, the available work days and labour charges calculated, and the variance factors identified and computed, the cost and effort (measured as time spent) of each task may be estimated. The effort is best estimated for the individual rather than for the job itself since different individuals will have varying knowledge and skill levels. The task list developed initially can be referred to for time estimates to be incorporated into the estimation of effort. Computing the cost estimate for each task takes into account the labour charge rate for each job multiplied by the estimated effort. Additional costs include hardware and software, the involvement of others outside the study team, special education and training required, facilities, supplies, and travel.

The estimating process, especially the personnel proficiency ratings, may, at first glance, appear to be an inordinate amount of work. The fact is, however, that before one can tackle a problem, one must know what resources are available to assist with the tackling. When undertaking a study, the staff personnel which make up the study team are the major resource. If the average proficiency level of the staff members is relatively low, the entire study is going to take longer because a learning curve is a time-consuming factor.

Scheduling

Scheduling is no more than planning to accomplish a task or objective at a certain time or date — a deadline. But within that simple definition lie the details for meeting that deadline. A well-thought-out schedule can result in evenly-paced activities leading to satisfactory study completion. A poorly-developed schedule, by comparison, can result in cut corners and/or missed milestones leading to dissatisfaction with the study and the people performing it.

Scheduling is the process of assigning resources to tasks. The schedule for a particular study should identify each task — its sequence, dependencies, assignee, duration, begin and end dates, and acceptable slack time. Schedules are driven by time, resources, or budget, so these and other constraints, such as task dependencies, planned (and unplanned) time off from work, personnel turnover, relocation, and hardware or software changes or upgrades must be considered.

One of the most popular scheduling tools is the scheduling chart. A scheduling chart graphically represents the entire study process. Two types of charts commonly used are Gantt and PERT. Because information regarding these (and other) charting techniques is readily available in the management literature, only a brief explanation will be provided here.

A Gantt chart (the name comes from its originator, Henry L. Gantt) is basically a horizontal bar chart showing the chronological flow of tasks in order of task initiation. It can also be used to show the allocation of work days to an individual or group working on a particular task. (See Figure 4.1.)

A PERT (Programme Evaluation and Review Technique) chart is much more complex in that it is designed to indicate both task dependencies and the critical path (the segments with the longest duration) through the project. Rather than just indicating various task starts and finishes independently, each task is shown in its relationship to other tasks. (See Figure 4.2.)

A scheduling chart is a good idea for most studies. The complexity of the chart, however, should be commensurate with the complexity of the job being charted. Generally, PERT charts are useful for scheduling large multi-faceted projects such as designing and implementing a major computer installation or constructing a records centre. For routine studies of office systems and procedures, a Gantt chart is usually sufficient. Persons with microcomputers will find that there are several commercially available software packages which will automate the scheduling process and ease the project monitoring task.

UNDERSTANDING AS THE KEY TO PROBLEM SOLVING

The most basic question in management analysis is, 'Does the job need to be done?' By job, we do not mean the individual functions of typing, filing, or processing microfilm, but the final result of all systems functions combined. If the system (and perhaps even the organization) being studied does not have to exist, it stands to reason that the individual functions being performed are superfluous.

If there is one area that could be said to cause inexperienced management analysts the greatest problem, it is accepting the philosophy that nothing should be taken for granted. But the fact is that performing useless work more efficiently does not increase the corporate margin. Far greater benefits can be derived from eliminating an unnecessary operation than from improving it.

It is not outrageous to begin an assignment which calls for reviewing a filing scheme by questioning the value of the files. It is not inappropriate to start a study for a potential microfilm conversion by asking why the paper documents are kept in the first place. It is not heretical to begin a feasibility analysis for an automated reporting system by asking what would happen if the manual system were merely abolished.

If an activity were not performed at all, what would be the result? If an activity must be performed, could it possibly be reduced in scale? A successful management analysis effort requires that everything be challenged, and the analyst must always keep in mind that just because something is, does not mean that it should be.

Systems and procedures must be studied from the perspective of those operating or performing them and also from the perspective of the persons or organizations being

Figure 4.1 Gantt chart

Activity/Tasks	Timeline – weeks from project start																		Level of effort			
	1	2	3	4	5	6	7	8	9	10	11	12	13	14	15	16	17	18	SIT	JIT	TE	GA
Develop manuals for records and management information studies course																						
1 Review and develop content																			5			
2 Draft and review design																			5			
3 Draft and review sample sections																			4	1		
4 Develop first draft of instructor and student manuals																			15	2		
5 Develop final draft of instructor and student manuals																			6	2	3	24
6 Produce final copy of manuals																			5	2		
																			40	7	3	24

30

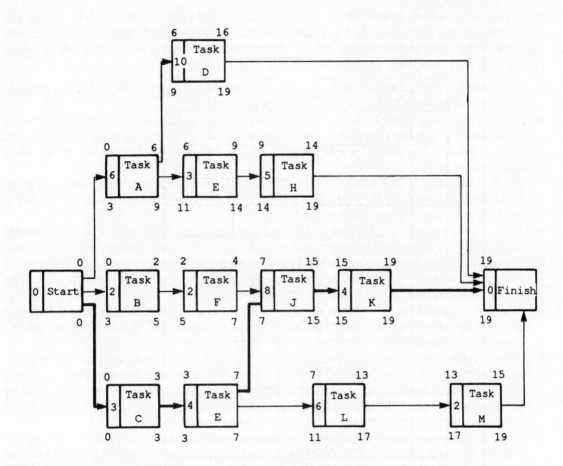

Figure 4.2   PERT chart (critical path shown by heavy line)

served. It is not always easy to balance the various needs and wants, but only with a full appreciation of all requirements and all points of view will it be possible to adequately determine if improvements can be made that will truly benefit those involved.

Assuming that the operation is to remain (which will be the situation the vast majority of the time), the total system should be reviewed generally at an early stage to see whether there are simpler ways of performing the various tasks. Not all problems are major ones, and often it is possible to make improvements simply by studying the basic operational requirements. For example, a system might have been well-designed initially and subsequently became inefficient because of a workload increase.

Obtaining the overall picture is not always a simple task. It is often difficult to get a general understanding of the work methods and procedures because a great many people simply cannot explain what they are doing in any coherent fashion. Moreover, there may be great differences between the duties as officially described in the position descriptions and those actually being performed. Nevertheless, it is essential that the analyst clearly understand the entire mechanism before beginning to work on the component parts. Once the general understanding is obtained, the detailed gathering of data can begin.

Selective questioning

A large part of management analysis work consists of gathering facts. As important as facts are, however, they must be collected selectively because excessive fact-finding results in an accumulation of information which is difficult to analyse. The sole criterion for collecting facts is their relevance to the problem. In that context, the analyst should ask specifically about the nature and amount of work, its purpose, the people who do it, the methods used, and the structure of the organization within which the work is being performed. The following are typical questions:

- *What work is being done?*   Ask about the process — are people typing, filing, copying, writing, answering phones, attending meetings, etc.?
- *Why is the work done?*   Is any part unnecessary? What would happen if it were eliminated? What are the results? Work on one process may seem to be justifiable yet when considered as part of a total system may be found to be duplicative, overly time consuming, or just unnecessary.
- *How much work is being done?*   Are the activities measurable? If so, have they been measured? If not, how do managers know when workers produce enough? Is there a backlog and, if so, when did it begin?
- *Who does the work?*   Is the work efficiently and equitably distributed? Are the people sufficiently qualified and experienced? Could any of the work be done by persons of a lower grade, or, should higher-graded personnel be employed for greater effectiveness? Is there adequate supervision? Is there too much supervision? (These questions will tie in with those relating to organization structure.)
- *Where is the work done?*   Is the work centralized or decentralized? Would a different location be advantageous? Are working conditions adequte? Is necessary equipment conveniently located?
- *When is the work done?*   Does the work proceed in a timely manner? Are there inordinate delays in the process? Are deadlines reasonable? Is the sequence of events correct? Could steps in the later stages of the process be simplified or eliminated by modifying or extending an earlier step? Are inspections or quality control checks performed at the right time?
- *How is the organization structured?*   Is the overall organization properly balanced? Are the lines of authority clearly defined? Is the supervisory span of control reasonable? Is the work divided evenly and logically? Are authorities and responsibilities delegated to the lowest level possible? Is there co-ordination between managers and staffs of the various units which must interact to get the job done? Are the downward and upward communication lines open?

By asking the correct questions the analyst can often encourage others to provide meaningful information. Often the presence of an objective outsider who appears sympathetic to problems and eager to remedy them will stimulate people to think about their jobs in new and different ways and may also get them to offer valuable ideas and suggestions.

There is one other question that needs to be asked regarding an intangible, yet extremely important, area. The issue of staff morale is often an underlying factor behind office system deficiencies. No 'people system' (and almost all office systems are people systems) will function effectively if the people are discontent. The human mind, being as creative as it is, can find extraordinarily subtle ways to throw a wrench into the organizational works. Often employees may not even consciously realize that the spanner is being thrown, but the fact is that, given the same working conditions, people who feel good about their jobs and their employers will outperform those who do not.

A morale problem is usually the easiest difficulty to spot and the hardest to remedy. No amount of new paint, carpet, furniture, or equipment will adequately substitute for an evenhanded supervisor or a fair salary. Moreover, managers frequently do not want to deal with what are usually very uncomfortable or delicate issues. Providing specific recommendations for improving the morale conditions in an operation is usually not within the scope of the management analysis effort. However, it is necessary that an analyst who uncovers such a problem report it to management either as a part of the formal report, or, if more appropriate, in a special meeting called to discuss the situation.

Information sources

The ways in which a management analyst can obtain information are many and varied. The following are the most often used sources:

- *Existing documentation* Documentation such as organization charts, work distribution reports, production statistics, procedures manuals, and previous studies of the system or organization should be readily available and provided by management or senior staff members.
- *Direct observation* The management analyst should examine the operational work methods and procedures and should discuss the job with those concerned. Occasionally, the analyst may perform some or all of the tasks to get a feel for exactly what is involved in the process.
- *Records* Information should be obtained about processes, actions, or decisions from both active and inactive records. Sometimes it will be found that employees are keeping 'personal' copies of correspondence, indexes, files, and other records in addition to the official ones. This type of personal material often contains a wealth of information. Its very existence may suggest that people have reason to believe that the official records are inadequate.
- *Outside Research* Materials prepared by others outside the organization that relate to the subject. For example, when preparing a records retention schedule, applicable laws must generally be researched in a law library.
- *Questionnaires* These are useful to obtain data over a wide area (such as an interdepartmental study) or where one needs to know detailed information from geographically-remote locations (such as branch or field offices). Questionnaires are better for collecting statistical information than narrative. It is difficult to word questions so that everybody will interpret them the same way, and people generally have neither the time nor the inclination to write meaningful responses to philosophical open-ended enquiries.

  When questionnaires are used, specific response deadlines should be established and clearly indicated to the respondents. The deadline should be set in advance of the time when the data will actually be needed because people will inevitably be late with their submissions. Response times should be reasonable, yet not overly long. A short deadline will provoke complaints, and a long deadline will result in the questionnaires being put aside and forgotten.
- *Forms and logs* Often there is no relevant or accurate data on the system. When this is the case, such data will have to be collected as part of the study in order to have a baseline from which to make comparisons or projections. Because the data collected varies from study to study, forms and logs are usually not available as stock items and are, therefore, developed on an as-needed basis by the management analyst. An experienced analyst maintains a master set of such data collection devices used on previous studies or, at least, knows which reference materials contain model examples.
- *Interviews* Information about goals and objectives, relationships, authorities, attitudes, and general organizational atmosphere can often only be obtained by direct questioning. Interviewing, therefore, is one of the most important aspects of the management analyst's job. Successful interviewing requires a high degree of skill, because the purpose of an interview is not only to obtain raw data, but to get the ideas of the person being interviewed regarding potential system improvements.

  Arrangements for an interview should always be made with the knowledge of the manager or supervisor in charge of the particular operation. Information regarding the general nature of an individual's job should be obtained beforehand so that the analyst can plan the course of the discussion. The interview should be conducted informally and in a relaxed atmosphere. Questions should be carefully phrased so as to avoid implying criticism of the interviewee or his work. The person should clearly understand that it is the system being studied, not the people. While analysts must guide the conversation with their questions, they should listen more than they talk.

As much as possible, interviews should be scheduled so as not to interfere with work requirements. Some interruption, however, is expected. If the situation is at all likely to inhibit discussion, the management analyst must arrange to have an area where interviews may be held in private.

The length of the interview will depend, to a large extent, on the interviewee. The analyst should be aware of signs (body language, facial expressions, etc.) that the person has had enough. Several short sessions are better than one long one. Even under the best of conditions, people being interviewed often feel pressured and are apt to give inadequate or erroneous information if the discussion goes on too long.

Additional points to be considered are:

- *Avoid leading questions.* Encourage the interviewee to express his own thoughts. If there is hesitation in answering, be patient. Do *not* answer for the person.
- *If the person does not know the answer to a question, leave it.* The goal should be to collect accurate information, not information based on guesses or suppositions. Often the key question 'why' can only be answered after the interviewee has been given substantial time to think about it.
- *Ask for comments and suggestions.* Elicit ideas on methods, systems, procedures, or organization. A question such as, 'If you were in charge, what would you do differently?' can provide interesting results.
- *Check the facts.* Before the interview ends, review the ground covered to ensure that the information provided has been understood.

Note-taking during an interview is up to the judgement of the analyst. If the goal is to get a lot of detailed information, taking complete notes as the discussion progresses may be necessary. If the aim is to get general impressions, short notes may suffice. Tape recorders should be used with caution. They often tend to inhibit people from engaging in free and open discussion, and, additionally, can create more work for the analyst if the tapes have to be transcribed, edited, or summarized.

Fact-finding guidelines

There are no hard and fast rules to follow when collecting information. Analysts must be flexible and modify their techniques to fit the environment in which they are working. The following guidelines, which are applicable regardless of the methodology used, will help to ensure that accurate data are obtained:

- *Be organized* Information should be collected systematically and verified as soon as possible after its collection. Notes should be neat, legible, and clearly identifiable. Files for the data obtained should be logically organized so that the information is easily referenced.
- *Obtain first-hand information* Except at the beginning of a study when it is necessary to meet collectively with several of the principals who are concerned with the system or operation, the group method of fact-gathering should be avoided. It is better to have individual conversations with people so that information is more openly and accurately given, and sensitive issues are more honestly discussed. Supervisors should not be present during interviews with their employees. Although supervisors may wish to help by giving their own versions of how the work is being done, this information is often only valuable for comparison and should not be used in lieu of that which can be obtained from the worker.
- *Do not confuse facts and opinions* Facts are facts and opinions are not. This does not mean, however, that all opinions are invalid. Opinions may be the result of much thought and experience and may provide information that is not available from files or

statistics. The analyst should carefully weigh the value of any statements of opinion, regardless of the source, and accept only those which seem to have exceptional validity based on other factual information obtained or situations observed.

- *Obtain complete information* The data collected must be truly representative of the overall situation. If the workload has significant cyclical fluctuations, collecting only data relating to one phase of the cycle will not be adequate. It may be necessary to work at certain times, on various days, or at certain points during a month or year. There may be great variations in the work methods used during the different periods.
- *Use definitive terminology* The terms people use to describe work are often indefinite. Vague phrases such as 'co-ordinates', 'deals with', and 'handles' are not meaningful in an analytical context. The analyst should challenge such descriptions and find out what is really happening.
- *Do not overlook the obvious* Operations of a routine nature, which may seem unimportant and mundane to the person who is doing them, may be quite important to the smooth functioning of the overall system. The analyst should carefully observe the working areas and question the purpose of all files, records, reference materials, or office machines which have not been specifically referred to and explained by the persons performing the work.

COSTING

When determining the cost of a system or operation, there are four types of resources that must be considered. These are:

- direct personnel costs
- direct equipment, materials, and supplies costs
- other direct costs
- overhead costs.

Personnel costs

These consist of direct labour and fringe benefit costs. The direct labour cost is that portion of employee salaries that is chargeable to the system. The fringe benefits cost (which is expressed as a percentage of the salary cost) consists of allowances and services provided to employees in addition to their salaries.

To compile the direct labour cost for a system, two items of information are needed: firstly, the amount of time it takes to perform the system activities, and, secondly, the rate of pay of the personnel performing them. The amount of time can be expressed in either work-hours or work-years. When determining the direct labour cost, the actual salary rates should be used for existing positions if they are obtainable. If they are not obtainable, the median salary rate for the particular grade level should be used. Table 4.1 shows one

Table 4.1
Direct labour operational cost

Activity	Grade	Annual salary (£)	Hourly rate (£)*	Time required per year	Total direct cost (£)
Source document preparation	230	24 500	11.77	50 hours	589
Source document coding	125	12 600		1 year	12 600

*The hourly rate is determined by dividing the annual salary by the number of working hours in a year (2087 used here).

method of computing the direct labour costs when the amount of time spent on an activity and the grades of the personnel performing the activity are known. Although the example used is for operational activity costs, the same procedure may be used for computing development and user costs.

The fringe benefit cost consists of retirement/disability, health and life insurance, and other employee benefits, such as work disability, unemployment programmes, bonuses, and awards. The fringe benefit cost is expressed as a percentage of the salary cost expended on the activity. Fringe benefit costs vary considerably from organization to organization and should be determined on an individual basis. This percentage factor should be obtainable from an organization's budget office which determines the actual fringe benefit costs annually. Table 4.2 shows the procedure for compiling the fringe benefit cost.

Table 4.2
Calculating fringe benefit cost

Direct labour cost (developmental, operational, and user)	×	Fringe benefit cost factor	=	Fringe benefit cost
£500 000	×	10.5 per cent	=	£50 000

Equipment, materials, and supplies costs

These refer to costs that are directly expended on a reporting system or activity. Examples of the types of equipment that may be included are computers, word processors, printers, microfilm readers, copiers, and calculators. Examples of the types of materials and supplies are magnetic tape, paper, microfilm, copier toner, printer ribbons, etc. In cases where equipment is used for more than one system, the cost should be pro-rated so that only the share used specifically for the system being costed is included in the calculation. The equipment cost should include acquisition as well as transportation and installation costs. This cost should be amortized over a period of years depending on the useful life of the equipment and consistent with the organization's accounting procedures. The annual equipment maintenance charges should also be included. Table 4.3 shows the procedure for determining equipment cost.

Table 4.3
Sample calculation of annual
equipment cost

Item	microcomputer
Acquisition cost	£5000
Annual cost on 5-year amortization (£5000 ÷ 5 = £1000)	£1000
Percentage of time used for reports operations	95 per cent
Annual equipment cost (except maintenance) (£1000 × 0.95 = £950)	£950

Other direct costs

These consist of purchased services, and operations and activities for which fees are charged, such as ADP and printing charges. An example of this is the charge-back user fee imposed on an office for the time spent using a terminal to access a mainframe computer data base.

Overhead costs

These are costs incurred by an organization to support the accomplishment of its overall purpose. These costs are called overhead, or indirect costs, because they apply to activities which benefit the entire organization rather than any one particular function or section. Included in overhead costs are the following:

- Supervisory personnel salaries and fringe benefits
- Clerical and technical personnel salaries and fringe benefits
- Supplies and common distribution items such as telephones and electricity
- Space and utilities.

Each organization concerned with developing a system for determining reporting costs should compute its own overhead rates. Before that rate can be computed, however, it is important to establish what overhead base to use in terms of the organizational levels to be included. This determination is based on the levels included in the system being costed. For example, if a system had been developed for a particular section, division, or office, the overhead base would be established at the commensurate organizational level. However, if the system encompasses the entire organization, the overhead would consist of all the organization's supervisory, technical and clerical, common supplies, space, and utilities costs.

There are several ways of determining the overhead rate factor. One method is to obtain the ratio between an organization's direct purpose costs and its overhead costs. The steps for calculating this rate factor are as follows:

- Obtain the total overhead cost for the organization affected by the reporting system. Be sure to *exclude* that portion of supervisory, clerical, and technical personnel costs attributable to the reporting system itself. For example:

	£
Supervisory (salary and fringe benefits)	760 000
Clerical/technical (salary and fringe benefits)	170 000
Supplies	135 000
Common distribution (telephone and other common terms)	88 000
Space and utilities	83 000
Total overhead cost	1 236 000

- Obtain the total amount of the annual budget for that organization and subtract the total overhead cost from the budget figure. The remaining portion is the amount expended *directly* on the accomplishment of the organization's purpose. For example:

	£
Total budget	3 200 000
Total overhead	1 236 000
Direct mission cost	1 964 000

- Compute the overhead rate factor for the reporting system by dividing the total overhead cost by the direct mission cost, as follows:

	£
Total overhead cost	1 236 000
Direct mission cost	1 964 000
Overhead rate factor	0.63
	(63 per cent)

These costing procedures are applicable to any system, manual or automated. Care must be taken to use a consistent costing method when figuring the cost of old and new systems activities to ensure that the subsequent analytical comparison of the two will be accurate.

ANALYSING AND DRAWING CONCLUSIONS

There comes a time in every study when the data collecting ceases and the intensive data analysis begins. Analysis is the most important aspect of the work.

During the analysis, thinking and reasoning are not confined to any particular stage of the assignment. As the work proceeds, the analyst is always comparing one bit of information with another, all the while keeping in mind the overall goals and objectives of the system or organization being studied. At the end of the data collection phase, however, the analytical effort becomes the predominant activity and is therefore considered as a separate function.

When analysing office systems and procedures, there is no set of formulae which can be used to find the answers to the problems. While there are certain managerial theories which have been developed over the years on subjects such as supervisory span of control, and centralization versus decentralization, generally one will find that those theories are more easily studied than applied.

Effective analysis of information systems (whether manual or automated) requires that a common-sense approach be taken. The principles and techniques that one must know to design information systems (filing rules, forms design, data-base concepts, microfilm reduction ratios, etc.) can only be applied effectively in an overall environment of rationality. The underlying factor to consider is that the system must work, not just look good on the drawing board.

Essentially, analysis is the mental process of reviewing all data which has been collected by questioning, asking additional questions, and then drawing conclusions. Figure 4.3 illustrates this process.

Although it is impractical to try and explain how one should think during this requestioning period, the following briefly describes the basic thought process which may be engaged in to achieve successful results:

- Define the purpose of the work. Ensure that you have a complete understanding of exactly what is trying to be accomplished.
- Without any limitations, think of all the ways the work might be performed. Be imaginative, creative, and consider even idealistic schemes.
- Identify the problems inhibiting the accomplishment of the work and the situations that need to be changed.
- Consider how the ideas that you had in the second thought phase could help to overcome the problems identified in the third. Think of different methods for carrying out the entire procedure. Think of ideas that will improve both efficiency and effectiveness.
- Identify the restrictions and mitigating circumstances which would preclude implementation of the ideas proposed (for example, corporate policies, monetary limitations, legal requirements, etc.).

To get the facts – ASK:	ASK – WHY?	To make improvements – ASK:
NEED What offices and what people recieve the information? What recipients use the information? What procedures describe the origin, distribution and use of the information?	WHY this need?	**NEED** How is the information used? Is it absolutely essential? How much does it cost? Is it worth the cost? Is there another source for all or a portion of this data?
PEOPLE Who requires this data? Who enters information on the basic document? Who extracts or manipulates data from the source document? Who analyses the data? Who makes the decisions?	WHY by these people?	**PEOPLE** Can the work be done by someone else? Can some or all of it be done by machine? Can any of it be done co-operatively? Do employees know their procedures? Is work performed at the right grade/level? Are duties related or varied? Are supervision and training adequate?
PLACE Where is the source document prepared? How many copies are made? Where are completed documents sent? How are they transmitted? Where is the information used? Where is the information summarized and published?	WHY here?	**PLACE** Is this the best place to prepare the source document? Is it closest to the source of information? Is it best equipped to do the job? Is equipment utilized for a variety of jobs, or just used for source data jobs? Could another office do it as well or better? Would another location speed transmission and use?
TIME What is the time schedule for obtaining the data? What are the deadlines for the final products? How much time is allotted to each process?	January WHY at this time?	**TIME** Is the time factor critical? Can peak loads be levelled by doing the job at a different time? Is the time factor realistic? Should frequency be altered? Can timing of related events be changed?
METHOD How is the source document prepared? What machines or tools are used? How is the information processed? Are there quality or production standards? Are production and quality controlled?	MEMO WHY this method?	**METHOD** Is there a better or faster way for entering data on the source document? Can data on the source document be prepared in a machine language? Are processing steps taken in a logical order? Can any processing steps be eliminated? Can parellel processing be substituted for serial processing?

Figure 4.3   The analytical process

- Determine the most *practical* solution.

While the effort, as stated, is a mental one, it does not mean that the analyst is confined to dealing with only mental images and abstractions. Spreadsheets (computerized or otherwise) may be used; statistical formulas may be applied; mathematical models may be constructed; and a whole host of other techniques are available for employment as the situation requires. If the situation does not require the utilization of complex methodologies, however, it is better to leave them unused.

Although some analysts like to include esoteric equations and convoluted diagrams in their reports because they think such things are impressive to management, the practice is one that is best avoided. The sophistication of the analytical process should be irrelevant to the manager who is seeking a solution to a problem. The only significant concern is that the solution be sound and workable.

Simplified flowcharting

There is one analytical technique that is invaluable to the management analyst, and that is simplified flowcharting. Yet, unlike subjects such as statistics or organization theory, on which a myriad of reference materials can be found (and which are, therefore, not detailed in this book), simplified flowcharting has been generally ignored in management literature. The method is therefore presented here.

A flowchart is a graphic representation of a process; in effect, a picture of a system. With an ordinary flowchart, symbols are used to represent documents, actions, and machines. A template designed for ordinary flowcharting might have 18 to 21 symbols or more. Because everything that is happening in the system is represented, and because the symbols are not specifically identified throughout the diagram, the picture can get very confusing. Simplified flowcharting, by comparison, uses between five and eight symbols representing only documents and machines. The action is described by brief narrative statements placed below the symbols, and each symbol is specifically identified every time it is used. Figure 4.4(a)-(d) clearly explains the process.

A simplified flowchart is helpful to the analyst not only for analytical purposes, but also for illustrative purposes when conducting a management briefing to present the results of the study. 'Before and after' flowcharts are often much more effective than lengthy explanations for describing improvements made.

THE REPORT

When the analysis work is completed, the management analyst must write a report to management detailing the findings and providing recommendations for improvement. Depending on the nature and complexity of the study, the report could take on the form of a two-page memorandum or a 100-page volume. One should not make the mistake of equating size with usefulness, however. As a general rule, smaller is better. Astute managers do not care how much a report 'weighs'. What is important is the information that a report contains.

A complete and effective survey report covers topics such as:

- *Background/Rationale* — Why the study was done. For whom, by whom. Include begin and end dates. Add other significant data as appropriate.
- *Methodology* — Identify the universe (organization, geographic location, etc.). Identify the principals (study team, department heads, etc.). Explain the techniques used (questionnaires, interviews, sampling, on-site processing, etc.).
- *Findings* — Summarize the facts obtained which relate directly to the problems being solved. Except for explaining special circumstances or unusual occurrances, do not go into great detail. Rather, identify trends and patterns and generally outline the process.

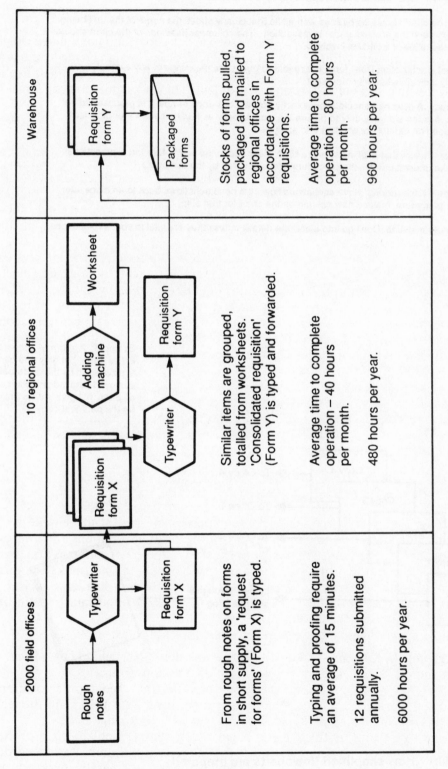

Figure 4.4(a) Simplified flowcharting. This example shows a basic manual system for processing requisitions for forms

41

Only a few basic rules are involved in simplified flow charts.

- Title The chart should be headed with a title that clearly states the name of the unit being surveyed and the process under investigation. The columnar headings of the chart should show the office or work unit involved.

- Symbol identification Don't force the reader to guess the meanings of any symbol. Clearly indicate what they represent.

- Accuracy A flowchart should show exactly how a job is done or how it is proposed to be done. It is the analyst's duty to picture the work exactly as he/she sees it – or proposes it – based on careful observation and analysis.

- Brevity Ensure that explanations are brief, clear and to the point. Use the explanations to make understandable the procedural steps covered by the symbols.

- Eliminate backtracking Have continuous flow. If a document flows back to an office later in the procedure, make a new column on the chart for that step.

    Eliminate minutiae Don't go into elaborate details unless they are vital to your explanations.

Example: If a form is prepared in five parts, but only one part is processed by the office being surveyed, show distribution of all parts, but give details only for the pertinent copy

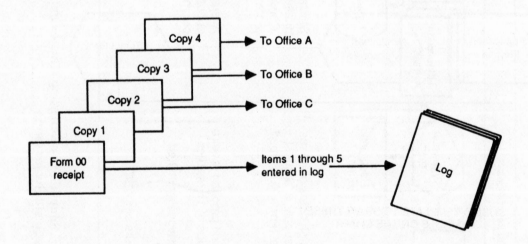

Figure 4.4(b)   How simplified flowcharts are prepared

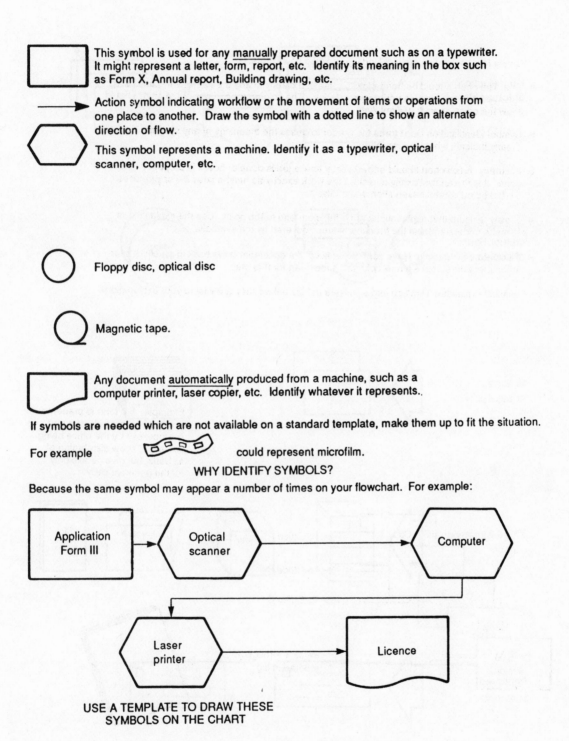

This symbol is used for any <u>manually</u> prepared document such as on a typewriter. It might represent a letter, form, report, etc. Identify its meaning in the box such as Form X, Annual report, Building drawing, etc.

Action symbol indicating workflow or the movement of items or operations from one place to another. Draw the symbol with a dotted line to show an alternate direction of flow.

This symbol represents a machine. Identify it as a typewriter, optical scanner, computer, etc.

Floppy disc, optical disc

Magnetic tape.

Any document <u>automatically</u> produced from a machine, such as a computer printer, laser copier, etc. Identify whatever it represents..

If symbols are needed which are not available on a standard template, make them up to fit the situation.

For example could represent microfilm.

WHY IDENTIFY SYMBOLS?

Because the same symbol may appear a number of times on your flowchart. For example:

Application Form III → Optical scanner → Computer

Laser printer → Licence

USE A TEMPLATE TO DRAW THESE SYMBOLS ON THE CHART

Figure 4.4(c)   The use of symbols in simplified flowcharting

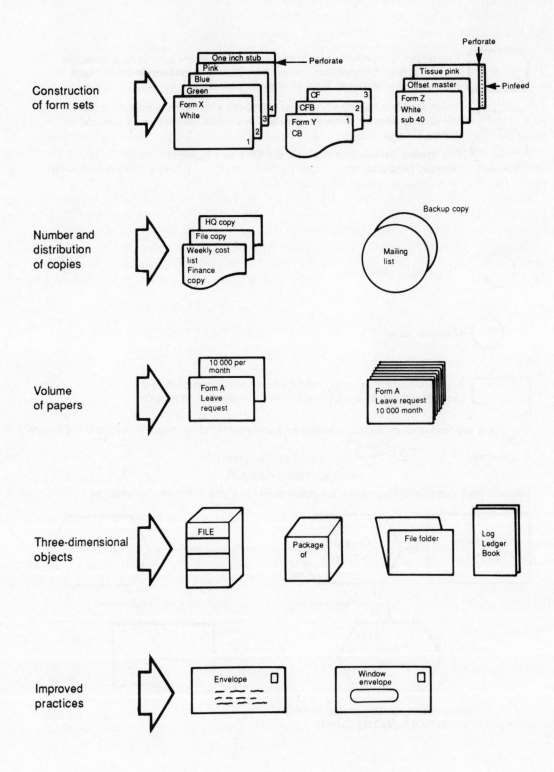

Figure 4.4(d)   Simplified flowcharting — what symbols may illustrate

- *Analysis* — Summarize the analytical thought process which led to the conclusions. Explain everything in an organized and logical manner so that the conclusions will be identified by the reader before reaching the next section.
- *Conclusions/Recommendations* — Outline specific steps to be taken. Present alternatives if appropriate. Include potential resultant cost savings when applicable.

The information in each section should be well organized and clearly presented. The above is general guidance. It may not apply in all instances and should be modified as necessary. For example, in a very short report the methodology section might be eliminated entirely. In a lengthy report, appendices might be added to provide supporting detail. Many analysts like to combine the findings and analysis sections as that often makes for a more easily followed presentation. For relatively long reports, an additional executive summary section may be added which compresses the essence of the entire presentation into several pages for review by top-level management.

Formats, type styles, bindings, cover sheets, and other packaging specifications should be consistent with organizational standards. Unlike weight, the appearance of the product is important. A sloppy-looking report may never even get read.

Management analysis techniques are an integral part of records management, and are used constantly in the process of solving records and information systems problems. The first and most comprehensive exercise of these skills will be in the information survey.

5 The Information Survey

Originally, a records survey (or inventory) was done in order to identify all record series and the extent of their use, for the purpose of devising retention/disposal schedules. Records series are groups of records arranged in accordance with a filing system or maintained as a unit because they relate to a particular subject or function, result from the same activity, have a particular form, or because of some other relationship arising out of their creation, receipt, or use. The survey was also focused on the systems used for maintaining and filing active records, and on gaining the information necessary for the establishment of forms and reports control programmes.

This kind of survey was centred around the filing cabinet and the mail room. Questions were asked about the title of a record series, the type of documents it contained, what method of filing was used in what kind of equipment. The records analyst wanted to know who originated documents, to whom they were sent, how important they were, how long they were needed in the office and later in storage, and when they could be destroyed. The records analyst would look through files and interview staff until he/she understood the purpose and actual use and value of the record series and its documents. Incidentally, this person would have a fuller understanding of the records flow and use in the organization than would any other person in that organization.

Now, it is this very understanding, this view of the whole, that is the true goal of records analysts. Before they can consider devising retention/disposal schedules, or making improvements in filing equipment or systems, they must consider the whole information structure of the organization. Who creates or brings in what kind of information? How do they use it? Why? Do they get all that they need? Do they share it? Can they benefit from information used by another department? Do the communications systems support or inhibit the transfer and use of information? Most importantly, what are the goals of the whole organization and what are its information requirements in order to achieve them?

The procedures of the records survey are altered little by this change of emphasis and broadening of scope. More, it is the awareness of the analyst that must change, so that every question asked, while it may be about a small detail, will aim at an understanding of the full information structure.

The initial information survey is a gathering of all available information about existing records in an organization. This type of survey is done not just to design a system, but to design a records management programme for the whole organization. The survey is the primary source of the information necessary to plan programmes on retention scheduling, vital records protection, reports management, forms control, indexing systems, and records storage. It is an opportunity to discover all current recordkeeping problems and to anticipate future ones.

Later, when a records management programme is established and operating, surveys of a smaller, more specific, scope may be necessary. Examples of purposes for such surveys might be to:

- provide a basis for establishing a vital records programme;
- gather information to determine what records should be microfilmed;
- help plan the information requirements for a new building;
- serve as a basis for evaluating the effectiveness of active filing systems;
- identify all historically significant records in order to establish an archives;
- survey all equipment and supplies used for active records;
- provide statistics for evaluating commercial versus in-house records centre storage;
- assess the appropriateness of a new technology, for example, optical disc, for the management of certain information;
- determine the need for a policy regarding official records maintained in machine-readable form on executive work stations;
- gather information pertinent to a feasibility study for organization-wide office automation.

The survey must be planned carefully, so that all needed information will be obtained. It must be executed with thoroughness while causing as little disruption as possible. It can be expected to be time consuming; and also disconcerting if personnel are not properly informed in advance. In spite of the difficulty of doing a survey, it is absolutely crucial to the creation of any records management programme and, as the sole opportunity for gathering so much detailed information about the organization, it cannot be omitted.

WHY DO A RECORDS SURVEY?

The greatest value of the survey is that it gives, as one's first view of an organization's information, a reasonably objective and complete overview of the records, their real uses, and of the organization itself. Other reasons are:

- To know what information exists — While everyone will have a good approximation of what information they produce, no one will know all that exists in the entire organization. Before any changes can be suggested, the records manager must have a thorough knowledge of what actually exists.
- To know what the records are and the procedures for working with them — It is necessary to identify and have at least a basic understanding of the function of each type of record, including its path flow, who produces it and why, who needs it, what is done to it, the purpose it serves.
- To learn the users' information needs — No one will provide better (or worse) suggestions than some of the users. They know the information thoroughly and can give a history of how it was used, and of failed or successful programmes in the past.
- To know all of the available storage media — Changing media is expensive. An organization may have just made a big investment in a particular medium of information storage, or may refuse to do so, or may have disparate and incompatible media. No suggestions or proposals can be made before there is a catalogue of existing media (paper, microfilm, discs, etc.) and their uses.
- To obtain preliminary retention periods — Traditionally the main reason for performing the survey, the preliminary retention periods allow one to begin preparations for a records retention programme as soon as the survey is completed.

Thus, the survey will be the tool used to find out everything necessary for the design, justification, and establishment of a records management programme.

MEMORANDUM

To: All employees
From: The Managing Director
Subject: Records Management Survey

Our company has a serious filing and recordkeeping problem, and we have begun to take steps to find a solution. Starting next month, John Smith and a team of assistants will conduct a survey of all files, computers and microfilm, within the company. They will ask all of you questions about your information and filing needs and problems. They will also require your attendance while they look through the files. Please give them all of your assistance. We apologise for the inconvenience but we are certain that the resulting improvements will make it all worthwhile.

Figure 5.1   The pre-survey memorandum

Management support

Because even a well-conducted survey is somewhat disruptive and intrusive, many people will object to it. Without the full support of senior management, the survey will not be a success. This holds true for all records management programmes generally. They usually require major reconsiderations and changes, and these are often resisted. The records manager should find an ally in at least one senior manager, who will, when it becomes necessary, use authority to ensure co-operation.

Before the survey can begin, the senior manager or permanent secretary should send out a general memorandum to all employees, announcing plans for a survey and records management study. This memo should explain when and why the survey will take place, that it will require some time and co-operation from all employees, that confidential and even secret files on paper and computer will have to be seen and explained, and it should ask for the full compliance and co-operation of all employees in the study (see the example shown in figure 5.1). If a records management directive or mandate has already been produced, this memo may not be necessary, but it can't hurt and it could help.

At the same time as this memo is sent, the records manager should obtain the necessary clearances to view any confidential or secret information. It may be necessary for others on the team to have this clearance as well, if there are large amounts of confidential files. Copies of the clearance or authorization should be kept at all times while doing the survey, and given to anyone who asks to see it. The same should be done with a copy of the senior manager's initial, authorizing letter. Many people will say that they have not seen it or have lost it. Rather than let this be an excuse for delay, simply give them a new copy from your supply.

SCHEDULING THE SURVEY

Because a records and information survey can be very disruptive, it must be carefully scheduled with all departments. Introductory and explanatory appointments need to be made:

- Introductory appointments — it will be necessary to make a brief appointment with each department, simply to explain the purpose and procedures of the proposed survey.

Give to each one a copy of the authorizing letter and one of the survey forms to be used. After explaining how the department will be surveyed, ask for the names of key people within that area to be questioned. These will be the contacts who will escort and assist the surveyor. Once the procedure is fully explained and discussed, ask what problems the department head has with the records and information used in the department.

- Explanatory appointments — meet with each of the contacts to explain again, and in more detail, how the survey will proceed. Again, give copies of the authorizing letter and the survey form. Ask that all staff in the area be fully notified that the survey will take place and when. At this time, make the dates for surveying that department or area. Base the number of days spent in each area on the number of employees, giving approximately one day for every 8 or 10 employees.

Be sure to follow this schedule precisely. Allow one free day a week for compiling notes, rescheduling appointments for people who missed the scheduled one, etc. Much of this scheduling can overlap with the actual survey, for example, make initial appointments and start surveying Department A; when nearing the middle of that survey, make initial appointments and schedule for Department B.

Traditional view has it that the survey should begin with the stored records, as a trial run, and there is nothing terribly wrong with this procedure. However, the stored records, in basements or remote buildings, are often mysterious, too old, too peculiar or idiosyncratic to understand. Trying to survey them first often leads to a frustrating failure at the beginning of the project. It is better to do the stored records last, after becoming familiar with all of the active records, and then be able to make quicker and more accurate guesses as to what they might be. The best place to begin the inventory is in a small department that does not have urgent work, and in which at least one secretary or clerk has been working for a few years. In this environment, there will be enough time and knowledge to answer the questions about the records. The environment should also be relaxed enough so that those new to doing the survey will be able to make a few mistakes without dire consequences. Departments with unique documentation, such as the accounts department, should not be one of those first to be surveyed.

STAFFING THE SURVEY

When the organization is large and there are many analysts there should be a project manager. This person will be the primary liaison between the survey team and the staff of the department being surveyed.

SURVEY TASK FORCE

Because records management involves every part of the organization it is helpful to establish a task force for planning and overseeing the records survey. The task force acts in an advisory capacity during the survey planning. It also acts as a resource to the project manager throughout the survey. Depending on the survey's objectives, this task force might consist of the records manager, legal counsel, head of administration, and data processing manager.

INFORMATION COLLECTION

After the letter of authority has gone out, and any specific management briefs concerning the survey have been received, it will be necessary to decide exactly what type of information is to be obtained from the survey, and for what reasons. If the object is to regain space from files, then the space taken by files and equipment will be important to quantify. If the main reason is to reduce costs, then the costs of files storage must be ascertained. Generally, the necessary information to find will be:

- Volume — The amount, in linear or cubic feet, of records and files, the number of terminals and word processors, the number of filing cabinets. The amount of storage space used on the mainframe computer, and the number of floppy discs used.
- Media — The different media on which information is stored, and how, if at all, they are linked: paper, microfilm, discs, audio-cassettes, etc.
- Creation — How and why is information created? Who creates it?
- Paths of distribution — To whom is the information sent, how often, why? Are people receiving reports and letters that they no longer need, that they no longer understand?
- Age — How old is the information on computer, in files, on microfilm? How old is the information in storage?
- Usefulness: active/inactive — How long is the information or record series needed in the office, how long in storage? When can it be destroyed?
- Document/Report/Form types — What kind exist? Who designs them? Who orders them?
- Organization — What kind of filing systems, codes, indexes are used?
- Legal requirements — What are the legal retention periods for any of the reports, forms, documents? What other legal requirements are there, such as specifications of what must be asked, how it must be stored, etc.
- Vital records — What records or information are absolutely vital to the survival and reconstruction of the organization.
- Problems — What problems do the users have with their files and information?

METHODS FOR PERFORMING A RECORDS SURVEY

There are three basic ways to perform a survey: by questionnaire, by committee, and physically. The first two are of less value because they provide the least amount of accurate data, but are here described for information purposes.

Questionnaire

In this method, a questionnaire, asking about all of the topics in the list above is sent to each employee, or in some cases to each section head, asking him/her to describe the information and files that he/she creates and uses. There are many flaws in this method. Users see their work in the most narrow of contexts and cannot understand questions of a more general view. They may not understand certain terms, such as 'retention period', and so provide incorrect or insufficient answers. Questionnaires also take time, and everybody professes to hate them, so usually only 50 per cent are returned. A last, and more serious, failing of this method is that the records manager will often have a very difficult time understanding descriptions of information that was never seen or discussed. However, if used as a preliminary exercise to the physical survey, this can give an initial map to the office and its problems, helping the records manager to plan the focus of the survey more precisely. In very large organizations, of five thousand employees or more, such a preliminary survey by questionnaire could be extremely helpful.

Committee

In this method, representatives from each department meet with the records manager to describe and discuss what exists in the department and to apply preliminary retention periods. This almost never works as it takes a long time for the records manager to explain the reasons for the meeting, to deal with the personalities involved, and to get them to think alike about the information that they use.

Physical survey

In this, the records manager and his/her assistants go from department to department, room to room, looking into every file drawer and video display unit screen, asking questions, and filling out the forms. This method is, by far, the most time consuming and labour intensive, but it does yield the best results, giving a full, clear overview of the organization, its information, and its politics. It cannot be stressed strongly enough that this method of doing the survey is the only one to be considered seriously.

PREPARING FOR THE SURVEY

Having decided on areas of emphasis and on the method of surveying, a form can now be designed. It is unimportant whether it is a box form or a list of questions. This form need not be perfect. It is a worksheet, will be used for this exercise only, and will not be used by anyone but the records manager and the assistants. Ensure that the form is not full of records management 'jargon', so that people are not being asked questions that confuse them. Group the questions by subject on the form, to facilitate processing the information. Leave plenty of room for comments. A too detailed form will be wasted. At times, the survey proceeds so quickly, that only the quickest notes, in shorthand, can be taken.

The records and information inventory form (see the example shown in figure 5.2) will certainly suffice for any survey of which the emphasis is on the reduction of space or costs.

The first section gives the name and location of the area surveyed, the date, and the name of the contact person in that area. To make things easier, this part can be filled in on one form, and that form photocopied, before beginning the investigation of an area.

In the second section the following is required:

- The record class/series title — The record class or series is that group of documents or files which is always treated together. Examples of these are personnel files, invoices, contract negotiations. They may contain many documents as well as correspondence, but the individual files would not be subdivided and separated.
- Dates — The earliest and latest dates of files in that record series. In some cases, where the series is arranged chronologically, this is easy to determine. In others, as with personnel files, it is necessary to examine a sampling of older files to make a guess. This is especially true of stored files, about which nobody can remember anything.
- Filing inches — Estimate the number of inches (or feet or centimetres) being used, on a shelf or in a drawer, by the files. If on microfilm or microfiche, how many rolls or sheets. If on floppy disc, how many discs, of what size, are used for each series? If on the mainframe, there may be a system that bills each department for its use and storage space. If not, it will be necessary to meet later with the computer group to discuss departmental use and storage on-line.
- Equipment — Note the type and size of filing equipment, reader-printers, terminals, word processors, personal computers. Include brand names and model numbers.
- Medium — Is the information stored on paper, microfilm, floppy disc, hard disc, a mainframe held internally or externally, a videocassette?
- Filing/control system — How are the files arranged: alphabetic, numeric, chronological, terminal digit, alphanumeric, etc. Disc and on-line directories will have to be examined, as will microfilm that is not blip-coded.
- Documents and content — List the type of forms, getting blank copies of each, and documentation within the files of the record series.
- Stored elsewhere — Are other files, including duplicates, from that series stored in any other location? Where?

The third section, 'Retention', is for gathering information on the use and requirements of the record series. How long is it needed in the office? How long in storage? Does the user know of any legal requirements? Is the information vital to the functioning of the

```
┌─────────────────────────────────────────────────────────────────────┐
│           RECORDS  AND  INFORMATION  INVENTORY  FORM                  │
│                                                                       │
│  Department group:                          Contact:                  │
│                                                                       │
│  Location:                                  Date:                     │
├─────────────────────────────────────────────────────────────────────┤
│  Record class/series title:                                          │
│                                                                       │
│                                                                       │
│  Dates:                                                               │
│                                                                       │
│  Filing inches:              of which      %    Medium:               │
│                              is inactive                              │
│                                                                       │
│  Equipment:                                 Filing/Control system:    │
│                                                                       │
│  Documents and content:                                               │
│                                                                       │
│                                                                       │
│                                                                       │
│                                                                       │
│                                                                       │
│  Stored elsewhere:                                                    │
├─────────────────────────────────────────────────────────────────────┤
│  **Retention**                                                        │
│                                                                       │
│  Office:                                                              │
│                                                                       │
│  Storage:                                                             │
│                                                                       │
│  Legal:                                                               │
│                                                                       │
│  Vital:                                                               │
│                                                                       │
│  Regular purging:                                                     │
├─────────────────────────────────────────────────────────────────────┤
│  **Data  protection**                                                 │
│                                                                       │
│  Source of information:                                               │
│                                                                       │
│  Purpose of holding:                                                  │
│                                                                       │
│  Future purposes:                                                     │
│                                                                       │
│  Released to:                               Countries:                │
│                                                                       │
│  How accuracy ensured?                                                │
│                                                                       │
│  Security ensured:                                                    │
│                                                                       │
│  Bureaux:                                                             │
└─────────────────────────────────────────────────────────────────────┘
```

Figure 5.2   Records and information inventory form

organization? Is the record series regularly purged or weeded? With electronic records, how often is outdated information deleted or archived? Is it done automatically? Who makes the decisions as to deletion?

The fourth section, 'Data protection', will help to provide the information on personal data necessary for compliance with the UK Data Protection Act 1984 and the US Privacy Act of 1974. However, for a deeper understanding of information requirements, it would be wise to use it for all record series. The source of the information may be the individual, published articles, supervisors, etc. The purpose of holding the information must be clear, for example in order to perform what task? Any future purpose that the user can imagine for holding the information will help in forward planning. The people to whom the information is released must be listed by name and job title. How the accuracy and security are ensured must be clearly detailed. List any bureaux which handle the information, and any countries to which it is sent.

The procedures form, (see the example shown in figure 5.3) should be used in conjunction with the previous form (figure 5.2), where more detail is needed about the use of the information. The first section requests: From whom is the record received, and what actions are performed to, or because of it? How long do these actions take and how often are they done? How often is the information referenced? How long does it take to find it, and to whom is it sent or shown?

The second section asks what reports are produced from this information, how often, and to whom are they distributed?

These two forms (figures 5.2 and 5.3) follow the standard questions asked for any basic records survey, and will provide all of the information necessary to begin records management programmes. However, for those who may have a broader brief, more technological offices or more forward-looking organizations, a slightly different approach should be considered.

The information survey and tracking form, see the example shown in figure 5.4, follows the same ideas as the other forms, but is applied to information rather than to a record. It contains the following sections:

- General purpose of the information in the record series? This is often, but by no means always, indicated by the title of the department or the job title of the person in charge, for example, accounting, finance, personnel, research, sales, production, planning, medical/health. Narrowed down, what is the general function for which this information was collected: To do the accounts? Pay invoices? To monitor full-time permanent personnel? To conduct research on the suitability of 'flying health clinics' in a particular region?
- What elements of information are needed to do this function? For example, names, addresses, dates of birth, bank account numbers, amounts of money spent, when, on what, etc.
- How is the information collected? For example, by forms posted or filled out in-house, by telephone, personal interview, hearsay, original research or research into published materials, external data bases sent by other departments. List all methods and sources. Get blank copies of all forms used.
- Is this information sufficient to do the job well? What else is needed? Why? Why is it not obtained?
- How is the information used or processed? List and understand each step of the use or processing. Understand what is done with the information in as much detail as possible. For example, accounts payable collects information on items or services purchased, including what, how much it cost, who ordered it, when, etc:
  - it is listed under the person or department that ordered it, and coded. Some of the information is entered into the accounts payable system;
  - the system produces monthly cheques. These, with an accompanying letter, are manually checked against the invoice and then posted;

```
┌─────────────────────────────────────────────────────────────┐
│                      PROCEDURES FORM                        │
│                                                             │
│                                                             │
│     Record Series Title                                     │
│                                                             │
│     From whom:                                              │
│                                                             │
│     Actions perfomed:                                       │
│                                                             │
│                                                             │
│                                                             │
│     How long does it take, per record?                      │
│                                                             │
│                                                             │
│     How often, per day, is it done?                         │
│                                                             │
│                                                             │
│     How long to find it again?                              │
│                                                             │
│                                                             │
│     How often record series referenced?                     │
│                                                             │
│                                                             │
│     To whom?                                                │
│                                                             │
│                                                             │
│                                                             │
│     Reports                                                 │
│                                                             │
│                                                             │
│     Title of those produced?                                │
│                                                             │
│                                                             │
│                                                             │
│     How often produced?                                     │
│                                                             │
│                                                             │
│     Distribution list?                                      │
│                                                             │
└─────────────────────────────────────────────────────────────┘
```

Figure 5.3   Procedures form

- the same information is used in reports to estimate future budgets, to control expenditure, to do random auditing, etc.

If there is time, draw a simple diagram or flow chart of these steps. If there is a procedures manual, get a copy, *but* be aware that most procedures manuals are outdated and are rarely used. Always ask to be shown the procedures and to have them explained. A listing of files and their method of organization is also useful.

Where information is entered on to a computer, obtain a blank screen print of each entry record. (On comparing these with the information collected, alternative answers to question 4 may be revealed.) Obtain a screen print of the list of reports produced from the information, small samples of searches on the files and samples of the reports. Ask how often the information comes in, is processed, and reported on.

INFORMATION SURVEY AND TRACKING FORM			
			Analyst:
Dept/Office title:	Location/building:	Contact:	

1 General purpose of the information in the record series:	2 Elements of information needed:		
3 How collected:			
	5 How is the information used or processed? List steps:		
4 Is this sufficient? Is more information needed? What? Why?			
6 How is it stored? Medium? Arrangement?	8 How long is it needed in original form? Subsequent arrangements: Summaries/reports only?	9 Who else uses/has access?	
7 Storage/medium changes:			
10 What laws or company policy pertain to it?	11 How old is it (earliest dates)?	14 How is accuracy ensured?	
	12 How much is there? % outdated:		
		15 What security precautions are taken?	
16 What training has the records user had?	13 Is any, old or new, stored elsewhere (include back-up archives tapes/discs)?		
17 What are the most serious problems? What, if any, improvements would the user make? Why?			

Figure 5.4   Information survey and tracking form

Where computers are used, it will be necessary, after surveying each department or, if the organization is small, after the survey is completed, to talk with the computer group about their understanding of information and procedures used. Note any differences between the two versions.

- How is the information stored? As with the other form (figure 5.2), note types, makes, models, and sizes of filing equipment, computers, word processors, terminals, reader-printers, etc. Note also the arrangement of the information; for example, paper filed alphabetically on open shelves, or, individuals' personnel files held alphabetically on microfilm that is not blip-coded, and the rolls of film are stored in chronological order.
- What changes are made in storage? Is paper microfilmed? How often and who does it? Is the paper destroyed? Where are the paper and film stored?
  Or are personal computer files always printed out? Are the discs kept? Where? Is the software kept with them? Are duplicates, back-up discs, run? How often? Where are they kept?
- How long is the information needed in the way it was originally collected? If it is altered, how long is the altered form needed? How long are the reports or summaries of it needed?
- Who else uses the information, whether all or part of it, inside or outside of the organization.
- Does the user know what laws or company policies pertain to the information collected and used, or which government agencies have contacts with the company?
- How old is the complete collection of that kind of information?
- How much of it is there? With paper, give the number of feet or inches/cm or metres; with electronic information give the number of discs or amount of space on the mainframe.
- Is any of the information, old or new, duplicates or originals, stored elsewhere? Where? Who controls it? How often is it sent there?
- How is the accuracy of the originally collected information ensured?
- What security precautions are taken against theft, fire, flood, power failures, tape or disc erosion?
- What records or information training has the user had? Include awareness seminars, courses through professional organizations, in-house talks, as well as pertinent academic education.
- What problems or areas of improvement can the user identify? Note as much as possible of what the user says about any aspect of his/her information.

Figure 5.5 shows a typical filing equipment survey form. It is used to make a quick tally of all the equipment in a room, area, or department. For some people this is one form too many and, rather than use it, they simply write the information on a notepad. What is important is to note:

- type of equipment (for example, four-drawer filing cabinet, 3-ft shelving bays, personal computer, etc.)
- dimensions
- number of drawers or shelves
- model number and make of electronic equipment
- number of pieces of each type and size.

While any of the forms shown in figures 5.2 to 5.5 can be used as they are, it is best to use them as guides for creating one that is appropriate to the goals of each organization's survey.

The following list gives some possible elements to consider when designing a survey form:

FILING EQUIPMENT SURVEY FORM

Date:

Inventoried by:

Dept:

Location:

Type of equipment	Number of drawers	Number in use	Number empty	Dimensions, if abnormal	Remarks (if personal computer, word processor or terminal, enter make and model no. here)

- record series title
- record series description
- purpose of record series
- documents in record series (component documents)
- record media/format
- report/form numbers/references
- record size/paper/tape/disc/drawings, etc.
- equipment used to store record series
- official copy designation
- official custodian of record series
- archival/historical value
- administrative need
- software/hardware requirements for machine-readable records
- location/area/building/room
- dates
- record volume (linear feet/cubic feet)
- person conducting survey
- date of survey
- record activity
- vital record classification
- department of record
- record range of dates
- sample of folder/item titles
- corporate entity
- physical description
- location of other copies of record
- record origination
- department's recommended retention.

ITEMS TO OBTAIN BEFORE THE SURVEY

Prior to the survey, a few items should be collected and studied beforehand:

- Costs of office space per square foot/metre, including taxes, rates, and insurance. The costs should be obtained for each building where any records will be surveyed. If the costs are not available, or are believed to be confidential, then it is best to contact local estate agents who handle similar commercial property in the area. The average figure, taken from two or three agents, should be close enough to be acceptable in any costings.
- Storage — the location and annual costs of any facilities used specifically for records storage, for example, the basement in the building belonging to another company.
- Maps of all buildings, showing not only room and cupboard arrangements, but furniture, filing cabinets and terminals, if possible.
- Copies of contracts with all service bureaux handling records and information for the company, such as commercial storage companies, microfilming bureaux, duplicating/printing/photocopying bureaux or rentals, computer services, etc.
- Equipment list showing all word processors, personal computers, photocopiers, mimeographs, microfilm cameras and reader-printers, computer terminals, etc.
- Filing costs should be broken down into the annual costs, per department or ministry if possible, for equipment and filing supplies. Again, if the purchasing department will not release these figures, they must be estimated from the average costs, as listed in catalogues, for the estimated annual purchase of equipment and supplies.
- Salaries for secretarial and clerical staff. If the annual, average salaries for these job classes are not available, those published in the local press for similar jobs will do.

- Employee internal telephone list — crucial for making and changing appointments, or for asking directions to oddly-placed offices.
- Staff structure charts — any diagram or list, showing reporting hierarchies, or connecting names with job titles, will be extremely helpful in understanding the flow of information.
- Procedure manuals — any procedure manual, for any function, will include valuable information on reports and correspondence procedures and titles.
- Forms — blank copies of all forms used will help with the establishment of a forms control file. While copies will be collected during the survey, any that can be gathered, in response to a requesting memo, and catalogued in advance, will give a head start to the project.
- Copies of previous studies — obviously, if a study was once done on files, records, computers, secretarial or clerical services, archives, efficiency, etc., it will contain useful information, and give a solid foundation to the records manager's understanding of the organization, and will help to avoid wasting time duplicating those studies.
- Copies of filing indexes and lists — even if outdated, these will help to understand not only the files to be surveyed in offices but those in storage.

DOING THE SURVEY

There is little step-by-step instruction that can be given for actually doing the survey. It requires persistence, alertness, curiosity, a certain thrill at sleuthing, and a great deal of diplomacy. Each department is different, with different procedures, personalities, equipment, needs, histories; and the records manager will have to deploy different techniques to discover the records and information in them all.

One of the typical problems encountered when conducting any type of survey is that files are not organized by record series. Many departments organize their files in a large alphabetical subject arrangement which contains numerous record series, official and convenience copies, record and non-record material, etc.

It is important to take the time to list each record series even though they are buried in the large subject file arrangement. Another problem area is a sub-series within large series of case files. Litigation files, personnel jackets, and certain types of project files are good examples where there may be five to ten different record series in one file.

When surveying inactive files there are often problems with how containers are packed, especially if there has never been a formal records management programme in the organization. A typical dilemma is presented in the survey with containers marked 'Jim's desk drawer contents'. If Jim were the employment permanent secretary, there may be very valuable historical records in the containers. If he were a middle manager there may be some official records, but the containers probably hold mostly unofficial copies and non-record reference materials.

In an effort to discover everything about the department's records, three criteria may be kept as guides:

Look at all files in all equipment on all discs, screens, films.

Ask every question necessary until you truly understand what is in the file, why it is kept, how it is used, where it comes from and goes, and any problems with it.

Find every storage place with records and information: in cupboards, down the hall, on top of cabinets, shelves, terminals, under desks, at home, in the safe, in another building, at an associate company's office, in commercial storage, in the car. Then go look at that too.

THE 'ALL-ENCOMPASSING GAZE AROUND THE ROOM'

At some point in each area, simply stop. Stand still in the centre of the bustling office, forget the detailed analysis, and try to comprehend the whole.

- Count the people
- Are they seated, walking back and forth to files, rushed, relaxed?
- Count the equipment
- Is it old, new, mixed?
- Count the heaps of paper
- Does everything look messy, cheap, frantic or clean, expensive, calm? A mixture?

It is very easy, in all of the information professions, to become obsessed with detail. The catalogue number assigned to a book, the correct finding aid in an archive, the best filing system in an office – all can take days of absorbed effort. But it is necessary to remember that this detail must fit well into and support the whole. The occasional exercise in perceiving the whole helps to maintain a balance between the microscopic and the global views.

The surveying of information held on a mainframe computer must be done by interviewing the data processing manager about each of the systems in use, how they work, who controls them, has access to them and what reports are produced. Find out which systems simply receive and process data, and which ones give the user creative freedom to design files and function. Find out how the time using the system and storage are charged, if to the individual workstation, the department, or as a central service.

Make friends with the data processing manager. Nearly every records management programme will affect or be affected by a data processing programme. The two departments must work closely together if the organization is to provide true information resources management.

THE SURVEY INTERVIEW

Who owns the information

This may appear to be a theoretical topic but it is crucial to the information professions. The conflict over ownership of information stems from very natural impulses and assumptions that we are only now, because of technology, being forced to clarify and articulate. It is appropriate to discuss here the problems and confusion surrounding the ownership of information because it is during the survey interviews, the numerous discussions with individuals who use, process, and store information to do their work, that the issue of ownership will arise time and time again.

At its very foundation, the whole concept of records and information management rests on the premise that the information collected and created by employees during the course of their work for an organization belongs to that organization. The records manager's function is to manage all of that information in its recorded forms for the benefit of the organization as a whole.

However, it is natural for people to consider that the products of their mind, coming from the very private source of their identity, belong to them. The information that they glean from publications or surveys and compile in an original way, the ideas of their own that they develop on a scratch pad or on a computer, the documentation of their work, the reports and studies they write, all quite naturally seem to them to be their personal property.

The question of ownership is further complicated when the subjects, if human, of the information consider themselves as the owner. It is, again, quite natural for people to consider that they own their name, the information about where they live, or how many children they have. Most people feel very strongly that, by right of ownership, they control access to information about themselves.

As an example: A man fills out a competition entry form, giving his name, address, and the fact that he owns two cars manufactured by the company running the competition. An employee of the car manufacturing company enters the information from the form into a data base he has created on a personal computer. Now, without going into the discussion of use or transfer of the information, who owns the man's name, address, and the fact that he has two cars? Does the man own it himself, because the information is about him? Because no one else could have it if he did not supply it? Does the employee of the car company own it because he collected it and created the data base that manipulates and stores it? Does the car company own it because it paid for the collection and storage of the information? Because it will award the competition prize? Because the employee could not get the information unless he worked for the car company? While it is true that any information created in any location by employees or agents (such as consultants) of the organization belongs to the organization, that does not necessarily apply to information *collected* by the employees of the organization.

The interviewing technique

There is no question that the interview of an individual about the information used and overseen requires tact, patience, perseverance, and diplomacy. The interview and survey will be the introduction to records management for most people in the organization. The impressions that they form on this initial contact are, thus, very important.

Prying into people's private working lives is a sensitive operation. Pointed questions, opening drawers, reading papers and screens, pressing for explanations, all tend to put people on the defensive. The surveyor should maintain an attitude of polite but firm efficiency, no matter how angry, insulting, or rude an interviewee may be. However, sometimes it will be wiser to stop, especially if an interviewee is visibly frightened by the whole process.

There will be numerous people who, because of fear, suspicion, or a generally obnoxious attitude, will refuse to co-operate with the surveyor. There will also be encounters with difficult personalities, and it is important to retain a sense of humour. For many people a records survey is too much like the inspections of their rooms when they were children. Like children, they try one's patience, but are smarter than you may think. While it is impossible to recommend the ideal persona for the surveyor to assume, there are a few basic steps and techniques which will help make an interview proceed smoothly.

Introduction

- Give a clear explanation of how and why the survey is taking place. Refer to the authorizing letter.
- Reassure that confidentiality will be protected, security clearance has been obtained, that no secret records will be examined without a contact person present; and *especially* that the ultimate goal is to improve records and information systems for everyone.
- If possible, and with the interviewee's permission, use a tape recorder. This minimizes the distractions involved with note taking and allows more free-flowing conversation.

During the interview

- Refuse to participate in 'power games'. Pride, superiority, winning an argument have nothing to do with the survey.
- Ignore the 'offence is the best form of defence' kind of behaviour.
- Do not fill silent pauses. It is an old defensive ploy to let sentences fade into excessively long periods of silence. The nervous analyst will fill these with senseless chatter and so, learn nothing.

- Always ask three basic questions:

  1 What do you like least about your current records system?
  2 What do you like best about your current records system?
  3 If given the opportunity, what would you change?

- Rephrase questions as many times as is necessary until they are understood and answered, however —
- Do not press a point too hard. Choose a different line of questioning for a few minutes, then gently return to the more difficult one.
- Verify everything by examining the records.
- Be sensitive to the reasons for fear of the survey. People's filing cabinets and computer files often can reveal many personal failings.
- Rephrase important points to ensure that you correctly understood what was meant.

Lastly

- Stay calm.
- Don't take anything personally.

COMPILING THE SURVEY RESULTS

If the survey is to be of any use at all, notes must be written up at the end of each day and again as each department, section or group is completed. It is important to include all first and later impressions on weaknesses and strengths in filing, space, systems, and procedures. These impressions have the benefit of being taken while looking at the organization as a whole, and they will necessarily be diluted with time, involvement in specific programmes, and in office politics. They will be invaluable when it is time to assess the practicability of any proposed programme in any area.

Once the forms have been completed the project manager should review the data collected. There may be two official copies of the same record in different departments when there should be only one official copy. The project manager may be able to identify two record series with different titles that are actually the same record series. The project manager's review will provide the necessary informaticn for the survey team to make all appropriate modifications or changes. Once these are made the entire survey should be given to the department to review.

Totalling

The purpose of totalling the statistics from the survey on a daily basis is to make them manageable, as well as to provide for the surveyor a running commentary on overall importance of each finding.

The form shown in figure 5.6 is a simple tally sheet to total the quantities recorded on the survey forms. It is designed to total the information gathered on the other forms, with an emphasis on inactive information and space used. A different emphasis, say, on types of electronic equipment used, would be reflected in a differently structured form. Before beginning the survey at all, it would be wise to consider the kind of totals desired on this form, to ensure that the original survey form includes the questions necessary to obtain that data.

The survey totals form should be completed at the end of each day, for each department, then for each division, and finally for the organization as a whole. This will enable the records manager to present the statistics in an understandable way in the report, both in

```
Date:                    Survey totals for the - Day:

Dept:                                            Dept:

Number of contacts:                              Group:

Number of buildings or floors:                   Ministry/
                                                 Company:
Number of record series/classes
or elements of information:

Earliest date:


Active records

Number of feet and inches of:          Paper:

                                       Microfiche:
Number of discs (wp):

Number of discs (pc):

Number of microfilm rolls:

Number of tapes:

Number of different arrangements/filing systems:


Inactive records

Number of feet and inches of:          Paper:

                                       Microfiche:
Number of discs (wp):

Number of discs (pc):

Number of microfilm rolls:

Number of tapes:
```

Figure 5.6   Survey tally sheet

Inactive records

Other:

Total time spent referencing paper information:

Average per linear foot:

Total time spent referencing wp and pc:

Average per disc:

Equipment	Total number	Sq. ft. used	Sq. ft. needed
2, 3, 4 or 5 drawer standard filing cabinets:			
2, 3, 4 drawer lateral filing cabinets:			
36-inch wide shelf files:			
36-inch wide lateral files:			
Circular files:			
Microfilm cabinets:			
Other:			

Number of files/information elements covered by
Data Processing Act:

Number of files/information elements considered vital:

% of files needing protection covered by security measures:

Number and names of storage companies used:

Number and names of service bureaux used and for what:

Figure 5.6 (cont.)

Table 5.1
Department totals

Dept	Linear feet
A	307
B	28
C	691
D	216
E	235
F	32
Total	1509

text, and in charts or histograms, as shown in Table 5.1. After completing, the survey totals forms should be batched with the survey forms to which they refer.

If, instead of, or in addition to, the tally sheets, a computer program is to be used to total and analyse the data gathered, the program must be fully planned, installed, and tested before the first day of the survey. Generally, it is inadvisable to set up a program simply to do the arithmetic for the results, or even for the graphics for the final report. However, if one of the packaged automated records management systems is to be used, much of the information gathered, especially that which would facilitate the production of preliminary retention schedules, could usefully be entered.

EVALUATING THE SURVEY RESULTS

Evaluation, like records appraisal, requires a little skill and a great deal of common sense. Two common mistakes to be avoided are:

- Data obsession — whereby the evaluator is convinced that every tiny datum gathered on all forms must be incorporated into the evaluation. It must not. An evaluation is a sifting, not a reproduction, of the whole.
- Data glorification — whereby the evaluator sees every datum and every tally as deeply significant to the function of the records or information system. They are not. Inevitably, much of the data collected turns out to be useless.

The evaluation of the survey results must be made with a use for that information in mind. Records management is meant to improve records and information systems for the people who use them. A survey that results only in a statistical report on completed forms is a complete waste of time. An evaluation should include consideration of the following:

- What records are useless and could be destroyed/deleted immediately?
- What records are inactive and could be removed to storage?
- What filing equipment could be emptied and removed or reused?
- What word processors and personal computers are improperly or inefficiently used?
- What records or information could be consolidated?
- What duplication can be eliminated or reduced?
- What records are insufficiently protected against loss?
- What records have archival value?
- What filing systems for paper, indexing systems for microfilm, and directory lists for electronic files need improvement?

Only when these questions have been considered can plans for improvement and new programmes begin.

Start by organizing the data gathered to provide the information necessary to meet the objectives of the survey. If the survey results are in machine-readable form this organization will be quite simple.

To meet most survey objectives the survey results should be organized by department first then alphabetically by record series within the particular department. If the survey data is already in machine-readable form, there will be many options for data organization for evaluation. Examples are:

- Record series — alphabetical by record series title for all departments; alphabetical by record series title for individual departments.
- Active filing equipment — by type of equipment for entire organization; by type of equipment for individual departments.
- Forms — by form number; alphabetical by form name; by form number and form name by department.
- Reports — by report number; alphabetical by report name; by report number and report name by department.
- Inactive records — by department by record series by volume; by department by record series by volume and destruction date.

COSTING EXISTING PRACTICES AND SYSTEMS

There is a strong case for ignoring cost as a justification for records management, and it rests on two points. The first is that the true value of records management is in the services it provides to the growing number of professional information users. As with many other staff functions, such as the data processing department, personnel, or the budget office, there is no question that they are legitimate and necessary regardless of whether they provide any 'return on investment'. The second point is that, if records managers sell their programmes on cost savings alone, then, once those programmes are established, they are often seen as unnecessary by management, which in many instances does not recognize the importance and value of 'managing' information.

While it is true that improved information services must be the goal and reason for records management, it is also true that managing directors and permanent secretaries look at costs. For this reason, some simple costing exercises will provide the extremely valuable information of what current systems are costing the organization. The following sections give guidance as to how various costs can be assessed.

Space costs per linear foot

1 Add the total number of linear feet from the inventory sheets to get the total linear feet.
2 Add the number of square feet used by equipment to get the total of square feet. (Use the chart in Figure 5.7).
3 Multiply the number of square feet by the annual cost per square foot to get the annual filing space cost.
4 Divide the total number of linear feet by the total number of square feet to get the average number of linear feet per square foot.
5 Divide the annual filing space cost by the total number of linear feet to get the annual space cost per linear feet.

Materials cost per linear foot

1 Take the total cost of all filing equipment (available from the purchasing department,

Equipment	Square feet of floor space		
Standard, upright filing cabinet, any number or drawers	3.5	-	closed
	7	-	open
	10	-	open, with room to stand in front of the drawer
36-inch long shelving any height, per bay	3.75		
	7.5	-	with workshelf out
	11.25	-	with room to stand in front of workshelf
Microfilm cabinet, standard, any number of drawers	4	-	closed
	8	-	open
	11	-	open, with room to stand in front of the drawer
Standard column, any height	25	-	closed
	5	-	open
	8	-	open, with room to stand in front of drawer
Circular file, 36 inches in diameter	9		
	14	-	with room to stand in front of it at any point

Figure 5.7   Floor space required by filing equipment

or from current sales brochures, with allowances for age of equipment, and the annual cost for filing supplies.

2   Divide the total equipment costs by the total number of linear feet to get the equipment cost per linear foot.

3   Divide the average number of linear feet increase per year (this can be obtained either from a storage facility or as an estimate from users during the interviews) by the annual supplies cost to get the annual supplies cost per linear foot.

Average storage costs per linear foot

1   Take the total number of years records have been stored in the offices. (From the earliest date of the inventory sheets.)

2   Divide the equipment cost per linear foot by the number of years records have been stored.

3   Add this to the annual space cost per linear foot to get the annual storage cost per linear foot.

Labour cost per linear foot

1   From the inventory forms, add up the total number of file references.

2   From the inventory forms, add up the total amount of time spent referencing.

3   Divide the time (no. 2) by the number of references (no. 1) to get the average time per reference.
4   Take the total number of linear feet in the office areas. (Do include storage cupboards, but do not include remote storage.)
5   Divide the number of references (no. 1) by the number of linear feet (no. 4) to get the average number of references per linear foot. (This may be a fraction.)
6   Multiply the references per linear foot (no. 5) by the average time per reference (no. 3) to get the average time per linear foot.
7   Take the average hourly secretarial pay (from personnel or published sources).
8   Multiply the average time per linear foot (no. 6) by the hourly secretarial pay (no. 7) to get the labour cost per linear foot.

N.B. Be sure to use the same amount of time in all your calculations: hours, days, weeks, or months.

These costings can be done for the organization as a whole and/or for each department or division. They will be useful as additional reasons for making improvements, but should not be given undue emphasis.

Where there is already a clear plan for improved systems or equipment in an area, it will be necessary to show how the current costs may be reduced by the new system, and what it will cost to implement it. The purchase, implementation, and running costs of any new system should be provided by the salesperson as a part of the bid (or quotation) to fill the order. Any salesperson who is not willing to examine an organization's systems and order, or to provide a fully costed bid, would probably not supply support after purchase, and so, the company should not be considered.

THE RECORDS AND INFORMATION SURVEY REPORT

The report should be either inductive or geographical in organization, the first stressing subjects across the organization, the second stressing each department's or division's records systems:

1   Inductive structure
    • Introduction
    • Problems in filing systems
    • Problems in retrieval
    • Problems in storage
    • Problems in protection of vital records
    • Conclusions
    • Recommendation for improvements
    • Appendices
2   Geographical structure
    • Introduction
    • Accounts department
    • Marketing department
    • Sales department
    • Production department
    • Summary of departmental systems
    • Recommendations for improvements

As the introductory publication from records management, the report should be formal in tone, clear in style, and standard in format. It should begin with a brief, one page, synopsis of the contents (see Figure 5.8). Graphs, tables, and appendices should be kept to the minimum necessary to explain clearly the findings, but not so much as to reduce the impact of the recommendations, or as to bore the reader. It should include a table of contents, a table of illustrations, and be presented with a standard letter.

SYNOPSIS

An inventory of the information held in Company A revealed that, in spite of a large number of word processors and personal computers, some 80 per cent of the information is still held on paper. There are 4011 linear feet of paper, of which 25 per cent, or 1003 linear feet, are inactive and could go to storage immediately.

The paper is stored in a variety of equipment types, from shelf files to heaps on bookcases and the floor, taking up 3071 square feet of office space. Approximately 750 square feet will be released by sending inactive files to storage and removing the emptied equipment. Of this information there are 743 different records series (documents which are always handled together) of which 37 per cent is duplication. Much of the duplication is on another medium.

There are no established retention periods for the storage, archiving, or destruction of the information. Neither are there sufficient protection procedures for vital records or for the information on personal computers and word processors. The organization of the information, in filing systems and on word processors particularly, presents a serious problem which will become much worse as the company grows. There is extensive duplication, incorrect distribution and uncertain filing requirements of reports on all projects.

The following report details suggestions for the establishment of a complete records management programme to organize and protect all company information.

Figure 5.8 Synopsis of the contents of the records and information survey report

This initial report will be more important than any other produced by records management, for it will inaugurate all future programmes. Sufficient time and care must be taken to ensure its excellence and thus, the approval of its recommendations.

Part III
Creation, Maintenance and Use

INTRODUCTION

Until recently records creation, maintenance and use had tended to be forsaken in favour of records disposition. But, with increasing emphasis being placed by government and business on the need for quick and reliable information, records creation, maintenance and use are more and more receiving the attention they deserve.

Reports are an essential tool for any manager. They are the basis upon which important decisions in any organization are made. Their management, therefore, is a key aspect of the records management programme (Chapter 6).

In much the same way, no organization can operate effectively if it is not sure what it is meant to be doing and how procedures are to be carried out. Policy and procedure statements, or directives, require careful management. They must be part of an established system, classified, indexed, standardized, and controlled in order that everyone in the organization can see that its functions are carried out correctly and with proper authorization (Chapter 7).

With the increased emphasis on information requirements has come the increased use of forms, the tools which are commonly used to organize, collect, and transmit information. But if the forms themselves are badly designed or used unnecessarily, the quality of the information will suffer. Forms must therefore be properly managed, which includes control, analysis, design, reproduction, stocking, and distribution (Chapter 8).

As far as files of correspondence and papers are concerned, recent trends have been towards local filing arrangements for active records and centralized storage for semi- and non-active records. As with reports, directives, and forms, they are an important information resource for an organization and as such require effective management. Records managers must provide the expertise necessary to ensure that active records are properly housed and adequately classified for easy retrieval, and that staff are suitably trained to look after them (Chapter 9).

Certain records are essential, or vital, to the continued operation of any organization. These must be identified and given particular attention, including classification, appropriate protection, and agreed procedures for handling (Chapter 10).

If disasters occur, the organization must be fully prepared to deal with them. Records management will play a key role in the disaster recovery programme and its staff must be aware of the procedures that are to be carried out (Chapter 11).

6 Reports Management

Organizations are usually in existence for specific purposes. The way organizations accomplish their purposes is by dividing the necessary work among various departments or sections and by establishing a corresponding managerial hierarchy to run those organizational entities. The managers of the different departments have goals and objectives to meet to help the organization achieve its overall purpose, and they are given a variety of resources (people, facilities, equipment, etc.) to use in order to meet them.

One of the primary tools managers use to manage their resources is the report. Reports are used to convey information. In order for the information to be useful, it must go to the right person at the right time. In order for information to be economical, the cost of obtaining, formatting, and transmitting it should be less than the value received from its use.

Although this chapter is called Reports Management, we are really dealing with the management of reporting systems. No report exists in a vacuum. Even the most basic report, consisting of a single sheet of paper containing only a few items of information, is part of a system which has been developed to help someone obtain, process, and use that information for a specific purpose. If the same information were transmitted electronically, using electronic mail or networked computers with video screens instead of typewriters and paper, that arrangement would be neither more nor less of a reporting system. It would merely be an automated system as opposed to a manual one.

All reporting systems cost money. Because of this, and because managers who want information are not always cognizant of the most efficient and effective method of obtaining it, reports management programmes are established.

The goal of a reports management programme is to improve the quality and economy of reporting systems on an organization-wide basis. Specific objectives of a programme include:

- Identification of the information needs of managers at all levels.
- Collection , transmission, processing, and storage of information through the most economic use of personnel, funds, and equipment.
- Prevention, and/or elimination of invalid, inefficient, or unnecessary reporting.
- Co-ordination of reports management with other records management functions.
- Evaluation of reports and reporting systems on a continuous basis to ensure economy, efficiency, and effectiveness.
- Reduction of reporting costs.

There are two aspects of reports management: reports control, and reports analysis and design. Both are of equal importance. While the system improvements and resultant cost savings primarily come from the analysis and design functions, as a practical matter, when the control function is inoperative, the analysis and design work rarely gets done. An effective programme is one in which all functions are being performed.

REPORTS CONTROL

As with all records management programmes, reports management should have an authorizing directive which spells out the various authorities and responsibilities, and also clearly outlines the procedure to be followed when establishing a new reporting requirement or revising an existing one. This control mechanism ensures that no reporting requirements will get promulgated in an organization without first having been reviewed and approved. An effective way to ensure that no unauthorized reports exist is to establish the policy that a reporting requirement which has not been approved does not have to be responded to.

Another reason for the control mechanism is for periodic review. Although a report is static, the organization in which it exists is dynamic. Therefore, changing goals, objectives, and even organizational structures can reduce the need for and value of information which was once considered important. It does not necessarily follow that when a need for information is diminished, the requirement for supplying it is proportionately curtailed. Generally nothing is done about such a requirement unless a specific challenge to it is raised. The periodic review provides an automatic challenge mechanism.

At the time a report is evaluated and approved it should be assigned an expiration date. Some time (perhaps 60-90 days) prior to that expiration date the report should again be evaluated to ensure that the requirment is still valid. If it is valid, the report may be renewed. If not, action should be taken to correct the problem or the requirement may be allowed to expire on schedule.

Several tools can make the reports control job easier: an inventory (or catalogue); a history (or case) file; a functional (or analysis) file; and reports control symbols.

Inventory

To establish the inventory, a form such as the one shown in Figure 6.1 may be used. The form should be distributed to all organizational units with an explanation of its purpose and with instructions for its completion and submission. A copy of each report, the prescribing directive (or a reference to the directive)', and any associated forms should also be requested for use in the history file. All organizational units requiring a report from other offices, and all offices preparing a report should complete the appropriate parts of the form and submit the requested materials.

This second factor is quite significant. Although it is somewhat duplicative to have respondents as well as requirers complete the inventory forms, the effort, for the initial inventory, will ultimately prove to be worthwhile. Inevitably, the information received from the two sources will not match. The discrepancies can alert the reports management staff to problems regarding those particular systems.

Once the information is obtained, a temporary inventory listing of all reporting requirements should be created. The listing should include the:

* title
* control symbol
* associated form numbers
* frequency
* due dates

REPORTS INVENTORY		
Prepared by: **Name:** **Organization:** **Tel:**		**Date:**

Instructions
Submit an original and one copy for each report required or prepared by your office. All offices complete Section A. Complete Section B if report is required by your office. Complete Section C if report is prepared by your office. Attach sample copy of report and send to the reports management office

Section A – Identification Data		

1 Report title	2 Report control symbol
	   or number (if any)
		3 Form no. or format
		   (e.g. memo, tabulation
		   narrative, etc.)

4 Requiring directive or instructions	5 Frequency (monthly, quarterly, etc.)	6 Due date
		7 Expiration date

Section B – Requiring Office Data

1 Purpose and use of report (identify other reports for which this report is used as a feeder report)			

2 Offices required to submit report		3 Sources of information used by
		   preparing offices to complete
		   report (form no., report, file, etc.)
			4 No. of copies required

Type	Number		5 Distribution
6 Date report originated	7 No. of revisions since origination		8 Date of last revision
9 Estimated cost of developing report		10 Estimated annual cost of using report	

11 Current appraisal

		yes	no				yes	no			yes	no
N **e** **e** **d**	a Is this report still needed?			**D** **a** **t** **a**	h Is data best for the purpose?				**P** **o** **s** **s** **i** **b** **l** **e**	**i** **m** **p** **r** **o** **v** **e** **m** **e** **n** **t** **s**	o Combining with others?		
	b Is every item still needed?				i Is comparative data needed?						p Making easier to complete?		
	c Is the report needed as often?			**I** **n** **s** **t** **r** **u** **c** **t** **i** **o** **n** **s**	j Is report clear and easy to use?						q Using a form if not used?		
	d Is every copy still needed?				k Are there written instructions?						r Stopping negative reports?		
	e Is there another source?				l Are they clear, concise, complete, current?						s Using summary?		
Value	f Is it worth its probable cost?				m Are they issued in a formal directive?						t Using sampling?		
											u Reporting by exception?		
Date	g Does the due date give enough time?				n Are illustrations needed?						v Changing source?		
											w Changing sequence?		

Section C – Preparing Office Data		

1 Sources of information
   for completing report
	2 No. of copies
	   prepared
		3 Distribution (original and copies)

4 Estimated annual cost to prepare report	5 Estimated annual cost for collecting and maintaining information needed for report	

Figure 6.1   Reports inventory form

- requiring directive
- requiring organization
- respondent organization
- expiration date
- cost.

When all the reports have been analysed, those that remain should be listed in a final inventory which should be selectively distributed throughout the organization. For ease of use, the final inventory should be organized alphabetically by report title and also cross-indexed numerically by report control symbol.

History files

The history file should contain complete, historical documentation on each report, including:

- the original reports request approval
- associated forms and instructions for completion
- correspondence, worksheets, and other documents relating to the report
- a reference to, or a copy of, the prescribing directive
- a reference to feeder reports, if any.

A file should be created for each report when it is established and for existing reports identified in an inventory. History files may be arranged alphabetically by the report title, or numerically by the report control symbol.

Functional files

Functional files (which are really subject classification files) are used for comparing reports on the same subject or functional area, for identifying duplicate reporting requirements, and for eliminating unnecessary reports. Functional files assist analysts in understanding relationships between reports and reporting systems and in streamlining systems and procedures. The files contain report request approval forms or inventory forms and are organized by broad functional categories (personnel, budget, procurement). If the volume warrants it, functional files may be subdivided by subordinate subject headings.

For larger systems, a functional file may be automated by establishing an integrated subject classification data base which can then be used to identify reports in the same functional category along with associated directives, forms, and files.

Reports control symbols

A reports control symbol is a coded series of numbers and/or letters assigned to an approved report and which is usually printed on the report form or, at a minimum, contained within the prescribing directive. The symbol serves two major purposes: it indicates to respondents that the report is authorized, and it may also be used as a unique identifier.

The extent to which a reports control symbol is used as an identifier depends on how the coding system is structured. For example, the control symbol 63-PER-Q might indicate that the report was the 63rd authorized report in the control system; that the personnel department was the requiring office; and that the response was due quarterly. A symbol such as the one just described could be used with an automated data base functional file.

The expiration date of the report may be incorporated into the control symbol if desired. In fact, almost any type of identifying information might be included. It does not matter how lengthy a control symbol becomes as long as those using it can understand the coding.

Reports control process

The procedures for establishing new reporting requirements or revising existing ones should be part of the overall reports management directive. Basically, the control process operates as follows.

Whenever a report is initiated or revised, a report approval form, such as the request for clearance and evaluation of reporting requirement, shown in Figure 6.2, should be completed and submitted to the reports management staff. The form should provide a description of the proposed report and a justification for its creation, including its estimated costs and expected benefits. Associated documents, such as the requiring directive, additional forms, and a copy of the proposed report format should accompany the request. The reports management staff should provide any necessary assistance to the report initiator in completing the form and in obtaining the required information.

Having received the request, the reports management staff should co-ordinate with other organizational units having an interest in the information being requested and with those that will be required to respond. The proposed report should be reviewed by the reports management staff for adequacy, necessity, usefulness, and economy (see analysis and design section following), and should be approved only if:

- A valid need exists for the information required by the proposed report.
- The information requested is limited to items needed to satisfy the report's purpose.
- The information is not available elsewhere through an already existing reporting system.
- The value of the information exceeds the cost of obtaining it.
- The reporting frequency is consistent with the time by which the information is needed.
- Clear and complete instructions for reporting have been developed and are contained in the prescribing directive.

Assuming that the reporting requirement meets *all* of the criteria for approval, it should then be assigned an expiration date and a reports control symbol and entered into the inventory. This is the entire control process until there is a request for modification or the periodic review takes place.

REPORTS ANALYSIS AND DESIGN

Proper analysis and design of reporting systems are basic functional requirements for effective reports management programmes. Unfortunately, these functions are often only given lip-service or are overlooked entirely in many organizations. Without the critical analysis and design functions, a reports management programme manages nothing. The control function in such a deficient programme is diminished because it, of necessity, becomes 'rubber stamp' authorizing process, and the reports management staff personnel are little more than number assignment clerks.

Adequate reports analysis and design requires a significant investment of resources. This investment, however, is paid back substantially through the development of improved and more economical reporting systems. The methodology which may be used to achieve that payback has already been outlined in Chapter 4. The following additional information, however, is specifically oriented to analysing reporting sytems.

Needs assessment

The first step in the development of a report or a reporting system is to assess information needs. There are two ways of approaching this task. One is to determine the information needs on an organization-wide basis by identifying the needs at each level of the

REQUEST FOR CLEARANCE AND EVALUATION OF REPORTING REQUIREMENT

1 Submit to	2 Report (*check applicable boxes*)
	Action ☐ New ☐ Revise ☐ Exempt ☐ Cancel ☐ Continue

INSTRUCTIONS Complete and submit an original and two copies of this form to request the clearance and evaluation of all new or revised reporting requirements that are subject to the reports management programme. Attach a supporting statement that fully justifies the need for the requested information, a listing of responding offices, copies of worksheets used in costing the report, a sample of the report form or format, copies of the prescribing directive or instructions that would be available to respondents, and copies of the cost/benefit evaluation. This form will be used for the annual review of reports.

3 Office symbol of the originator/user	4A Person to be contacted for information	4B Corres. symbol	4C Telephone no.
5A Title of report		5B Current approval no.	

6 Frequency of submission of report (*check*)

Annually	Quarterly	Weekly	On occasion	Other (*specify*)
Semi-annual	Monthly	Daily	Contingent	

7 List cancelled or modified reports or forms

A Title	B Report approval no

8 Summary of estimated reporting workload

A Number of respondents	
B Number of times this report submitted annually by each respondent	
C Total number of reports submitted annually (A X B)	

9 Summary of estimated reporting costs (*attach worksheets used in cost report*)

Description (a)	Development costs (b)	Annual operational costs (c)	Annual user (d)
A Requiring office	£		£
B Responding agencies/offices	£	£	
C Totals	£	£	£

10 Name and title of requesting office approving official

11A Signature of approving official	11B Date	12A Signature of reports control officer	12B Date

Below for use of clearance and evaluation office

13 Clearance and evaluation results			
☐ Approved (*see below*)	Recommend disapproval ☐ (*see attached*)	☐ Exempted (*see attached*)	☐ Cancelled (*see attached*)

14 Assigned report title	15 Assigned report approval no.
	16 Expiration of approval (*date*)

17A Signature of approving official	17B Date

Figure 6.2   Request for clearance and evaluation of reporting requirement form

organization from the top down. The objective is to develop an overall understanding of the organization's information needs and to construct a set of interrelated systems to meet those needs. This approach is basic for the creation of an overall information management system. Although talked about a great deal, such systems are usually not established because of the time and effort involved in their development.

Another way to assess information needs is to focus on the requirements of individual managers and to develop systems to meet those requirements. Simultaneously, the possibilities for integrating those systems with other organizational systems are considered. When comprehensive systems design and integration is done at all, this second approach is usually the one taken.

Assessing information needs requires the involvement of persons possessing several different skills, including:

- Reports management analysts to co-ordinate the collection, analysis and synthesis of data into specific information requirements for affected organizational units.
- Programme managers and specialists to provide first-hand knowledge of the information needs and operations of their programmes.
- Senior managers to formulate policies.
- Automated data processing specialists to provide the necessary expertise in the formulation of, and possible integration of, automated systems and processes.

In assessing information needs, certain sources should also be reviewed to determine information requirements that are imposed by law or directive. These sources consist of legislation, regulations, orders and directives. Additionally, survey and audit reports should be examined to ascertain if information management problems have been previously identified.

Individual reports analysis

Each prospective report in a reporting system should be subjected to a comprehensive analysis. The analysis should ensure that each requirement:

- is necessary, meaningful, and useful
- does not duplicate other reports
- is designed to obtain information from the best source and in the simplest manner
- has a frequency consistent with the time when the information is needed
- is cost effective.

There is a myriad of questions to be asked when analysing a report or a reporting system. While some information should be available from reports history and functional files, most information for a new requirement will have to be obtained from the persons who require, prepare, process and use the particular report being reviewed. To facilitate the review process, a reports evaluation checklist, as shown in Figure 6.3, has been developed. The checklist is a summarization of the following 144 questions which must be answered for a complete reports review.

The report as a whole

- What information does the report provide?
- What is the stated purpose of the report?
- Who required the report?
- Who established the report?
- How is the report used? Is it used to take specific action, or to make plans and decisions?

REPORTS EVALUATION CHECKLIST			
Report title			Review date
Section 1 – Need			
Instructions. (Check either column (b) or (c). If questionable, show changes in column (d)) (a)	Questionable (b)	Satisfactory (c)	Proposed changes (attach additional sheets, if needed) (d)
1 The report as a whole: Who uses it? How? What is its purpose? Should it be continued?			
2 Use of each item: Is every item used? Any missing items to be added?			
3 Use of each copy: Are all copies used to good advantage?			
4 Functional relationship: Is the information within the scope of the office functions?			
5 Misapplication: Does the report try to solve a problem which should be solved by other means?			
6 Stand-by data: Is the data obtained for 'just in case' use?			
7 Sources: Is the data available in another report or office?			
8 By products: Is it possible to get the data by some other process?			
9 Direct use of records: Could actual records or 'last copy' of record be used instead of a report?			
10 Sampling: Would a sampling of a few offices give reliable data?			
11 Exception reporting: Would it be appropriate to report conditions only when other than normal?			
12 Combination: Could the report be combined with another report?			
13 Non-related material: Are non-related subjects included in the same report?			
14 Adequacy and suitability: Is scope or content tailored to meet needs?			
15 Value versus cost: Is the report worth its cost?			
Section 2 – Timing			
16 Reporting periods: Are reporting periods properly stated?			
17 Frequency: Is the present frequency suitable, excessive or inadequate?			
18 Due date: Is the due date specifically stated?			
19 Preparing office workload: Has this been considered? Can due dates be changed to avoid peak workloads?			

Figure 6.3   Reports evaluation checklist

REPORTS EVALUATION CHECKLIST (page 2)			
Report title			Review date
Section 3 – Style			
Instructions. (Check either column (b) or (c). If questionable, show changes in column (d)) (a)	Questionable (b)	Satisfactory (c)	Proposed changes (attach additional sheets, if needed) (d)
20 Report title: Is it the same as, or listed in the directive?			
21 Purpose of report: Is it clearly stated?			
22 Reporting instructions: Are reporting instructions clear and adequate?			
23 Integrated reporting: Are data needs of other levels included?			
24 Feeder reports: Are procedures for feeder reports provided to assure uniformity and simplicity?			
25 Reporting units: Are reporting units shown? Are there too many, too few?			
26 Negative reports: Are negative reports required? What use is made of them?			
27 Number of copies: Are number of copies specified?			
28 Routing: Are correct mailing addresses given?			
29 Format: Is the best format for this report used?			
30 Arrangement and size: Are items sequenced according to user need? Is spacing adequate? Are item captions clear? Is size adequate and practical?			
31 Standardization: Do all offices use the same forms or format?			
32 Summary information: Would a summary of information rather than statistics or a narrative be better?			
33 Cumulative data: Can data be maintained on a cumulative basis to eliminate last-minute workloads?			
34 Comparisons: Are comparisons made against goals, past performance or current performance of others?			
35 Graphics: Are graphics used to good advantage?			
36 Authentication: Are verifying or approving officials' signatures used only when necessary?			
37 Data sources: Are records from which reports are to be prepared identified?			
38 Arrangement of records: Should records be rearranged to simplify reporting?			
39 Report symbol: Is it shown after title of report?			
40 Style of presentation: Does the overall report provide clarity and simplicity?			

Figure 6.3   (cont.)

- What specific plans and decisions are based on the report?
- What would happen if the report was discontinued?
- Would a programme function be impossible to perform or severely hampered without the report?

Use of each item

- Are all the items used?
- How is each item of information used?
- Does each item fill a specific information need?
- Do any items fall into the 'nice-to-know' category?
- Are all items consistently reported by all preparing offices?
- Is the information being reported valid?

Use of each copy

- How many copies of the report are prepared?
- What is the distribution of the report?
- Which copies are actually used (action copies)?
- Which copies are information copies, and are they necessary?
- Should any recipient be removed from the distribution?
- Would broader distribution eliminate the need for other or summary reports?
- How is distribution accomplished? Is it adequate for the distribution volume?
- When was the last time the accuracy of the distribution list was checked?

Functional relationship

- Is the report within the scope of the recipient's functions?
- Have the recipient's interests or responsibilities changed?
- Have other offices acquired related functions or responsibilities?

Misapplication

- Is the report a substitute for taking action to improve a situation?
- Does the report attempt to solve problems that actually require administrative or other action? (It is possible that direct or better supervision would considerably improve a situation.)
- Is the real purpose of the report to create delay in hopes that a problem will solve itself?

Standby data

- Is data obtained just for standby or 'just-in-case' use?
- How often has it been used?
- Was the need critical at the time?
- Was the information up-to-date?
- Did it answer all the questions or was additional information required?
- Is it worth the cost to prepare and maintain this information just in case the need arises?
- Would a one-time situation report serve the purpose?

Sources

- Is another source of information available that will satisfy the reporting requirement?

- Is it possible to obtain the information from other available reports or records?
- If another office has the information available in a different form or format (for example, computer printout), can it be used or modified to provide acceptable information?

By-products of other activities

- Will the need for a report be eliminated by using by-products of existing operations?
- Can routine office procedures at the source of needed information be modified to provide by-product data during the normal work process?
- Can information be extracted from existing systems, procedures, or products by modifying existing forms, recordkeeping, or accounting systems?
- Can existing operating procedures be modified to meet information needs without requiring a new report?

Direct use of records

- If the information is obtained from a record or form, could it (or a copy) be used directly instead of creating a separate report?
- Could records photographed or otherwise copied quickly at the source be used instead of a new report?

Sampling

- Is complete coverage essential rather than a scientific sample?
- Would a sample of offices or persons provide sufficient data?
- If sampling is used, are the present respondents representative enough to provide accurate data when projected to the whole?

Exception reporting

- Is exception reporting feasible? (Can reports be made only when conditions are other than normal?)
- If exception reporting is being used, are instructions on timing and procedures well defined?

Combination

- Are there possibilities for combining the report with other records? (Use a recurring data analysis chart to identify duplicative information.)

Non-related material

- Does the report contain items of information unrelated to the primary purpose of the report?
- Can this information be included in other related reports or a separate report? (In contemplating changes, consider the effects on work patterns at the source of the information.)

Adequacy and suitability

- Is the scope or content of the report too broad or too narrow for its intended purpose?
- Does the data match the specific needs of the using offices?

Value versus cost

- Has a cost/benefit analysis been performed on the report?
- What are the developmental, operational, and user costs?
- Has the value been quantified?
- Does the cost exceed the value?
- Can the data be obtained in a less costly manner?

Reporting periods

- How long is the information needed?
- Indefinitely or only for a few weeks or months?
- Has the report been assigned an expiration date consistent with this need?
- Are reporting periods, such as work-days as opposed to calendar-days, properly stated in the instructions?

Frequency

- Is the frequency (monthly, quarterly, annually, etc.) of the report prescribed in the requiring directive?
- Does the directive state when the first report is due?
- Does the frequency fit the users' needs?
- Is it possible to lower the frequency without hurting operations? (The lower the frequency, the more economical the report.)

Due date

- Does the requiring directive indicate the date when the report should be received at its destination?
- Are the most distant preparing offices and the method of transmittal taken into account when assigning due dates?

Preparing office workload

- Has the workload of preparing offices been taken into consideration?
- Is there adequate preparation time?
- Are deadlines realistic?
- Have the heaviest workload periods, such as the end of months or quarters, been avoided wherever possible?

Report title

- Is the title brief and descriptive?

- If the directive concerns only the report, is the title of the report similar to the subject of the directive?

Purpose of report

- Is the purpose of the report clearly stated in the requiring directive?
- Is it clear to preparing offices what use should be made of the data?

Reporting instructions

- Are the reporting instructions sufficiently detailed and clear so they can be readily understood?
- Is a completed sample report included to clarify complex reporting?
- Do the instructions provide for uniformity of reporting?
- Do the instructions provide a clear picture of who is to report what, when, how, to whom and why?
- Is the directive organized so that it can be conveniently used by all those involved with the report?

Integrated reporting

- Where more than one organizational level uses the reported information, have the needs of all levels been tied into the reporting system?
- Is the pyramid principle applied? Is the information less detailed as it goes up the organizational ladder?
- Do the reporting instructions include specific data requirements for each organizational level?

Feeder reports

- Is the report a feeder report — does it provide information to be included in another report?
- What is the extent of feeder reporting?
- Would it be feasible to bypass intermediate feeder reports and furnish lower level data to the requiring office?
- Would additional feeder reports improve operations and the quality of information?

Reporting units

- Are specific offices required to prepare the report identified in the reporting directive?
- Are these offices in the best position to furnish the information?
- Are there more or fewer reporting units than needed?
- Is the existing number of reporting units sufficient for data comparison?

Negative report

- Is this a negative report?
- What use is made of it?

- Is it necessary?
- Is the requiring directive specific about the necessity of submitting negative reports?
- Where negative reports are required, what percentage of the total reports do they represent?
- Are the reporting units continually submitting negative reports?
- Can exception reporting be substituted?

Number of copies

- Is the number of copies to be prepared and distributed specified in the requiring directive?

Routeing

- Does the requiring directive contain the correct address of each recipient?
- Can the report be transmitted without a covering transmittal letter or memorandum?
- Is the method for distributing the report adequate?
- Is a copy of the report sent to everyone who needs and uses the information?
- Has the accuracy of the distribution list been verified in the last year?
- Have those who do not use the information been removed from the distribution list?

Format

- Is the format of the report prescribed in the requiring directive?
- Is the format suitable for the way the report is used?
- Is the report easy to prepare?
- If the report were changed to a form, would it lose its effectiveness?
- Do users have to search through the text to find the information they need?
- Does the report contain information which is repeated in successive reports? Could a code word, symbol, or number be substituted for this information?
- After identifying possibilities for converting narrative reports to forms, has the forms management staff been consulted?
- If a form is prescribed, has it been cleared with the forms management staff?

Arrangement and size

- Has the reporting form been designed according to established standards?

Standardization

- Do all preparing offices use the same form or format?
- Is the terminology used in presenting information standardized as much as possible?

Summary information

- Does the report require a time-consuming review by users to obtain essential data?
- Can selective or summarized high-lighting of certain elements be used to advantage?

Cumulative data

- Can last-minute workloads be eliminated by maintaining cumulative statistical data at the source?

Comparisons

- Should the report contain comparisons of data? (Reports that include comparative data are more useful than raw data or statistics.)
- Have production or performance goals been established to compare data against?
- Are the most meaningful comparative bases used, such as established standards, past performance, time-spans, trends, financial or production goals, and correlation with other schedules, programmes, or events?

Graphics

- Are graphics used in the report?
- Would graphics enable users to comprehend data faster?
- If illustrations, photographs, charts, graphs, and symbols are used, are they used to good advantage?

Authentication

- Are the signatures of verifying and approving officials required only when absolutely necessary?
- Are these signatures at the appropriate level of authority?
- Does each approval add to the information's reliability?
- Are these signatures collected merely for prestige?

Data sources

- Does the requiring directive specify the records from which reported data should be extracted?
- If no source records exist, of if they cannot be specified, does the directive prescribe how to develop or obtain the information?

Arrangement of records

- Are files or other sources maintained so that data can be easily extracted?
- Can records be arranged in the same sequence or order as the report format?
- If not, can the report format be adjusted to match the data sequence of records?
- Can file headings be matched with the report headings?
- Does the arrangement meet the needs of both the report and file users?

Report symbol

- Is the report symbol in the prescribed location?
- Is the symbol in a conspicuous place on the report?
- If the report title is the subject of the requiring directive, is the report symbol included in the directive title?

Style of presentation

- Is the report style suitable for its intended users (executives, technicians, the general public)?

- Is the tone of the report and the detailed statistics appropriate to the users' levels of knowledge and responsibility?
- Does the complete report reflect as much simplicity and utility as possible for the intended users?

An additional tool that analysts often find useful for reports review is the recurring data analysis chart, shown in Figure 6.4. This chart can be used to evaluate the possibilities of consolidating or eliminating duplicate reports and is particularly helpful in identifying repetitive data by functional category. Use of the chart involves selecting a functional category of reports, such as personnel, and listing the reports in sequence across the top, starting with the report having the greatest usage. Each information item required by each report is then listed down the left-hand column and checked off in the appropriate right-hand column whenever the item appears. When completed, the chart identifies information items that are common to various reports in the group, and provides the basis for reducing the number of reports or information items.

COSTING REPORTS

It hardly seems necessary to state that a comparison of two factors is not easily made if one of the factors is unknown. Yet, when managers are determining the value of a report or a reporting system, that truism is often forgotten. In organizations of all types and sizes reports are routinely considered to be justifiable in the complete absence of any knowledge as to how much they cost.

To ensure effective and economic reports management, organizations should determine the costs for all reporting requirements. Lest this be considered overkill, it should also be pointed out that the effort involved in developing a cost estimate for a particular report should be related to its probable expense. In determining the amount of effort to be expended in estimating reporting costs and the degree of accuracy needed, two factors should be considered. One is the probable cost of the report: the higher the cost, the more accurate should be the cost estimate. The second is the cost/benefit ratio, which can be used to determine the degree of accuracy needed by comparing the cost of a report against its value. The value can be expressed in either quantitative or qualitative terms. If the benefits of a report clearly outweigh its costs, it may not be necessary to achieve as high a degree of accuracy as when the costs and benefits appear to be more evenly balanced. When benefits are not clearly and substantially higher than probable costs, greater precision in cost estimates will permit a more valid evaluation of a report's cost effectiveness. The use of costing shortcuts, such as sampling or averaging, should be consistent with this general guideline.

Cost segments

The total cost of a report may be divided up into three distinct segments:

1. *Developmental costs* which stem from activities involving the establishment of a new report or the modification of an existing one.
2. *Operational costs* which are a factor of on-going activities such as data collection, processing, and transmitting.
3. *User costs* which result from activities performed by the office which imposes the reporting requirement.

All segments exist whether the report is manual or automated, the only difference being the type of activities which are included in the reporting process.

Although, ideally, all segments should be considered, it may not be possible to obtain all the data or to obtain it in the detail required for a complete costing effort. As always,

Page   of   pages

RECURRING DATA ANALYSIS CHART		Title, description, or source							
Subject of analysis or activity		Report x	Report y	Report z					
Personnel Reports									
Analysed by Ann ALIST	**Date** 4/88								**Total**
Item		No.	No.	No.	No.	No.	No.	No.	
1 Name		✓	✓	✓					3
2 Address		✓	✓						2
3 Phone No.			✓	✓					2
4 Birth Date		✓	✓						2
5 National Insurance No.			✓						1
6 Employee No.			✓						1
7 Organization Code			✓	✓					2
8									
9									
10									

Figure 6.4   Recurring data analysis chart

common sense should be applied. It is usually difficult, for example, to determine developmental costs for systems that have been in operation for several years when records had not been maintained during the developmental process. Operational and user costs, however, are available for an active reporting system, and should be recorded and updated periodically. Conversely, developmental costs are available for new systems while operational and user costs may not be, and only a projection or estimate of the latter costs may be possible. In these instances, estimates should be made as accurately as possible under the circumstances, and later revised to show actual costs when the information becomes available.

It may also be difficult to delineate reporting activities precisely. For example, the analysis of a reporting requirement and the design of a reporting system may overlap. Separating the costs of these two activities may be purely arbitrary, and, in such cases, the costs may need to be combined under a more general category. The following guidelines may be used to determine the various segments into which activities may be categorized for costing purposes.

Developmental costs

Specification of reporting requirements   including:

- Identifying the need for certain information.
- Determining the objectives and scope of the reporting system that could provide this information.
- Identifying the benefits of the system.
- Appraising the impact on existing and planned operations and systems.
- Conducting feasibility studies.

Analysis of the reporting requirements   including:

- Determining the specific data that should be provided.
- Identifying alternative methods for obtaining the data.
- Identifying data sources, processing requirements, and equipment.
- Describing inputs, reports, major functions, and the limitations of each alternative.
- Selecting the best alternative for providing the needed information.

Design of the reporting system   including development of system descriptions (specifications), including input and ouput documents, data collection procedures, data and document processing, contents of files, interfaces with other systems, and output distribution. For automated systems, this includes the development of technical specifications for the programmer and the writing of the computer program.

Installation of the reporting system   encompassing:

- Testing the new system procedures.
- Acquiring and installing new equipment or modifying existing equipment.
- Developing and issuing implementing instructions, users' guides, operations manuals, and forms.
- Converting existing methods and procedures to the new system.
- Scheduling and conducting orientation and training.
- Preparing the site (for large automated systems).

Operational Costs

Data collection   activities which include:

- Obtaining, assembling, and recording source data by the preparing units.
- Controlling the accuracy of source data.
- Forwarding the source data to the processing unit.
- Storing source data for future reference.

Data processing activities which include:

- Receiving and controlling source data documents at the processing unit.
- Preparing data for data entry — logging and batching input forms, transcribing data, manually editing data, correcting errors.
- Translating data to machine-readable form.
- Resolving data errors and obtaining missing data.
- Updating files and data bases.
- Performing system maintenance tasks — updating and upgrading system software.

Data transmission activities which include:

- Reproducing copies of reports.
- Delivering reports (mail, electronically, by hand, etc.).

User costs

- Interpreting and analysing the reported information.
- Reading, reviewing, and discussing the reported information.
- Using the information for the intended.

Basic costing requirements

In the development of a reporting system, estimates of reporting costs should include the resources expended on each of the three basic cost segments — developmental, operational, and user. For each segment, the direct personnel costs; direct equipment, materials, and supplies costs; other direct costs; and overhead costs should be developed as described in Chapter 4 and included in the calculations.

Costs to be excluded

There are two types of costs to exclude when estimating the costs of a reporting system — independent reporting costs and non-reporting costs. If a reporting system uses a feeder report as input and if the feeder report is an independent report that would continue if the reporting system did not exist, the cost of the feeder report should be excluded from the estimated costs of the reporting system. Likewise, costs that constitute an integral part of an organization's functions and would continue if the reporting did not exist are non-reporting costs that should be excluded from the estimates even though the reporting relies heavily upon, or could not exist without, such operations. For example, a reporting system that uses payroll data should not be charged with the cost of the data needed to produce the payroll or with the by-products of the payroll system such as payroll control registers, time and attendance cards, etc.

Alternative Data Gathering Methods

There are various methods for gathering data. The method used should be appropriate to

SUMMARY WORKSHEET FOR ESTIMATING REPORTING COSTS

Report symbol: Report title: Estimate prepared by: Date:

Factors		Costs (£)					
Reporting categories	Reporting activities	Direct personnel (a)	Overhead (% of column (a)) (b)	Direct equipment (c)	Direct material (d)	Other direct costs (e)	Total (a + b + c + d + e) (f)
Developmental costs	1 Specification of reporting requirement						
	2 Analysis of reporting requirement						
	3 Design of reporting system						
	4 Installation of reporting system						
	5 Developmental costs (add totals in column (f))						
Operational costs	6 Data collection						
	7 Data processing						
	8 Data transmission						
	9 Operational costs for one report (add totals in column (f))						
	10 Annual operational costs (cost for one report multiplied by frequency per year)						
User costs	11 Refining, interpreting and analysing information received						
	12 Reading, reviewing, discussing and documenting information presented						
	13 User costs for one report (add totals in column (f))						
	14 Annual user costs (cost for one report multiplied by frequency per year)						

Figure 6.5 Summary worksheet for estimating reporting costs

the degree of accuracy required to evaluate a reporting system for cost effectiveness. The following alternatives should be considered:

- *Pilot testing* This method provides actual costs and may be worthwhile in high-cost reporting networks with fully-mechanized systems including data banks, a large number of data elements, or a new data collection system. Pilot testing may also be useful if respondent costs are needed for budget purposes.
- *Factoring* A comparison may be made with a similar report or reporting system for which costs have already been established. Assuming that the estimator is experienced, this method can provide data at a medium to low cost with a high degree of accuracy.
- *Sampling* This method is best applied when the report is new in concept and will have a large number of respondents. Obtaining a representative sample is the key to success, and care must be taken to ensure sample accuracy. Costs may be low to high.
- *Technical estimates* A low-cost method of data gathering based entirely on the estimator's experience and judgement. Best applied only to low-cost reporting systems such as those with few respondents or a short life.

Data Summarization

To simplify the summarization of data, the summary worksheet for estimating reporting costs has been developed. This worksheet, shown in Figure 6.5, aids in summarizing and presenting information in a clear and systematic manner, and helps to ensure that all pertinent information is collected and that no significant reporting activity or cost items are overlooked. Summary worksheets should be supported by working papers showing detailed computations and including the source and basis for the data used. This material should be retained until the cost of a reporting system is again estimated, which should be done whenever a major change occurs in the system, or (in an abbreviated manner) during the periodic review.

7 Directives Management

The word 'directives' has been used here to describe policy and procedure statements issued by an organization. They have different titles in different countries, sometimes even within countries. Essentially, what is covered in this chapter are office notices, bulletins, board notices, management statements, circulars, etc., all comprising the policies and procedures of a particular organization. In many offices these are consolidated into a manual or staff handbook, which can itself be described as a directive.

In the absence of written guidance, people will perform an operation in the manner they think is best — or at least the easiest. Few of the methods, if any, will be identical. Some will be efficient and some will be inefficient. With written guidance, the 'approved' way of operating (which hopefully is efficient) is clearly spelled out so that people know exactly what to do and how to do it.

What a person should do is called policy. How it should be done is called procedure. Policies and procedures originate at practically all levels within an organization. What usually happens is that the various entities at each level — and sometimes even within a level — develop their own methods for disseminating policy and procedural information. This way of operating is both the easiest and the hardest. It is easiest on the policy and procedure originators because they can sit in a vacuum and think up instructions and have them printed. It is hardest on the organization as a whole, because inevitably this sort of non-system leads to duplication, conflict, increased workload, and poor decision-making.

Policies and procedures are types of directives. Directives are issues that guide, instruct, or inform people in an organization about their work. It is important to have procedures documented in directives to achieve consistency of decision-making and uniformity of operations. It is also important to have the directives themselves organized in a logical manner so that the people who originate guidance and instructional information have a way of disseminating it, and so that those in the organization who need to refer to the information can easily obtain it.

Because most people within an organization are generally unaware of how to design and operate directives systems, directives management programmes are established.

To establish a directives management programme an authorizing document is prepared outlining objectives, responsibilities, and authorities for the programme, and procedures for operating the directives system.

There are two aspects to a directives management programme:

- establishment and operation of the directives system;

94

- directive analysis and control.

DIRECTIVES SYSTEMS

The basic types of directives systems are:

- Single-level — where one system exists for an entire organization and all issues must conform to one standard;
- Multi-level — where a principal system is established at the highest administrative level and individual systems are allowed at lower levels, but with a standard subject classification scheme.

The single-level system is generally used in a small- to medium-sized organization and the multi-level system is most appropriate in a larger organization, especially one that is highly decentralized.

Regardless of the system used, there should'be two types of directives: permanent and temporary. Permanent directives have continuing reference value and long-term significance, whereas temporary directives are of a transitory nature. The distinction between permanent and temporary directives is made to reduce the volume of material retained in the overall directives system.

Permanent directives

Permanent, in a directives context, does not have the same meaning as the term permanent in an archival context. Archival permanence means forever. Directives permanence, however, means until specifically cancelled or superseded. It is the use of a directive that is the determining factor in deciding on its permanence.

A directive should be issued as permanent if it:

- Establishes or changes the organizational structure
- Delegates authority or assigns responsibility
- Establishes or revises policy
- Prescribes a method or procedure
- Establishes standards of operation
- Revises or cancels other directives
- Promulgates a form or report.

Directives containing information to be retained for reference and guidance should be issued as permanent directives, as should handbooks and manuals which are part of the directives system.

Specific names should be given to permanent directives so that they are easily distinguished from the temporary type. Among the most common names used for permanent directives are orders, instructions, and regulations.

Temporary directives

Temporary policies and procedures have no continuing reference value. They are used to establish short-term programmes, to test or establish interim procedures, and to make announcements. Temporary directives remain in effect for a fixed period of time, usually not exceeding one year. They are self-cancelling in that they are assigned an expiration date when they are issued, and they should be destroyed upon expiration or cancellation. Only in emergencies should a temporary directive be used to modify a permanent directive, and in such cases a revised permanent directive should be issued as soon as possible thereafter.

A variety of names can be used to identify temporary directives. The most widely used terms are notice, bulletin, and circular.

ESTABLISHING A SYSTEM

The development and establishment of a new directives system requires the review and updating of all policies and procedures that have been issued regardless of form. The existing methods of communicating policy and procedure should be evaluated, and any deficiencies remedied.

All organizations should ensure that there are particular staff responsible for the management of directives. These staff should be an operational unit of the records management programme. In addition, copies of directives must be placed in files. There are two main types of directives files:

- *History file* A permanent, continuous record of directives that have been issued by an organization. This file provides an easy reference source to past directives that have been cancelled, revised, or superseded, and can provide the means for tracing the development of a policy or procedure on specific subjects. History files are generally organized by subject classification code. Essential documents to be included in them are the original copy of the directive, each draft version sent out for clearance, significant working papers, the document containing signatures of officials who concurred during the clearance process, notations regarding regulatory source materials, and the signed original of the authorization for cancellation.
- *Master reference file* A copy of each directive should be filed by subject classification code. When a directive is cancelled, it should be marked as such with the cancellation date and cross reference to the cancellation notice indicated. When a directive or page is revised, the new material should be filed in front of the superseded portion, plainly marked as revised.

Directives indexes

Indexes serve as finding aids for users and help the directives management staff locate all issues in the system. There may be two basic indexes — a numerical index and a subject index.

A numerical index is a list of all current directives arranged by control number, and is often referred to as a checklist or inventory. This index supplies information on the most recent version of each directive and on each revised page or change. The numerical index should be issued periodically and should contain the control number, date, and title of each directive. It may also include the originating office symbol, the distribution code, and the review date.

A subject index contains an alphabetical list of keyword subjects with corresponding control numbers for the directives in which those subjects are discussed. A subject index should be issued as a user finding aid when there is a sizeable amount of related material in the directives system.

Classification

In addition to the general category names (that is, notices, orders, bulletins), directives are more specifically identified by a subject and classification code. The development of a subject classification scheme provides a uniform, systematic method of identifying and locating directives and ensures that all directives on a given subject are in one place. By grouping directives by subject, all existing policies and procedures can be evaluated in

```
ENERGY POLICY AND EVALUATION
RESOURCE APPLICATIONS

      Petroleum

        Natural gas
        Coal
        Uranium
        Shale

      Power marketing

      Geothermal

ENERGY CONSERVATION
SOLAR APPLICATIONS
CONSTRUCTION AND ENGINEERING

      Construction

      Engineering

      Design criteria
```

Figure 7.1   Part of subject classification table

order to prevent duplication, conflict, procedural weaknesses, or gaps in coverage. A classification scheme should be:

*   Complete — containing a category for all existing directives.
*   Flexible — allowing for expansion or reduction of subject areas.
*   Logical — grouped so that the reasons for the arrangement will be obvious.
*   Restrictive — with subject titles mutually exclusive of each other.
*   Precise — so that each subject is clearly identifiable.

The complexities of an organization must be understood before a directives subject classification scheme is proposed. Regulations, organizational charges, functional statements, delegations of authority, and position descriptions are possible sources for gaining knowledge of organizational operations. A detailed analysis of administrative and programme files should be completed to identify the subjects on which an organization would be preparing directives. Conceptually, the classification scheme should follow the major functions of the organization.

When the subjects have been identified, a subject classification table should be developed. This hierarchical classification listing divides broad groups of interrelated subjects into primary categories, and subdivides the primary categories into successive levels of subordinate categories as shown in Figure 7.1. Subordinate subjects must logically relate to each appropriate primary subject, and some primary categories will, of necessity, have more subordinate categories than others. In preparing a subject classification table there are a few factors to be considered.

Various organizational entities may want separate sections/subdivisions to cover their particular operation, even though their functional responsibilities fit quite well within one primary subject. If a classification scheme is devised according to the wishes of each organization, the results will be an organizational classification scheme, *not* a subject classification scheme. Splitting primary subjects increases the chance for overlap and conflict.

In a similar vein, an effective subject grouping cannot be achieved if portions of the subject classification table are reserved for the exclusive use of one organizational unit. Each directive must be classified and assigned to the most appropriate subject area. In any directives system the requirements of the user should always be given preference over the convenience of the originator.

Coding

Coding consists of assigning symbols or abbreviations (numbers, letters, alphanumeric combinations) to the subjects listed in the subject classification table. Prime considerations in selecting a codification pattern are concise identification, easy retrieval, expansion, indexing, uniform reference sequence, and control.

There are many patterns for numbering the subjects in the classification table. The most common are numeric, alphabetic, duplex numeric, alphanumeric, subject numeric, and decimal. Examples of these six types are shown in Table 7.1.

When coding a classification scheme, a determination should be made about the number of code characters necessary to provide complete coverage and room for expansion. While three characters may adequately cover some arrangements, four characters may be necessary to completely pinpoint identification and allow for future expansion. Using one of the examples in Table 7.1 the secondary subject, Employment, may need to be further broken down into tertiary and quarternary categories as follows:

Personnel	3000 (Primary)
Employment	3100 (Secondary)
Recruitment	3110 (Tertiary)
College programme	3111 (Quarternary)
Special programmes	3112 (Quarternary)

The numbering pattern should provide for specific identification of different directives in the same subject area. Procedural practices may dictate that several directives are required to implement various segments of a particular operation.

Revised directives

A common method for identifying a revised directive (a complete rewrite of an existing directive) is to add an alphabetical suffix to the originally assigned subject classification code. For example, OA-144.1A would indicate the first revision of OA-144.1. The next revision would be indicated as OA-144.1B.

Another method used to identify directives which are periodically revised is the addition of a hyphen or similar mark to the original assigned classification code along with a sequence number. Using this method, the first revision to the original OA-144.1 would be designated as OA-144.1-1 or OA-144.1/1.

Manuals

Some organizations incorporate directives on specific subjects into sets of manuals. In the administrative areas, for example, there may be manuals on such subjects as accounting, office services, and personnel. A different approach would be to combine these functional directives into one manual called the administrative manual. Where directives are collected in a manual arrangement, identification is usually accomplished by manual title and sequential numbering, with each manual assigned the appropriate primary subject classification number for the specific functional area it covers.

Table 7.1
Codification of directives

	Numeric	Alpha	Duplex numeric	Alpha numeric	Subject numeric	Decimal
Personnel	110	A	3	A	PERS	1.
Employment	110	Aa	3-1	A/1	PERS-1	1.1
Recruitment	111	AaA	3-1-1	A/11	PERS-1-1	1.1.1
Appointment	112	AaB	3-1-2	A/12	PERS-1-2	1.1.2
Promotion	113	AaC	3-1-3	A/13	PERS-1-3	1.1.3
Demotion	114	AaD	3-1-4	A/14	PERS-1-4	1.1.4
Separation	115	AaE	3-1-5	A/15	PERS-1-5	1.1.5
Veteran	116	AaF	3-1-6	A/16	PERS-1-6	1.1.6
Special	117	AaG	3-1-7	A/17	PERS-1-7	1.1.7

99

Temporary directives

Temporary directives are usually identified by sequential numbers. A common method used is a series of consecutive numbers preceded by the originator's symbol and a reference to the calendar or fiscal year (for example, PER-88-2).

Documentation

A complete outline and explanation of the directives system must be prepared and issued so that users can understand and utilize the system effectively. One possible method is to incorporate the material into the original programme document. However, the following information should be included:

1   The complete subject classification table (titles and numbers).
2   A listing of organizational symbols for those entities authorized to originate directives.
3   An illustration showing how to completely identify a directive by its code, for example:
    0A   .... Originator's symbol
    2010   .... Subject classification number
    .2   .... Consecutive number
    B   .... Revision designation
    Chg 1   .... Change number

FORMAT AND STANDARDIZATION

The adoption of standards for the format and contents of directives is essential to ensure their economical production and effective use. The most basic question is whether the system will be manual or automated.

Automation technology has provided many options that were formerly unavailable. Although the basic manual system consisting of looseleaf papers filed in three-ring binders is still the most popular format for directives issue, there are now alternative methods such as micropublishing using computer output microfilm (COM), and complete on-line systems wherein the text of all directives is centrally stored in electronic form and may be instantaneously accessed through remote terminals.

A frequently seen hybrid system is the issue of directives text in hard-copy manual format combined with a corresponding automated keyword index. The automated index greatly speeds up the referencing process which is the most time consuming aspect of directives utilization.

The advantages of automated directives systems are many and varied. Whether the technology utilized is micrographics, computer, optical disc, or a combination, the result can be substantial increases in the timeliness of the information issued (a key factor in any directives system) along with commensurate decreases in document storage space, system maintenance, user reference time, and overall costs.

An automated system must be carefully planned for and designed. There is a risk in stating this because the interpretation could be made that a manual system, in contrast, might be thrown together haphazardly. This is not true. All systems require great thought and intensive analysis if they are to function effectively, efficiently, and economically. Yet there are definite differences between automated and manual systems. Because a directives system is organization-wide in scope, if there is the slightest doubt as to whether an organization is ready to automate, in terms of capital investment, user acceptance, managerial support, or a host of other areas, automation should not be undertaken. Any system which is only half-finished or half-used is a mess. And an automated mess is worse than a manual mess.

Regardless of whether the system is automated or manual, a basic format for presenting the information must be developed. All directive material should be organized and arranged in a logical manner to enable the user to locate the desired information quickly. There are a variety of formats which have been developed to present directive material. The most commonly used are the outline format and the playscript format.

Outline format

As its name implies, the outline format arranges information in outline form within an alphabetic and numeric hierarchy. The outline is a highly-structured format and is useful where a policy or procedure must be broken down into its component parts with each part individually described.

The outline could be considered the all-purpose format. Policies, procedures, instructions, etc. can all be presented in outline form. It is described in some detail, but one must keep in mind that structure and consistency are key elements of an effective directives system. Whether the system is manual or automated, the manner in which the information is presented is critical. (See Figure 7.2).

A directive page heading should be brief and simple in order to give maximum space for text. The appearance of the heading should be different from the organization's letterhead in order to avoid the possibility of confusing directives with correspondence.

The head of the first page should include the identification items listed and described below. This information enables the users to quickly determine if the directive applies to them.

1   *Issuing point/organization*   Identification of the issuing organization is essential for organizational management purposes, for directive users who may need to contact the originator, and for archival reasons. The name and short address of the issuing organization should be shown in the heading of the first page of a directive. This name should also be shown on each succeeding page.

2   *Directive identifier*   When developing or revising a directive, the originating office must consider all related directives on the subject and should know how and where its directive will fit into the overall system. Originators should be responsible for assigning a subject classification code to each directive issued. This code will:

- make it easier to locate
- establish uniformity of sequence
- provide an automatic grouping of subjects
- simplify control.

Because directives are filed by subject classification code it is important that the code appear in the upper corner of each page. On even-numbered (left side) pages the code should be in the upper left corner. On odd-numbered (right side) pages, the code should appear in the upper right corner.

3   *Originating office code*   Identifying the specific office within an organization that originates policy or procedure can greatly assist the researcher. A code, abbreviation or short name may be used.

4   *Date of approval or effective date*   Unless otherwise stated, a directive is effective on its approval date. When it is necessary to make the provisions of the directive effective on a date other than the approval date, a paragraph headed 'Effective date' should be included. When dating directives, take into account the time needed for printing and distribution.

5   *Subject line*   Each directive is given a subject line to briefly identify the area addressed. The subject identified should generally agree with the appropriate subject in the classification scheme.

6   *Distribution code*   The office that develops the directive should know exactly who will carry out the required action and should, therefore, determine the distribution. The distribution code is usually placed at the bottom of the first page of the directive.

The format of a notice is the same as the one shown here with the exception that the word 'notice' will be substituted for the word 'instructions'.

The addresses shown in the 'To' line will be indicated by a collective title such as 'field office personnel' or 'senior staff' or the words ' all company personnel'.

The subject line must be selected from and generally agree with the appropriate subject in the subject classification chart.

Paragraph titles will be used for all major paragraphs and may be used for subparagraphs. If one subparagraph is titled, titles must be included for other subparagraphs of the same subdivision.

Text. Paragraphs will be numbered consecutively throughout the text. If a paragraph is subdivided, it must have at least two subdivisions. Paragraphs will be indented as shown.

The sequence of paragraphs in directives is at the discretion of the originating office.

Page numbering. The first page will not be numbered. The second page will be numbered '2' and the remaining pages numbered consecutively throughout the text and attachments, if included. Page numbers will be centered at the bottom of each page.

Identifying number taken from the subject classification chart.

Date of issuance. This will be the effective date of issue, unless otherwise specified in the text.

Originating office. The above items will be carried on the upper right of odd-numbered pages and upper left of even-numbered pages.

The purpose of each directive will be stated in the first paragraph.

The second paragraph of an instruction which cancels another instruction will contain the statement of cancellation. However, in a notice whose sole purpose is to cancel an instruction, the statement of such cancellation may be made in the purpose paragraph.

If applicable, the last paragraph of each instruction and the next to last paragraph of each notice will indicate any reports required and any forms prescribed for use and will state where required forms may be obtained.

The last paragraph of each notice will state when or under what conditions the notice is to be cancelled. In all cases a specific cancellation date will be provided.

Distribution will be shown as the last item on the first page.

COMPANY NAME
COMPANY ADDRESS

AB/B 500.1
9 January 19xx
M:KS

Company Instruction 55b. 1
To:
Subject: Company Directives System

1. Purpose.
   ....
2. Appropriate heading.
   ....
3. Appropriate heading.
   a. Appropriate heading.
      (i) Appropriate heading.
         (a) ....
         (b) ....
      (2) Appropriate heading.
   b. Appropriate heading.
      ....
7. Appropriate heading.
   ....
8. Appropriate heading.
   a. Appropriate heading.
   b. Appropriate heading.
9. Appropriate heading.
   ....

DISTRIBUTION: C

Figure 7.2   Outline format directive configuration

7   *Subsequent page identification*   Not all identifying items included on the first page of a directive are needed on subsequent pages. It is usually sufficient to include only the name of the issuing organization, the subject classification code and the date of the directive.

8   *Approval or signature block*   Each directive must be approved or signed by an authorizing official. The most common area for indicating this approval is on the first page.

Playscript format

The playscript format is entirely different from the outline format. It is modelled like the script of a play with the names of the characters (responsible persons) on the left side of the page and the corresponding lines (actions) listed down the right side of the page. The format is simple to write and easy to use because it goes through an entire operation from beginning to end. It is very useful for detailing procedures. The disadvantages of a playscript format is that it is not hierarchical and does not break down a function into routines and sub-routines as would an outline format.

Organization of directives

The basic unit of text in a directive is the paragraph. All paragraphs require a number or letter designation. Each main paragraph should have a brief description heading to assist the reader in identifying the subject matter. Subparagraphs should be used to divide long paragraphs or to list conditions, exceptions, or procedures. Headings may also be used for subparagraphs, and they may be underlined to highlight the text.

Lengthy directives such as manuals or handbooks should be divided into chapters. Chapters may be further divided into parts and sections.

When using the outline format, the basic rule for outlining is followed. That is, whenever a unit is divided, at least two sub-units must be established. Paragraphs are alternately numbered and lettered at each level of subordination.

1   *Paragraph sequence*   The format of the directive must be prescribed so that there is a standard presentation of information in a logical sequence. The following paragraph headings are commonly used:

- Purpose (should be stated in the first paragraph)
- Scope/applicability
- Cancellation (other directives, related forms and reports)
- Authority/background
- References (other directives or documents)
- Policy
- Objectives
- Definitions
- Responsibilities
- Substance paragraphs
  Information
  Instructions
  Procedures
- Effective date (if other than approval date)
- Forms prescribed
- Reports required
- Expiration date (for temporary directives).

2   *Margins/indentations*   The margins and identations for each page should be estab-

lished to provide maximum readability. These format specifications may be quite different depending on whether the system is manual or automated.

3 *Page numbering* The first page of a directive should not be numbered. The second page (left-hand page) should be numbered '2', and the remaining pages numbered consecutively. All left-hand pages should contain even numbers and all right-hand pages should contain odd numbers. If chapters are used, pages should be numbered consecutively within each chapter. Numbers should be centred at the bottom of each page so that they will not be confused with the identifying subject classification code. Directives material is usually referenced by paragraph number rather than by page number. Page numbers are primarily used for inserting revised pages or removing obsolete ones.

4 *Supplementary materials* Materials such as appendices, attachments, and exhibits should be placed at the end of the chapter to which they relate or at the end of the directive, whichever will be most convenient to the user. Each page of the supplementary material should be identified clearly showing the subject title, classification number, and issue date.

5 *Figures* Figure numbers may be used to identify illustrations, charts, and tables placed within the text of a directive. If figures are small (one page or less) place them as close as possible to the paragraph to which they relate or where they were first mentioned. Place longer illustrative materials at the end of the appropriate chapter. All figures should be captioned and numbered consecutively.

6 *References* These are used when the material being referenced relates directly to the subject matter, makes a significant contribution to understanding the text, or eliminates the need for repeating lengthy material. Although references can be useful, they should be used sparingly. When first cited, the complete designated title and identification number should be included, and the reader should be told why the referenced information is needed.

7 *Transmittal sheets* Transmittal sheets may be used to forward directives to users. Directives can be self-transmitting, however, by supplying the pertinent information on the first page. Directives having fewer than five pages are usually issued without a transmittal sheet. The transmittal sheet is used to give a summary of the contents of a directive or to outline the changes that have occurred in a revision. It can also be used as a cancelling device, to cancel directives, forms, or reports.

8 *Revisions* The process for making revisions should be standardized to prevent confusion. Revisions and changes should be given exactly the same distribution as the directives they amend. If extensive changes are required, the entire directive may be revised and reissued. If only minor changes are necessary, issuing a few revised pages may suffice.

Revised pages should carry the change number and the revision date. This information should be placed at the top of the page near the subject classification number. Time may be saved by the users in comparing an old directive page with a new one if a distinguishing mark is placed in the margin opposite the changed portion of the text, or at the beginning and end of the changed sections.

If an additional page is needed to incorporate a revision to the body of a directive, the page numbering scheme may be adjusted by adding a letter to the applicable page number (for example, 14, 14a, 14b). At such time as the directive is completely revised or reissued, however, the pages should be renumbered consecutively to conform to the original pattern.

Often, minor typographical errors can be corrected by instructing the directives recipients to make pen and ink changes to the printed text. Substantive changes, however, should not be made in this manner.

9 *Supplements* Supplements to directives are often allowed in order to enhance managerial flexibility by enabling managers to issue specific instructions on procedures or to interpret policies for their particular organization entities. Such guidance usually

applies only to a specific area within the organization and should only be issued within that area. All supplemental issuances should be numbered with the same subject classification code as the basic directive, and should complement the basic directive, not conflict with it.

REPRODUCTION, DISTRIBUTION AND STOCK

The most comprehensive and well organized directives are of little value if they are not available to the persons who need to use them. Therefore, reproduction and distribution of the directives material is considered to be an integral part of the directives management system.

Reproduction

The method of reproduction will depend on the type of directives system which is being used. For the common looseleaf manual type of system, original, camera-ready copy must be prepared for printing. Many organizations use specially-designed format sheets, preprinted with non-photographic blue ink, for preparing reproducible directive material.

Although it is not uncommon to find the original copy is prepared by the directives management staff, this is not necessarily the most efficient way of operating. As long as the material is prepared using consistent formats and type styles, it can be prepared satisfactorily by the originating office, word processing facility, or other unit.

When an automated system is involved, the situation is somewhat different. In order to maintain control and guard against errors, directives text should only be entered into the system by the directives management staff. This is not to say that the material could not be typed by another unit and electronically transmitted to the directives staff, or that a floppy disc could not be transferred to achieve the same purpose. If the organization has a sizeable directives system, but without organization-wide automation, there is also the possibility of having directives material keyboarded on standard electric typewriters and optically scanned into an automated directives system by the directives management staff.

Once the information has been entered into the system, it can be electronically photocomposed and prepared for printing; it can be output in a microform through use of a COM system; or it can be stored for electronic access by users through remote terminals.

Distribution

A good directives system provides timely distribution of the required number of copies of directives on a 'need to know' and 'need to use' basis. In establishing or revising a distribution system, the following principles should be considered:

- Distribute selectively — send directives only to those who require them.
- Distribute directly — send directives directly to the organization level that uses them rather than through 'official channels'.
- Distribute consistently — send revised directives or notices of cancellation to the same organizations that received the originals.
- Distribute to titles — distribution lists that use organization or position titles are easier to keep current and are less subject to change than those using individual's names.

A directives distribution system is usually based on the structure of the organization. This framework is familiar to most employees within the organization and the hierarchical terminology used (that is, office, division, branch, section, unit) remains fairly constant over time. Further refinements of distribution patterns could be made based on factors such as geographical locations, functions, employee titles, or combinations of the above.

Even with a manual directives system, the distribution function is one that can probably be automated. Mail (distribution) lists seem to naturally lend themselves to computer applications. A microcomputer with basic, commercially-available file management software can handle most smaller distribution systems, and many larger, more complex systems can be handled by using commercially-available data base management software programmes. It is more than likely that the productivity increase and resultant cost savings from automating the directives distribution function alone would be sufficient to justify the purchase of both the hardware and the software necessary, and the equipment would then be available for automating other functions as well.

The orderly operation of a distribution system requires a uniform way of requesting changes in distribution lists. The method of requesting and approving changes and a description of the operation of the system should be documented in the basic directive and made available to users and originators.

Stocking directives

With a manual directives system, additional copies must be available for users. The number and location of the stocking points will vary with the size of the organization. Generally, extra copies to be stocked should be a part of the initial reproduction order, although stocking reproducible masters may be more convenient and economical in some instances. The cost of stocking reproducible masters should be compared with that of stocking extra copies. The availability of reproduction equipment, the length of time required to reproduce extra copies, and the possible savings in space and personnel costs should also be considered.

Where central stocking occurs, the initial stocking levels may be recommended by the directives originators. Replenishment of the stock would be determined by the stocking unit and by the directives management staff based on requisition experience, frequency of revision, cost, and the time needed to print additional copies.

DIRECTIVES ANALYSIS AND CONTROL

The directives analysis and control process includes analysis of the directive's content, editorial assistance for directives originators, co-ordination of proposed new or revised directives with various organizational entities, assignment of control numbers, and maintenance of the entire directives system.

Directives analysis

A proposed new or revised directive should be analysed by the directives management staff for timeliness, readability, format consistency, and accuracy. While most of these factors are self-explanatory, the accuracy factor requires some explanation.

The responsibility for writing a directive belongs to the directives originator. Therefore, the responsibility for the accuracy of a directive belongs to the originator as well. The directives management staff can review the directive's content to determine if forms or reports referenced are still current, if organizational references are up to date, and if there is a conflict between the proposed material and that contained in a directive already in existence on a related subject. It is unrealistic, however, to expect the directives management staff to know every procedure for every system in the entire organization. The accuracy review, therefore, is done for much the same reason as the editorial review — to assist the originator, not to do his/her work.

Editorial assistance

To ensure that all organizational directives can be understood by those who must use them, the directives management staff should provide editorial assistance to originators as required. Often directives originators know exactly what they want to say, but have a great deal of difficulty in determining exactly how to say it. Help from persons who are skilled in the art of simple writing is usually welcomed.

Co-ordination

Each proposed new or revised directive should be cleared with all organizational entities that will be affected by it or that have a functional interest in its content. Insufficient clearances may result in inadequate directives which have to be prematurely revised and reissued. When the proposed directive prescribes forms and/or imposes reporting requirements, co-ordination with the units managing those functions should be included in the clearance process.

To facilitate the clearance process, a directive clearance form such as that shown in Figure 7.3 may be used to obtain concurrence or comments from the reviewers. The directives management staff should forward the draft directive and the clearance form together to each reviewing office. Routeing copies to several clearance offices simultaneously speeds up the clearance process while allowing more time for thorough review and analysis. A reasonable deadline for the completion of each review should be provided.

After receipt of the reviewing offices' comments and concurrences, the directives management staff and the originator should jointly consider the comments and determine their impact on the proposed directive. Where the comments or recommendations will improve the directive, changes reflecting these comments should be made. Where they are not considered essential for improving the directive, an explanation should be given to the office(s) concerned. If differences between the originator and the reviewers persist, the problem should be taken to the next higher authority for resolution. Directives should ordinarily not be transmitted for final signatory review without reconciliation of the comments. If the differences absolutely cannot be reconciled at the programme level, the directive should be forwarded to the approving official with a written staff analysis outlining the nature of the dispute.

Control numbers/issue dates

Assignment of a directives control number that is consistent with the subject classification scheme should be done after all clearances have been obtained. The official date of issue should be assigned with the control number.

DIRECTIVE CLEARANCE RECORD	Kind of document	Identification (if any)

| Subject | Person most familiar with attached | | |
| | Name | Routeing symbol | Extension |

Reason for attached: what does it do? (Continue on reverse)

Proposed distribution (Spell out – do not use code)

ORIGINATING OFFICE CLEARANCE

Routeing symbol	Init.	Routeing symbol	Date	Signature and routeing symbol	Date	Office forms approval	Office reports approval

CLEARANCE ROUTEING

Routeing symbol	Internal clearance			Signature and routeing symbol	Date	Deadline date			
	Init.	Routeing symbol	Date			Concur substance and distribution		Non-concur	Comment accepted
						No comment	Comment attached	Comment attached	Changes made
	Final administrative clearance								
	Final approval (authorizing release)					Date approved			

After approval send to:

Figure 7.3   Directives clearance form

8   Forms Management

If four people were asked to supply their name, address, telephone number, and date of birth on a card, the likely results would be the following:

1. John Jacob Jones
   123 Anystreet
   Anytown, USA 54321
   (109) 876–5432
   January 1, 1950

2. John Jones   1/1/50
   123 Anystreet
   Anytown, USA
   876–5432

3. J. J. Jones
   123 Anystreet
   Anytown, USA 54321
   (109) 876–5432
   January 1

4. Jones, John J.
   123 Anystreet
   Anytown, USA
   876–5432
   1/1/50

Of the four responses, only number one provides complete information in the order in which it was requested. At the risk of over-simplifying, that is why forms management is necessary.

Forms are tools which may be used to organize, collect, and transmit information. When properly analysed and designed from a systems perspective, forms can:

- enhance the flow of work through an office or an entire organization;
- increase operational efficiency and effectiveness;
- reduce costs.

A form is a fixed arrangement of captioned spaces designed for entering and extracting prescribed information. Traditionally, these captioned spaces were preprinted on paper and the person supplying the information would merely fill in the blanks with a pencil or typewriter. Today there are other options. For example, with computer technology, a form can be stored in memory and called up as needed on to a video screen so that input data may be entered into the system through the terminal keyboard. A form may also be stored in memory and produced via a high-speed laser printer as output with the rest of the processed data. Additionally, a form may be photographically placed on a glass slide and optically enlarged on film along with the processed data as a simultaneous exposure for computer output microfilming (COM) generation.

Regardless of the type of form, however, it must always be carefully analysed and designed if it is to be effective, and available in the proper place if it is to be used. Because the various forms management functions require knowledge that most people do not have, forms management programmes are established and staffed with specialists who are able to use their expertise to organization-wide advantage.

The specific objectives of a forms management programme are to:

* Determine that forms are necessary and up-to-date
* Design forms to enhance information processing
* Ensure that instructions for use are adequate
* Specify the most economical method of reproduction
* Ensure that forms are available when and where needed.

There are three aspects to a forms management programme which, when combined, enable the objectives to be met. These are forms control; forms analysis, design and composition; and forms reproduction, stocking, and distribution. If the first two of these sound similar to the aspects of a reports management programme, it is because they are. In fact, in many respects, forms and reports management programmes function almost identically. The basic difference between the two is that forms management personnel must have the highly-specialized forms design knowledge and an understanding of the printing, stocking and distribution functions in addition to the more general analytical expertise which is a basic requirement for all records management professionals.

It would be reasonable to assume that the forms and reports programmes could be combined. Their functions are often inextricably intertwined and there is a great deal of overlap. As a practical matter, the primary vehicle for transmitting reported information is a form!

However, since there are many information processing systems which use forms and which are not reporting systems, and since there is the requirement for the specialized knowledge, the programmes are usually established as separate entities.

Nevertheless, there is no question that the staff of both must work together and continuously co-ordinate their efforts.

For a forms management programme to be effective, all of the functions must be performed. If there is good control and no analysis, then the programme is controlling rubbish. If there is good design and no distribution and stocking plan, then the well-designed form will not be available to the people who need it. A complete programme is an absolute necessity.

FORMS CONTROL

Control over the proliferation of forms in an organization is one of the major aspects of a forms management programme. When people feel the need to create a form, there is usually little hesitation about doing so. This willingness to create, combined with the readily available means to create (all that is needed is a piece of paper, a pencil, and a copying machine) means that the unauthorized or 'bootleg' form is a fact of life in most offices.

Theoretically, all forms should be subject to control and all forms should be analysed, designed, inventoried, etc. Practically, that principle is ridiculous. If an individual working on a project creates a worksheet that only he (and maybe a few other people also working on the project) will use, and if the total number of those worksheets will probably not exceed 25, and if the life of those 25 copies will be four months, and if the cost of the entire thing is £43.00, a real question exists as to the necessity for the forms management staff to become involved in that effort.

Forms managers who insist on absolute control over everything that fits the form definition without regard to the practicality of the situation, quickly become people to be avoided in organizations, and are seen as obstacles to progress rather than facilitators of it. Obviously, dismissal of the control responsibility is not being advocated; merely a pragmatic approach to its implementation.

A forms management programme should have an authorizing directive that spells out the various authorities and responsibilities and clearly outlines the procedures to be followed for creating a new form or modifying an existing one.

Generally, unauthorized forms should not exist. An effective way to inhibit their creation is to establish the policy (in co-operation with both the print unit and the procurement authority) that no form will be produced or purchased until it has been approved by the forms management staff. Simply initialling the printing or procurement requisition is a convenient way to indicate approval.

Control is also necessary so that forms are subjected to periodic review. Each time a form is reprinted it should be reviewed to ensure that it is still necessary and adequate for the purpose for which it was created. By co-ordinating the periodic review schedule with the reprint schedule, necessary changes can be made in a timely manner so that stock shortages are prevented.

The tools available to make the forms control job easier are the history file, the functional file, the control number, and the catalogue. In order to create these tools, a forms inventory must first be taken.

Inventory

To conduct a forms inventory a letter or memorandum should go to all organizational units requesting copies of *all* forms currently being used and the estimated annual usage for each. It is helpful to include the definition of a form and an explanation of the collection effort in the letter, along with a due date for the submissions.

The result of this request will be lots of forms, indeed, more forms than are needed. However, only by incurring this one-time duplication can a complete picture be drawn regarding organization-wide forms usage.

As the forms are received, copies should be filed both numerically by control number and alphabetically by subject. If the forms do not contain control numbers, assign numbers sequentially even if only as a temporary measure. The numerical file will become the basis for the forms history file and the subject file will be the basis of the functional file used for control purposes.

History file

The forms history file contains historical information on each form including:

- copies of the current and previous editions
- working papers showing stages of development
- a copy of, or reference to, the prescribing directive
- the original request for approval and subsequent requests for revisions
- documents containing specifications and showing reproduction/procurement action;
- documents relating to stocking and distribution.

The history file is organized numerically by forms control number.

Functional file

The forms functional file is a subject classification file used in the analysis process for comparing forms in the same functional area in order to avoid duplication. The file should be arranged alphabetically by function (subject) which, of course, necessitates that a comprehensive list of organizational functions (that is, apply, authorize, certify, order, request, etc.) be developed. The following is a basic list of functional file catgories:

- Acknowledge
- Agree
- Apply
- Assign
- Attest
- Authorise
- Bill
- Cancel
- Certify
- Claim
- Estimate
- Follow-up
- Identify
- Instruct
- Layout
- List
- Notify
- Offer
- Order
- Record
- Report
- Request
- Route
- Schedule
- Transmit
- Verify

Use of the functional file allows the forms analyst to:

1   Avoid creating a new form that duplicates an existing one.
2   Identify existing forms that can be eliminated or consolidated.
3   Identify forms that can be standardized throughout the organization.

Control number

The forms control number is a number assigned to an approved form and, preferably, printed on its face for identification purposes. Each form subject to the control system should have a number and, ideally, the numbers will all be part of the same sequential scheme. When modifying an existing forms control system, however, it may be necessary to have forms with different numbering schemes or to have two numbers assigned (new and old) for some period of time.

The simpler the numbering scheme the better. For example, a number such as 123-PRO-85 would indicate that the form was the 123rd in the system, that it originated in the PROcurement department, and that it was created (or revised) in 1985. That is sufficient information for identification purposes. Attempting to include data such as functional file codes and retention periods into the form numbers will only confuse the users.

A simple log should be kept of form numbers issued and the titles corresponding to them. Although that information is obtainable by looking in the history file, a log provides a much more convenient reference.

Catalogue

A forms catalogue is not an absolute necessity for a control programme (as are history and functional files) but it is often helpful to have for quick reference purposes. Catalogues vary greatly in both size and format. In some instances they consist of hundreds or thousands of pages, each containing a facsimile of a particular form and instructions for its use. In other (more frequent) instances, a catalogue is merely a listing of forms and contains only basic information such as title and number. The development and use of a forms catalogue is dependent on the number of forms in the system. Generally, for a small organization, a catalogue is not required.

Automated control

So far, all of the control tools described have been manual. These paper-based systems are entirely adequate for most organizations. While automated control systems have been developed for some extremely large organizations, they are generally not cost effective for use in a less expansive environment.

The developmental costs alone for a computerized functional file system could well exceed £150 000, and, even with the most advanced system, there will still be substantial work required of the forms management staff to determine if consolidation or elimination of forms is desirable and to decide how such actions should be accomplished.

Forms control process

The forms management directive should contain the procedures for establishing a new form or revising an existing one. Basically, the control process should operate in the following manner.

A request for a new or revised form (shown in Figure 8.1) should be completed and submitted to the forms management staff along with a rough draft or sketch of what the requestor thinks the form should look like. Associated documents such as instructions and a draft of the requiring directive should also accompany the request form. If necessary, the forms management staff should assist the requestor in completing the request form and in producing the associated materials.

The forms management staff should review the request and analyse the proposed form for necessity, adequacy, usefulness, and economy (see following sections). Approval should come *only* after it has been determined that:

- all items on the form are needed
- all copies of the form are needed
- the design is functional
- clear and complete instructions have been developed
- stock levels have been determined
- distribution patterns have been established
- printing and construction specifications have been developed
- the form is cost effective.

When the form is approved it should be assigned a control number and sent for composition. No further control is necessary until the form reaches a reprint point at which time the periodic review should take place. It should be noted that the forms management staff initiates the periodic review, not the form originator. The originator, however, must be contacted during the review process.

ANALYSIS AND DESIGN

The analysis and design of forms is, by far, the most important part of the forms management process. If all forms were going to be analysed and designed properly by their originators, the rest of the management and control process would be almost unnecessary, inasmuch as the primary reason for controlling is to achieve efficiency and effectiveness — precisely what properly analysed and designed forms do.

Forms design is such a highly specialized and technical area, that entire books could be written on the subject. Indeed, such books have been written and are readily available. This text, therefore, will not cover forms design, but will only deal with the analytical aspects of the analysis and design process.

The general subject of analysis is covered in some detail in Chapter 4. Specifically regarding forms, however, analysis seeks to answer the following questions:

- What is the work that creates a need for the form?
- How is the work done or how will it be done?
- Why is the work done or why will it be done in a particular way?
- Who does the work?
- What are the processes, operations and documents involved?
- What are the purposes of the form?
- In which operations and in what procedures is the form used?

REQUEST FOR APPROVAL AND DEVELOPMENT OF FORM
(If *more space is needed, use reverse and identify by Item No.*)

To: (*forms management office symbol*)	From: (*office symbol*)	Project officer: (*typed name and phone no.*)

1 Type of form ☐ New ☐ Revised	2 Form title		

3 Form designation and no. (*Leave blank if new*)	4 Form update	5 Report control symbol	6 Controlled forms ☐ Accountable ☐ Safeguard

7 Use			8 Used within					9 Method of completion			10 Recommended size
Permanent	Test	One time	One office	One area	One region	Nation wide		Type writer	Hand	Machine (*see item 21*)	

11 Type of file						12 Date form must be available/ implemented (*line one out*)	13 Prescribing directive
Visible	Vertical	Folder	Ledger	3-ring binder	Other (*specify*)		

14 Explain purpose for which form will be used (if proposed form replaces an existing higher level form prescribed for the same purpose, attach a written waiver from the originator)

15 Type(s) of using activities	16 Frequency of preparation (*daily, weekly, monthly, etc*)

17 No. of copies filled in at one writing	18 Distribution of original and each copy indicated in item 17	19 Initial issue quantity	20 Estimated monthly use

22 Superseded forms   ☐ Yes   ☐ No   (*if yes complete A and B. Complete C If stock is to be destroyed*)

A Number(s)	Date(s)	B Existing stock		C Justification for destroying stock (*explain why superseded form(s) cannot be used*)
		Use	Destroy	

23 Concurrences (*office symbol, name and extension of individual outside the immediate organization who concurred in accepting the workload this procedure will impose on his/her organization*)

25 Date of approval	25 Typed name, grade and title of approving official	26 Signature

For use of Forms Management Office							
27 Unit of Rqn	28 Const/ Pkg	29 Trim size	30 Carbon interleaved sets			31 Carbonless paper	
			No. of parts	Colour of carbon	Carbon coverage	No. of parts	Colour of paper

32 Punching						33 Binding		
No. holes	Diameter	C to C	Kind	Position		☐ Staple	☐ Glue	Other (*specify*)

34 Paper			35 Print						36 Forms stocked by (*if other than publications distr. centre*)
Basis weight	Grade	Colour	Colour ink	One side	Head to				
					Head	Foot	Left side	Right side	

37 Additional specifications attached ☐ Yes ☐ No	38 Total quantity to print	

39 Functional code(s)	40 Date processed	41 Forms management office approval (*signature*)

Figure 8.1   Request for approval and development of form

- Are there related organizational activities that should be considered?

By answering these questions, the forms management staff will be able to determine the following points:

- Is a new form really needed? The form may be the wrong tool for the purpose. Perhaps an existing form can be used.
- Can the form be used in a different way? Perhaps a form can be designed to serve several purposes and meet the needs of various users throughout the organization.
- Does the form meet the needs of those who will have to supply the requested information? For example, the users might be handicapped or speak a different language.
- Have the working conditions under which the form will be completed, processed and used been considered? Handling can be facilitated by simplified or improved design and construction.
- Have special features such as automated use been considered?

Quantitative data should also be collected. The following information will help in developing a complete picture of the form and what needs to be done with it.

- Number of forms completed in a given period.
- Time required to complete and process the form.
- Costs of activities involved in completing and processing the form.

Composition

Forms composition, which is the process of preparing a form for printing, is a technical area of specialization closely aligned to the graphic arts function of camera artwork production and the printing function of typesetting. In fact, many organizations have found it more cost effective to contract-out the highly labour-intensive composition work to graphic arts or typesetting firms rather than to develop and maintain the capability in-house.

With rapidly expanding computer technology, however, forms composition is virtually becoming a completely automated process that can be performed with much less technical knowledge and in much less time than was previously required. Using an equipment configuration consisting of a text entry and editing terminal, a composition and make-up terminal, a phototypesetter, and a processor as shown in Figure 8.2, an analyst can completely design a form on a video display screen and reproduce camera-ready artwork in up to two-thirds less time than would be required by the manual composition method. Although such equipment is still relatively expensive, larger organizations with a substantial number of forms might easily be able to justify the investment.

The forms management staff is responsible for production (or procurement) of camera-ready artwork and for proof-reading to ensure accuracy prior to printing.

Reproduction

If an organization has a printing facility, many forms will probably be reproduced in-house. If there is no such facility, or if the form is such that it requires a special manufacturing process (such as marginally-punched continuous forms or carbon-inter-leaved sets), the reproduction job will be contracted out.

The key to success, whether dealing with an internal printer or a contracted manufacturer, is to provide complete, written specifications so that there is no question as to exactly how the form is supposed to be produced. While specification writing can be somewhat complex, it can be greatly simplified by using a printing specification worksheet as shown

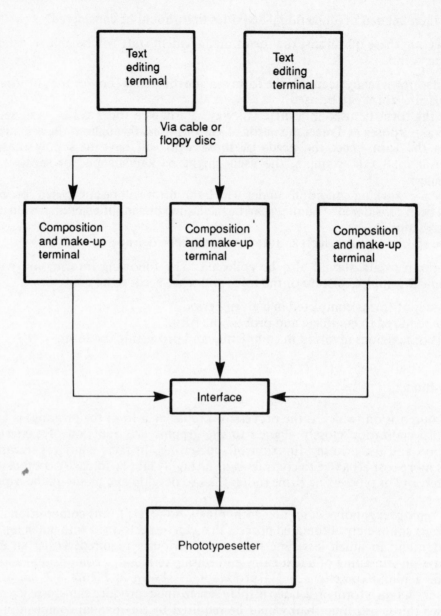

Figure 8.2   Electronic composition equipment configuration

in Figure 8.3. By entering all the appropriate data and submitting the worksheet along with the printing requisition, chances of error due to misunderstanding are greatly reduced.

It is not possible to provide too much information to a printer. For forms with unusual construction, a printer's dummy (shown in Figure 8.4) may also be submitted. A printer's dummy is a mock-up version of the form, clearly indicating the exact placement of folds, perforations, margins, etc.

If a specialized form is to be manufactured by a contractor, it is possible that the composition will be included as part of the contract. If this is the case, the forms management staff will be responsible for proof-reading the camera artwork received as well as for following-up to ensure that the job is produced and delivered in a timely manner.

STOCKING AND DISTRIBUTION

If a form is not where it is supposed to be, it might as well not be at all. To the person who

PRINTING SPECIFICATION WORKSHEET
(Cross out items in left columns which do not apply)

1 Form no. and title	Form no.		Title		
2 Size	Specify width first				

3 Paper and ink	Kind	Grade	Substance	Colour	Colour of ink

4 Grain	Direction □ Parallel to top of form □ Parallel to left of form

5 Print	□ One side □ Two sides	If two sides, print □ Head to head □ Head to foot	Head of front to □ left of back	Head of front to □ right of back

6 Margins	Front Top Left	Back Top Left

7 Register	□ All sheets □ In sets □ In pads □ With form no.

8 Number	Singly, in duplicate, etc.	Starting no.	Ending no.	Skips □ Not acceptable	Acceptable □ if listed

9 Perforate	No. of perforations	Direction □ Horizontal □ Vertical	Location Inches from top	Inches from left

10 Score	No. of scores	Direction □ Horizontal □ Vertical	Location Inches from top	Inches from left

11 Fold	No. of folds	Direction □ Horizontal □ Vertical	Location Inches from top	Inches from left
	After folding the following should be on the outside			

12 Punch	No. holes	Diameter	Kind	Location (top left)	Inches centre to centre	Inches center of hold to edge of sheet

13 Round corner	Radius	No. corners	Location □ Top right	Top □ left	Bottom □ right	Bottom □ left

14 Collate	No. sheets to set	In order shown □ Under paper □ Other (specify)

15 Pad	No. sheets to pad	No. sets to pad	Location of padding □ Top □ Bottom □ Left □ Right	Reinforce with □ Chipboard back

16 Dummy attached	□ Fold	□ Punch	□ Other (Specify)

17 Wrap	No. sheets per package	No. sets per package	No. pads per package	No. cards per package	Best □ method

18 Label	Label each package on one end showing form no., title, quantity in package, special nos if any

19 Special	*(Information not specifically provided for on worksheet, such as make and model of machine on which form is written)*

20 Prepared by and date	Name Date

Figure 8.3   Printing specification worksheet

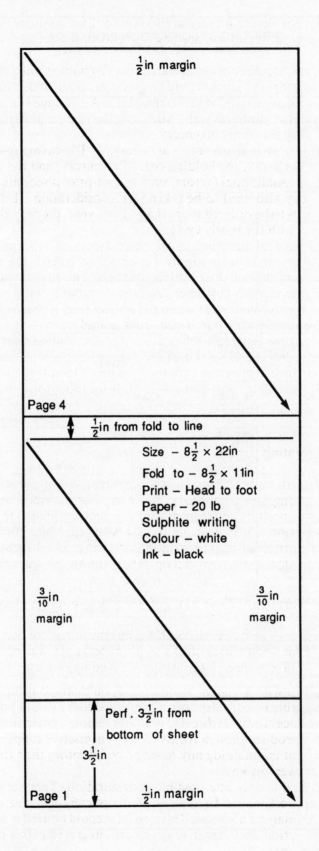

Figure 8.4   Printer's dummy

needs to use a form, the fact that there are 13 000 of them on order is irrelevant. Proper stocking and distribution, therefore, are key elements of a successful forms management programme.

If all supply cabinets, stockrooms, and warehouses contained twice the number of forms that were needed, shortages of stock would virtually be eliminated. That, however, would be an expensive type of security blanket to maintain. All storage space costs money and, obviously, the forms cost money as well. Additionally, there is always the possibility of a form revision rendering the costly inventory obsolete.

The question, then, is 'How many forms are enough?' The answer may be determined by considering the cost per order, the holding cost of inventory, and the value of the annual number of forms used. Additional factors, such as unit-price discounts and transportation quantity discounts may also need to be taken into consideration. If the determination is made that a form needs to be ordered more than once a year, the periodic review should be scheduled to coincide with the yearly cycle.

The amount and time of ordering is only one aspect of stocking and distribution. Arrangements must be made with supply personnel to receive the stock and make it available through organizational distribution channels. This may involve setting limits on the quantities available to each customer, and most certainly will involve timely notification to the forms management staff when the reprint level is reached.

In larger organizations, forms purchased from manufacturers or printing contractors may be shipped to multiple geographical locations for distribution to local offices. In some instances, the entire ordering and stocking function may be decentralized. When operating in a decentralized environment, extra care must be taken to ensure that the overall forms control responsibilities remain centralized — at least for those forms used on an organization-wide basis.

On-demand forms printing

The foregoing deals with the traditional methods of reproducing, stocking, and distributing forms. Modern computer technology, however, has provided new alternatives. By composing forms electronically and transmitting the digitized images to a remote processor hooked into a laser printer, it is possible for users to reproduce forms as required and thereby eliminate the processes of bulk printing, stocking, and distributing.

One way in which a demand system can operate is shown in Figure 8.5. The key steps in the process are:

1 Forms design — through the use of a graphic workstation or electronic composition terminal.
2 Image transmission — through telecommunications to remote user sites.
3 Image storage — on floppy discs until a hard (paper) copy is needed.
4 Reproduction — via low speed laser printer hooked up to a user's computer.

In all probability, even with a system as described, on-demand printing would not truly exist. It is not reasonable to consider that all terminal users would have laser printers at their disposal to produce forms. However, with the remote system illustrated, workers in small offices could reproduce enough forms to keep themselves supplied for a few days or weeks at a time without maintaining any more of an inventory than they would normally keep in their desk drawer anyway.

The system described is only one possible configuration. There are many others. For example, camera artwork could be created and optically-scanned into the system to produce the digitized image; a high-speed laser printer could be used at a regional centre for decentralized reproduction on a larger scale; or an integrated offset press could be used instead of the laser printer.

While demand printing can eliminate the problems of bulk reproduction, stocking, and

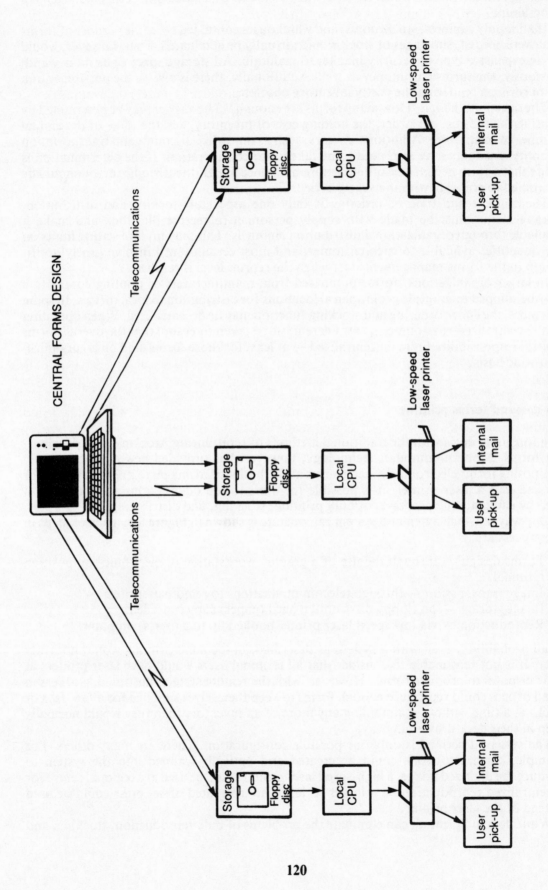

Figure 8.5   Printing forms on-demand at user sites using low-speed laser printers

120

distributing, it can also create problems of a managerial nature which are not present with the traditional methods. Among the problems are:

1 Control of the print image — to ensure that the design is not modified at the remote site and that the latest version is the one being used.
2 Allocation of printer time between various functions (forms printing, word processing, convenience copying) — since a laser printer dedicated to forms production would probably not be justifiable.
3 Additional staff training — so that forms can be produced by users on demand.

PCs and forms

In addition to the methods of composing already described, there is also commercially available software for personal computers (PCs) which allows anyone with access to such a computer to perform the composition function. For printing forms designed and composed by such 'end users', there is, obviously, the copying machine.

The problems involved with this type of operation are many, and are much more far reaching than the problems listed for a controlled, on-demand printing set-up as just described.

First, as already explained, composition is a process that should only take place after a thorough analysis has been performed and a functional design created. Use of composition software by the untrained individual will all but eliminate these two vital steps. Secondly, control with such an operation is completely lost. From a practical standpoint, it is neither possible nor reasonable to monitor everyone's computer. Thirdly, if by chance an adequately analysed and designed form happens to be prepared, printing it on a copying machine will render it inadequate. Most copiers either enlarge or reduce the original image, and the spacing on the form will be adversely affected.

Use of forms composition software by a properly trained analyst can be an expedient and relatively inexpensive method for composing forms. Indiscriminate use of such software by untrained persons throughout an organization will produce forms chaos.

9 Management of Files

As stated in the Preface, filing systems have been dealt with extensively within the records management literature. Because of this, a conscious decision was made not to cover the same material within this text. However, the authors believed that they would be remiss if they failed to include a brief filing overview within this book and to provide some information on the subject of *functional filing* which has not been adequately dealt with elsewhere.

Additionally, the subject of registries is covered in this chapter. Although *registries are not used within the US*, these files management organizations are important within the UK and throughout much of the third world as well, yet have not been dealt with by other records management publications.

The most important aspect of the management of active records is their use as an informational source. Without adequate management, the organization can neither obtain the information it wants nor at the proper time. Such a situation can lead to weak judgements, bad decisions, and uncertain policy, with all the serious implications that these might have for the efficient and effective running of the organization. Filing systems are the heart of information storage and retrieval activities.

FILING METHODS

Many complicated and intricate filing methods have been invented over the years — many unnecessarily so. The most efficient and economical method is the one that works for the department or organization (not that for which the department or organization itself has to work or adapt) and which is easily understood by its users. Very often the simplest method is best.

There are a number of factors to bear in mind when establishing a filing system:

- Ready identification and retrieval of individual records and files.
- Appreciation of functions and operational requirements of the offices served.
- Segregation and security of information requiring special protection.
- Ease of understanding by users.

These factors may also be important in determining whether there should be a centralized file area or whether there should be a number of different areas for various parts of the organization (see p.127).

Essentially there are three types of filing methods: numeric, alphabetical, and alpha-numeric.

Numeric

With this method the reference is a series of numbers, which may be allocated according to function, series, subject and item (in which case each part of the reference, up to four parts, would be a separate sequence of numbers — a hierarchical arrangement), or which may be one continuous sequence (particularly for one homogeneous series).

Hierarchical arrangement

All subjects dealt with are contained in one large series of numbers, for example 90000 to 99999. Blocks of the series are allocated to broad categories of the work:

93001 — 93400   Public Health Administration and Finance
94151 — 94200   Central Health Services Council

Within each block, specific numbers are allocated for specific subjects:

93202   Public Health Administration and Finance: Blind Welfare
93211   Public Health Administration and Finance: Maternity and Child Welfare

Sub-numbers are then allocated for specific aspects of the subject matter:

93202/5   Public Health Administration and Finance: Blind Welfare: Legislation
93202/6   Public Health Administration and Finance: Blind Welfare: Workshops

Continuous numbering

As each file is raised it is given the next number in the sequence, regardless of what its subject matter is, for example:

641   Research Stations: Out Letters
642   Meetings of the Agricultural Experimental Committee
643   Maize: Price Regulation

Such a system must be supplemented by an alphabetical index of key words in the file titles. If no such index is compiled, files can only be traced or retrieved with the greatest difficulty.

This method is frequently used for staff personal files, where the subject matter is essentially the same but where each file relates to a different person, for example:

1051   Green, R. J.
1052   Jones, A. I.
1053   Stone, C. A.
1054   Andrews, M. D.

An alphabetical index would also be required.

Alphabetical

Such a system would be rare and could only be used in a very small organization where the number of files is also small, for example:

Accounts
    Payable
    Petty cash
    Receivable orders
Audit
    External
    Internal
Budgets
    Allocations
    Control
    Requests
    Revision

Each main subject is in alphabetical order, and each item within each of those subjects is also in alphabetical order. No numbers are allocated to the files. Although this type of filing method is most easily understood, that is only the case if there are very few users. Alphabetical filing systems do not work in large organizations because people will file information under different subject headings.

Alphanumeric

This is the most common filing method and the positions of the letters and numbers might vary considerably. The permutations are almost endless. For example:

1   A letter or letters indicate the main subject:

    DP   Disabled Persons
    IR   Industrial Relations
    Y   Youth Employment

A subject number is added:

    IR 5   Industrial Relations: Shipping Industry
    IR 6   Industrial Relations: Transport Industry
    IR 7   Industrial Relations: Conferences

A serial number is added for a particular item:

    IR 6/1   Industrial Relations: Transport Industry: 1962 London Bus Strike
    IR 6/2   Industrial Relations: Transport Industry: Annual Meetings with Trade Unions
    IR 6/3   Industrial Relations: Transport Industry: Unofficial Strikes

2   A combination of letters are used to indicate the main origin of the file:

    PHC   *P*ermanent Secretary for *H*ealth, *C*onfidential File

                 Another letter (or letters) is added to show the main subject:

    PHC/L   Losses
    PHC/P   Promotions
    PHC/ADM Administration

A number is added to indicate a specific subject:

    PHC/P/4   Promotions: Clerical staff
    PHC/P/7   Promotions: Senior staff

A further number may be added to indicate a more specific item: (this is not recommended, but is included for illustration purposes).

PHC/P/4/1   Promotions: Clerical staff: Interviews
PHC/P/4/2   Promotions: Clerical staff: Appeals

3 Each division and/or each department/branch within the division is allocated a numeric code, which will appear on all the file covers originated by it:

9   Airworthiness Division
30   Aircraft Projects Department

Each main subject area (in this example a company) is allocated an alphabetical code:

ADH   De Havilland Aircraft Company

Numbers are then allocated to specific subjects and specific items:

3   DH 106 Comet 1 aircraft
02   Flight characteristics

Thus file 9/30/ADH/3/02 contains papers from the Aircraft Projects Department on the flight characteristics of the Comet 1 aircraft, manufactured by the De Havilland Aircraft Company.

4 A number may be prefixed to the reference to indicate the year or period of years when the file was opened:

84/DP 4/1   file opened in 1984
2/FIN 3/1   file opened in the five-year period 1981-85, indicated by the number 2 (the number 1 would indicate the previous five-year cycle, that is 1976-80).

In general, the number of elements to a reference should be restricted to four. Any more than this and the reference becomes unwieldy, difficult to remember, and an unnecessary complication of the system itself.

FUNCTIONAL FILING

The simple fact that records are the result of functions and are used in relation to them establishes the principle that they should be grouped and maintained according to the functions to which they relate. The functional categories delineated will reflect an organization's purpose, missions, programmes, projects and activities. The scope of the functions determines the breadth of the categories.

As the 'common language' of an organization, the vocabulary of functions is ideally suited to communicating the content of a group of records. Moreover, when records are arranged functionally, additions, deletions, or modifications may be made easily *without* changing the remainder of the file plan. Functions can be transferred from one office to another with only slight modifications — or possibly no modifications to the overall file structure. The final, but by no means least, advantage is the convenience of using functional charts when developing the file structure.

Each office or department within an organization has a function and these functions are generally carried out through a series of major programmes. These major programmes are often divided into subprogrammes and these subprogrammes may be further divided until one gets to the individual project level. A functional filing system which supports this natural programme structure is described below.

Functional filing system

One of the easiest understood and most efficient functional filing systems uses the

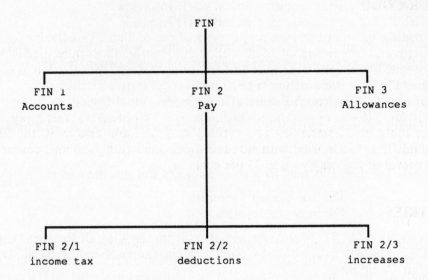

Figure 9.1   Hierarchical file series (functional)

alphanumeric filing method where the alpha element is a simple indicator of the function or part of the organization served by the contents of the file. Some common elements are:

FIN   Finance
ACC   Accounts
ADM   Administration
PUB   Publications
IT   Information Technology
ADP   Automated Data Processing
RD   Research and Development
SE   Staffing and establishment

This element would be limited to a broad function and there should be only a handful of such alpha elements in any one system. A large number of codes would not only lead to difficulty in distinguishing functions if they were minutely described but might also lead to an unnecessary lengthening of the codes in order to make such distinction clear. In any case the complementary numbers in the reference will help towards a closer definition of the contents of the file.

One number will represent a broad description of the series of files within the broad function indicated by the code, for example:

FIN 1   Accounts
FIN 2   Pay
FIN 3   Allowances

There is no need for these series to be in alphabetical order of the subjects. A further number will define more closely the subject matter within a series, for example:

FIN 2/1   Pay: income tax
FIN 2/2   Pay: deductions
FIN 2/3   Pay: increases

It can now be seen that the file series is built up in a hierarchical fashion, rather like a family tree (see Figure 9.1).

COLOUR-CODING

Colour-coding is *not* a filing system, but is a method of identifying the file folders within a filing system and preventing misfiles. Although colour-coding can be used with alphabetic filing systems, it is usually used with numeric filing systems, the selection of colour-coding being generally dependent on the type of numbering system used.

Colour-coded labels can be easily affixed to individual folders to convey the folder's identity in large letters or numbers which are visible from several feet away. These labels allow for more easily retrieving and refiling materials and also assist the filing staff in spotting misfiles. When used with side-tab, open shelf filing systems, colour-coding can speed retrieval of folders by up to 33 per cent.

REGISTRIES

Active records in the United Kingdom are generally managed in organizations through units called registries. As the machinery of government and the conduct of business make it increasingly necessary to have information to hand when and where it is wanted, the value of an effective registry organization becomes increasingly important.

The contents of a registry depend very much on the nature of an organization, but generally they will consist of files, arranged in some kind of referencing system. More modern registries will store information in the form of microfilm or magnetic disc.

Records management should supervise records creation, including one or more of the following:

- the provision of advice
- the co-ordination of policies
- the establishment of standards
- the inspection of premises and procedures
- the development of classification schemes for current filing and retrieval systems
- the training of staff.

In governments, national archival institutions, through their records management departments, fill this role. From wherever these functions emanate there is an increasing emphasis on central guidance and assistance to ensure economical and efficient management of records.

Registry systems should match the needs of the user; these needs should be the prime consideration in selecting the type of registry organization. Good communication is essential if problems are to be identified and solved. Users of the system should be invited to comment on proposed systems and they and records managers need a good understanding of each other's requirements and constraints.

In deciding whether the registry system should be centralized (one registry serving the whole organization) or decentralized (a number of registries each serving one functional unit of the organization), the following factors should be taken into account:

1 The speed of service required (quicker service is usually possible with decentralization).
2 Type and complexity of material to be classified and indexed (material will be more manageable with decentralization).
3 Volume of filing, numbers of files, file movements, etc. (a decentralized system will clearly have less files to manage).
4 Availability of storage space (for the organization as a whole a centralized registry will require less space).
5 Staffing needed (overall in the organization less staff will be needed in a centralized registry).
6 Number of units requiring access (less units would require access to a decentralized registry).

Not all papers in an organization need to be registered — that is, placed in a purpose-designed file cover and classified and indexed. It costs money to open a registered file and to file each paper or document. Ephemeral documents and copies for information only should not be put in registered files; they can be disposed of at the end of their active life. Even original papers that are of no archival interest and which have a finite life within a section/branch can be treated more economically as unregistered papers. Generally, too much paper is retained unnecessarily in organizations, consuming staff resources, impeding retrieval of the more important material and taking up valuable space.

A filing system is essential to a registry to ensure swift and accurate access to information. Much depends on this system. Above all it has to be understood by its users, and in this respect the simplest and most straightforward system is often the best. It is all very well constructing an intricate system to embrace all facets of the information contained in the registry, but if it cannot be understood or used by staff and management, access to vital information is effectively denied.

In addition, a programme for the orderly, periodic destruction or transfer of inactive files to archival custody, requires a filing system that permits the easy identification, appraisal and segregation of record series and files.

It is also desirable to aim for a standard system throughout an organization, be it a government department or a company. If there is to be a co-ordinated records management policy in government or in a business, then a standard registry system goes a long way towards achieving that aim. It also makes for less complicated training; it is much better to teach one system than a number of different ones. In many larger organizations there may be separate cadres of staff for records work, with a separate career structure. Movements of staff are encouraged and indeed enhance career opportunities. This becomes unnecessarily complicated when each part of the organization has its own unique filing system as, whenever a member of staff moves to another part of the business or department, he/she has to be retrained.

REGISTRY ORGANIZATION

Equipment

Registries should be clean and properly arranged in order to reflect the importance of the service which they provide to the rest of the organization. Equipment must be of adequate standard — information in the registry is vital to the organization and it must be well cared for. Filing units should be made of steel, be open, compactly arranged, and give due allowance for the easy extraction and replacement of files. Registries should never be omitted from the ergonomic programmes and activities in an organization. Questions that must be asked are:

- Is the layout the most economical in terms of space?
- Are the files closest to the people who use them most?
- Does the layout accommodate the flow of documents?
- Is the type of shelving the most economical and efficient for the types of files/papers being used?

There are many kinds of filing units:

1 Cabinets, with drawers (vertical) — by far the least economical. Space is required to open the drawer and further space to stand and extract/replace files. Access to files is limited since only one person can work at the cabinet at any one time.
2 Cabinets, with drawers (lateral) — these offer some space saving over the traditional filing cabinet because they do not pull out as far. They are not, however, space efficient, particularly for large amounts of files.
3 Cabinets, with shelves — these are only a half-measure towards achieving economical

storage in that they are not fully open yet use up less space than drawer cabinets. They are, however, useful if highly-confidential material is kept which needs to be locked away separately from the normal file series.

4 Open shelves — a very economical and productive way of holding files in a registry. Shelf systems can be of any height and many of them allow the shelves to be adjusted, allowing space savings and flexibility for future needs. Files are stored on the shelves horizontally so that reference numbers can be seen easily (see Types of file cover, p.131). It has been estimated that files can be retrieved 30 per cent faster than with drawer cabinets.

5 Mobile shelving — the most space efficient way of storing files, particularly for large volumes of material. The system yields the largest capacity while using minimal floor space. One shelf unit is stationary while the other units can be moved (manually or electrically) each along its depth to enable access to the files. While not in use the shelf units are kept tight up against each other.

When choosing a mobile storage system, records managers should consider a number of factors:

- Ease of installation — should be permitted without major modification of the floor.
- Stability of equipment — if the shelves are likely to be filled unevenly or if the material that is stored can move, the centre of gravity will change with the movement of the units along the tracks, thus causing a possible overturn of the equipment.
- Future needs of the organization — system manufacturers usually prescribe maximum loading limits. If more and more material is stored, the units may become overloaded, causing the mechanical parts to fail.
- Floor loading capacity — the increased capacity allowed by mobile systems will increase the load pressure on the floor.

The physical arrangement or layout of a registry must take into account the degree of access, if any, permitted to non-registry staff. It would generally be more efficient and less liable to disorganization (albeit quite innocently caused), if handling of files and papers in the registry were restricted to registry personnel only. In some organizations, or parts of organizations, this would be of paramount importance if the registry were limited to the storage of confidential material, and just as important if both open and confidential files were stored there.

Unless special considerations apply, it is far more efficient to keep confidential and open files in the same registry — less staff and less accommodation would be required. (See sections on Filing methods, p.122 and Types of file cover, p.131.)

Training

Training of personnel is an important element in helping to produce quality staff to effect a quality service.

In a registry hierarchy of, say, three or four levels (for example, supervisor, retrieval and replacement, filing, post opening), training courses of increasing technique and responsibility can be introduced and staff would not be permitted to progress to a higher grade unless they passed a particular level, be that by assessment on a training course or by examination. In addition, staff could be awarded a certificate at the successful completion of a course and/or examination — a goal to reach and an achievement of which they could be proud. Since they are dealing with files and papers from various parts of the organization (particularly in a centralized system), staff in the registry should also learn something of the overall functions and organization of the government ministry, business, or agency. They would then be better placed to deal with the filing of papers or the retrieval of files. It would be hopeless if a registry clerk were confronted with jargon or technical phrases on a paper and be asked to file it, or trace related papers, if he/she had little or no idea about where to start looking for the appropriate file.

Duties and grading of staff

The duties of staff in a registry and their grading depend to a great extent on the overall functions of the organization. However, there will be a number of different functions that will have to be carried out and these may be graded at different levels:

- Receiving and opening mail
- Placing mail and other papers on correct files
- Extracting and replacing files
- Opening new files
- Closing files
- Keeping a record of file movements
- Retrieving lost or missing files.

Consideration should be given to rotating duties among staff of the same grade so that no part of the operation might break down or fall into disuse at any time.

REGISTRY OPERATIONS

Storage

To a large extent the referencing system will dictate the classification and arrangement of files in the registry. Storage could be in subject order in a very small registry, but generally the best method is to store numerically, with an alphabetical index.

Thus, if there are a series of files — GEN, DP, FIN, ACC — in a registry they may be kept in the order ACC, DP, FIN, GEN. This, however, is not so important as the necessity to keep each series in numerical order, and confine each series to its own section of shelving, avoiding any breaks in the run of files. In a file series with three elements added to the main subject code (as in the example FIN 2/1 in Figure 9.1), the second element would be in numerical order within the first. Thus files would be stored in the sequence:

FIN 1			FIN 2	
FIN 1/1	FIN 1/2	FIN 1/3	FIN 2/1	FIN 2/2

Occasionally, a figure or figures may appear in front of the series code, as in the example 9/30/ADH/3/02 above. The hierarchical arrangement would still be maintained in that 9/30/ADH files would be arranged before 9/31/ADH but after 9/29/ADH.

A few file series might be considered more conveniently stored in subject order. This arrangement could suit personal files. If they are kept in strict alphabetical order of surnames there would be no need for an index; indeed there might be no need to give numbers to the files. In this order, however, there are difficulties in fitting new files into the sequence; files would have to be moved to create room for additions to the series. If the files were numbered and stored in numerical order — assuming that each file, as it is created, is given the next number in a continuous sequence, regardless of the name — there would be no difficulty in space allocation; the next file merely has to be added on at the end of the run of files. An alphabetical index would, of course, be required.

Indexing

Indexes of files should highlight key words in the title. The title itself must be as concise and as brief as possible while accurately reflecting the contents of the file.

It happens frequently that papers of a similar nature to an existing file will be created and care must be taken that, if they are added to a current file, the title continues to reflect the contents. At the same time it is unwise to change the title of a file unless it is absolutely necessary. Staff in the organization become familiar with file titles and changing them leads to considerable confusion. Generally it is better to create a new file for the new papers and, if necessary, make a cross reference to the file containing similar papers.

There are no hard and fast rules on what constitutes a keyword; only experience of the particular organization will help. The people producing the title must place themselves in the position of user and cover the most likely words in the title by which it might be requested and use these as the key words. For example:

- Health and Safety Committee: Minutes and Papers 1987.
  The key words here would be Health and Safety, but not Committee or Minutes.
- Wycombe General Hospital: Maternity Department: Policy Matters.
  Keywords: Wycombe, Hospital, Maternity.
- Industrial Relations: Transport Industry: 1962 London Bus Strike.
  Key words: Transport, Bus.

An index might be maintained on cards, on slips bound in a folder (commonly called 'dockets') or on a microcomputer.

File movements

The registry must know at any time whether it has a particular file or not, and, if not, in whose possession it is. Thus, a file location system has to be maintained and this can be achieved most effectively by replacing a file by a location card when it is taken out or sent from the registry. The location card (see Figure 9.2) would show the file title and file reference, the date on which it was taken out, or sent from, the registry, and the name of the officer/person who has it. One such card can be made out for every file (as it is created) and can rest inside the file cover when the file is in place in the registry.

An alternative method is to maintain a numerical list of files (in addition to the alphabetical index), which might also be kept on cards, dockets, or a microcomputer. Each entry in the list would show the same information as a location card.

The movements of files creates a conflict of interest between registries and their users. For registries they create headaches, but for the users whom the registries serve, the files exist to be moved and used. It is a frequent occurrence that someone in the organization requisitions a file and then passes it to another person without informing the registry. In such situations the file, to all intents and purposes, is lost. A way of avoiding this would be to instruct all persons in the organization to complete a file transit slip (see Figure 9.3) when they send a file to someone else. This slip would then be sent to the registry at the same time as the file is passed on.

Alternatively, there could be a standing instruction that all files must pass through the registry before being sent to anyone else. This, however, creates unnecessary movement of files, wastes time, and leads to frustrating delays.

Types of file cover

The type of file cover will depend to a large extent on the type of equipment that is used to store the files. There are, however, essential pieces of information which must appear on the cover:

- name of the ministry/department/agency
- file reference
- file title
- date on which the filed was opened.

FILE LOCATION CARD					
Number: AD 4/10			Title: Administration of Welfare Services: Appointment of Deputy Welfare officer.		
Name	Branch	Date	Name	Branch	Date
J. White D. Steele	Estab. A cs(R) 2	25/12/86 15/1/87			

Figure 9.2   File location card

REGISTRY TRANSIT SLIP
File no: FIN 6|2
Title: Accounts: Reprographics
Has been passed to: A. Brown
Of: Accounting Section (A4)
Signed: D. Green   Date: 15|11|86

Figure 9.3   Registry transit slip

Of these, the position of the file reference is the most important. It must be seen easily regardless of the method of storage, and it must appear adjacent to the file title so that it can be seen clearly when reading the front of the file.

The reference must, therefore, always appear horizontally next to the title. If the files are stored in a drawer cabinet, it must appear parallel with the opening edge of the cover so that it can be seen when the contents of the filing cabinet are examined. If the files are stored on open, or similar, shelves, it must appear at the bottom of the cover parallel to the opening edge; this assumes that the file will be stored resting on its 'binding' edge — by far the best method in that it causes least harm to the contents.

Other information that can usefully be printed on the file cover is a disposal box and instructions on use, movement and closure of the file. There should also be a transit grid on the cover, a series of boxes to indicate to whom the file is to be sent next. The disposal box is used to indicate what is to be done with the file when it is closed. There is no hard and fast rule about when to close a file — it very much depends on the nature of the subject matter. For example, when dealing with accounts it is convenient to open a new file each year for a new year's accounts. Conversely, it would be pointless to close a personnel file after a specific period; it is more convenient to keep it open as long as the person is a member of staff, with the proviso that if it gets too bulky it should be closed.

Generally, if the subject matter does not end before, it is best to close a file when it is five years old or when it is 3 cm thick, whichever occurs sooner. A second, or succeeding, part can be opened (with a suffix 'Part B' or 'Part 2', etc.) if the subject matter is continuing. There are a number of reasons for choosing this criterion, and it has to be borne in mind that the file might possibly be selected for permanent preservation. With a 30-year closure period, for example, it would be iniquitous to the researcher to have an opening span longer than five years. The 30 years applies from the last date on the file and so the oldest paper on the file would not be more than 35 years old. This has to be balanced against the ideal position of wanting to open papers to the public on a yearly basis. If all files were closed after one year, it would be a gross waste of time and materials. A five-year closure represents a reasonable compromise. The 3 cm part of the criterion serves to prevent the file becoming too bulky, which could damage the papers contained within it. The measurement of 3 cm is chosen because that is the width of the gusset of the usual standard type of file cover generally available.

The disposal box must give alternatives to enable a decision to be made on what should become of the file having given due attention to the value of its contents. These alternatives will be:

```
┌─────────────────────────────────────────────┐
│                                             │
│           DISPOSAL RECOMMENDATION           │
│                                             │
│     This section to be completed by the nominated officer for │
│     the file series.                        │
│        The Registry Manual and Disposal Schedule must be consulted │
│     before marking the boxes below.         │
│                                             │
│                                  ┌───┐      │
│     1. DESTROY NOW               │   │      │
│                                  └───┘      │
│                                             │
│                                  ┌───┐      │
│     2. DESTROY AFTER             │   │  YEARS │
│                                  └───┘      │
│        (give a number in box, not more than 12) │
│                                             │
│                                       ┌───┐ │
│     3. RETAIN FOR 2nd REVIEW          │   │ │
│                                       └───┘ │
│                                             │
│                                       ┌───┐ │
│     4. RETAIN PERMANENTLY             │   │ │
│                                       └───┘ │
│                                             │
│                                             │
│     SIGNED ..................... DATE .............. │
│                                             │
│     DEPT./SECTION ........................... │
│                                             │
│                                             │
│        PLEASE  RETURN  FILE  TO  REGISTRY   │
│                                             │
│     Printed for HMSO by Remploy Ltd., Db. 8918384 9/86 7M │
└─────────────────────────────────────────────┘
```

Figure 9.4   Disposal box

- destroy immediately
- destroy after a specified number of years
- examine (review) after a specified period
- preserve permanently.

When the file is closed in accordance with instructions — either by registry staff or by the department/section of the ministry or organization who has created the file — a nominated officer in the latter will be asked to indicate the decision made on the contents by marking one of the alternatives and signing and dating the action. Due regard must be taken of previously agreed disposal schedules (see Chapter 12). (An example of a disposal box is shown in Figure 9.4). The file will then be returned to the registry. Those files which are marked for immediate destruction should be examined by the records manager to ensure that they do not contain material of historical value. The rest will be kept in a semi-current store (records centre or intermediate repository) (see Chapter 13).

Records appraisal is examined in detail in Chapter 12.

COMPUTERIZATION

Information technology for the registry may be beyond the scope of many organizations but it can go some way to improving records management and solving problems, particularly in indexing and retrieval.

The use of computers within registries, to monitor the movements of files, maintain an index, assist in selection for storage or destruction, etc., is well worth considering. In a centralized registry, a simple program on a personal computer will remove the need for many of the small location cards, index cards, registry books, etc. In decentralized registries, the computer can provide the best of both worlds — the speed and efficiency of decentralization with the central control of centralization. Where large amounts of information are held on personal computers throughout an organization, proper management of records has been hindered as individuals creating, manipulating and destroying records have failed to realize that they were doing so. While in the UK compliance with the Data Protection Act has somewhat helped this problem, it still remains a serious issue. One solution for records managers to gain control over records on personal computers lies in networking. Within the software that controls the network can be written procedures for ensuring that certain records are copied to a central file, that they be given retention periods, and so forth. This is already possible with information held on a mainframe, but such controls must be included within the software from the beginning. To do so afterwards is too costly, and the records manager is ultimately reduced to managing printout instead of files.

A fuller discussion of records management computer programs is given in Chapter 13.

10   Vital Records

A private airplane carrying a bank's daily volume of cancelled cheques and non-negotiable securities crashes, killing the pilot and destroying all documents beyond recovery. An explosion renders a building unsafe to enter, resulting in delays in retrieving the records stored inside. A disgruntled employee erases all the data on an organization's payroll system. A ministry is burned to the ground during urban riots, leaving nothing intact. A fire burns inside a vault damaging many engineering drawings before it can be extinguished. The water poured on to the fire causes further damage as the documents become soaked.

What do all these incidents have in common? They represent disasters that can strike an organization at any time and severely damage or destroy its records.

Businesses suffer a myriad of computer disasters every year, leading to serious monetary losses. These are only a small part of the many business disasters, nearly 40 per cent of which have been due to fire or explosion. In other countries, disasters caused by floods, vandalism, and warfare are also numerous, leading to the financial and operational crippling or even collapse of organizations.

The kind of disasters that can affect an organization's records are many:

- Power fluctuations causing corruption or loss of data on computers
- Rats eating through wiring causing shorts and fires
- Air conditioners breaking down causing computer failures
- Explosions in neighbouring buildings causing fires and damage
- Leaking pipes dripping water on to files
- Flash floods taking away whole file rooms
- Transport vehicles crashing or being stolen causing loss of files, letters and tapes
- Military or airport radar equipment causing computer data corruption
- Employee negligence or malice causing security leaks
- Vermin nesting in and devouring files
- A cup of hot coffee tipping over and into a personal computer causing a breakdown
- The incomprehensible minds of vandals causing any damage that is fairly easy to inflict.

The possibilities for disaster are endless and the means of protection against it limited. A vital records protection programme can be expected to use the limited means to protect against some disasters and to lessen the damage in the case of their occurrence, but it cannot be expected to serve as an absolute and sure defence against any and all disasters. Too many records managers spend far too much money and effort trying to secure all of an organization's records against total nuclear war, when their energy would be better spent protecting against the more common variety of disasters such as fire, flood and incompetence. Even so, whether the disaster is natural or man-made, the results can be devastating to an organization unless it has implemented policies and procedures which assure the protection of its vital records.

Vital records are those records essential to the continued functioning of an organization during and after an emergency and those records which protect the rights and interests of the organization, employees, stockholders, customers and the public. Vital records include such records as would protect material and human resources, the maintenance of public health, safety and order, and the conduct of civil defence. They can also include records relating to employee compensation and benefits, insurance, valuable research findings, proof of ownership, financial interests, and legal proceedings and decisions. For example:

- Accounting records, such as nominal ledger, accounts receivable and evidences of assets and liabilities
- Payroll and personnel records
- Contracts and agreements
- Deeds and mortgages
- Patents and trade marks
- Corporate and shareholders' records
- Engineering drawings
- Research and development records.

While commercial organizations view vital records protection from the aspect of survival of the enterprise, governments must have a larger view. A government's vital records protection programme must attempt to ensure not only the survival of the government but of its ability to govern. A full governmental disaster contingency plan will co-ordinate a large number of departments or agencies. Records management, through its vital records protection programme, must be a strong component of this plan, and must liaise closely with the government information and communications departments on it. Vital records protection plans must include the following:

1　Records which will be necessary and useable during the disaster (these may have to be paper if electricity and the presence of computer operators cannot be guaranteed).
2　Records necessary to reconstruct the government when the disaster is over.
3　Records necessary to protect the rights of individual citizens.

With few exceptions, vital records should not be the original records of an organization. They should be duplicates, located away from the area where the original records are kept.

As with any records management programme, vital records protection requires careful planning and implementation. The objectives for a vital records programme are to:

- define vital records
- assign programme responsibility
- identify potential hazards
- analyse and classify vital records
- designate appropriate protection methods
- select appropriate vital records storage facility or facilities
- develop operating procedures
- audit and test programme procedures.

VITAL RECORDS PROTECTION IS INSURANCE

Protecting vital records and designing and testing a disaster recovery plan is costly and brings no profits or cost savings. Consequently, some organizations are slow to authorize such a programme; but at their great peril. Not all organizations burn to the ground, but all have fire insurance, and those that need it are grateful. Similarly, not all organizations lose all of their records and systems overnight, but all should be protected against such a loss. Over 40 per cent of all companies that suffer a serious disaster fail.

To encourage full management awareness of the organization's vulnerability to the loss of records, data, and information, a few measures may be worth considering:

- Submit a preliminary report on weaknesses and vulnerabilities discovered during the survey, for example no backup for information on personal computers; no procedural manuals exist to explain processing and inputting procedures; payment systems are protected but without a supply of the necessary blank cheques or remittance advices; there are 17 copies of keys to the management central file room but only ten keys can be located; etc.
- Contact the organization's auditors, legal and financial advisors, and insurers to find out their recommendations, requirements and possible reductions in premiums for disaster planning.
- Ask senior managers to attend a sales briefing by a disaster planning consultant.
- Ask to attend a seminar or course on disaster planning and/or vital records protection. (Often, directors will pay more attention to someone who has just been on a course paid for by the organization.)

The vital records programme should be regarded as essential to the organization's contingency planning effort. Management must be cognizant of the rights and interests that the organization is responsible for protecting and of what records are necessary to protect them. It must also recognize what the essential functions of the organization are under normal circumstances and what records are necessary to continue to perform those functions both during and after an emergency.

For this reason, the authority for the vital records programme should be spelled out in a programme directive which clearly outlines the policy, objectives, and responsibilities for the management of the programme and which provides procedures and guidelines for maintaining the organization's vital records. The records manager should be responsible for the establishment and co-ordination of the programme.

In addition to the basic authorities and responsibilities, all operating and auditing procedures should be incorporated into a directive, either as part of the basic records management directive or as a separate vital records/disaster recovery document. The directive should also include a designation of individuals authorized to access the records, sample forms, and all pertinent standards, specifications, and procedures.

EVALUATING POTENTIAL HAZARDS

The extent of the vital records programme depends largely on the potential hazards to the organization and its records.

A clear evaluation of the type of disasters likely to happen will indicate what kind of protective measures need to be taken. Generally, disasters are either natural, via the weather, or man-made, accidental or intentional. Subjects to consider are:

- *Environment* What problems are common in a given area? Tornadoes, floods, bush fires, earthquakes, electrical storms, heavy snowfalls, insect invasions, power-failures, regular warfare or invasions, high winds, tidal waves, etc. By far the most common hazards to records safety in most places are fire and the water or chemicals used to extinguish it.
- *Enticing vulnerability* What, by the very nature of the organization, would make it particularly vulnerable to attack or sabotage? A bank in an area where people are starving, a military installation, an innovative research facility whose secrets would be valuable if stolen, a political organization, a key national utility or communications installation, a high publicity or glamour business appealing to lunatics, etc.

- *Unpopularity* (This is closely related to the above.) What organizations might be particularly unpopular to some people? The police, the tax collection agency, the courts, companies that have just made many people (or only one vengeful or desperate character) redundant.
- *Technical vulnerability* What part of the organization's equipment and technology is both vital and so highly sensitive that a minute occurrance could cause a major disaster? (For example, one human hair in a computer disc causing a total crash.)

Specific steps taken to protect against fire and the damage caused by fire extinguishing agents will be discussed in Chapter 13. Vital records facilities should be inspected regularly by local fire departments for the adequacy of alarms and detection systems and the condition of fire deterrents. Plumbers and electricians can assist in identifying other potential sources of damage to records.

The geographic location of an organization must be considered when establishing a vital records programme. Records in places with high humidity must be protected against mould and mildew. Insects and vermin are more prone to attack records in some environments than in others. Vandalism and theft may be more of a threat in an urban area than in a rural one.

Potential hazards and their risk to vital information can be identified and evaluated by answering the following questions:

1 Have the following hazards been identified as potential threats to the organization's vital records?

- Fire and fire containment materials
- Water (due to flooding, bad plumbing, or high humidity)
- Impact damage (resulting directly or indirectly from fire, flood, earthquake, violent wind, or bombing)
- Infestation by insects or vermin
- Theft, vandalism, or loss

2 Have the frequency and severity of these hazards been assessed?
3 Has the dispersal of duplicate vital records to a location not subject to these hazards been considered?
4 Does the existence of these hazards influence the choice of an appropriate vital records storage facility?

VITAL RECORDS APPRAISAL AND CLASSIFICATION

Only a small portion — roughly two to six per cent — of an organization's records can be legitimately classified as 'vital'. To determine which records actually fall into this category, *all* records, that is, both active and inactive records from all functional areas, should be appraised for their vital record value to provide the required depth for a meaningful programme.

In the appraisal of vital records, consideration must be given to:

- the type of information needed during an emergency
- the specific rights and interests that require protection
- the value of the records which meet this need
- the availability of the information elsewhere.

In addition, these questions must be asked:

- Do these records include records of debts owed *to* the organization but not of those owed *by* it?
- Do these records exclude those which support legal rights that can be re-established through affidavit and are well known to the affected individuals?

- Do these records exclude those which are routinely duplicated by another organization or entity?
- Does the organization classify as 'vital' only the minimum volume of records in accordance with the programme's objectives?

Vital records are generally active, reflecting the ongoing operations of the organization, although some inactive records are also protected. Certain original documents, such as deeds, contracts, or articles of incorporation, may require vital records protection if they alone will satisfy legal requirements.

Many types of records are of *great* importance but not of *vital* importance. Such records require much effort and expense to reconstruct if lost, or have intrinsic historical value. They could also include source records used to reconstruct vital information. The vital records programme does not involve these important records, although the standards and methods of protection associated with the programme may well be applied to them to the degree that the value, risks, and available resources for their protection are appropriate.

A useful guideline for the classification of records might be:

- *Operational or functional records/systems* — those without which the organization would collapse, unable to function. Such systems would include the nominal ledger and production systems; such records would include licences to operate, project drawings, procedures manuals.
- *Costly records systems* — those that may be of secondary importance but that, if lost, the time and money necessary to replace them would alone constitute a disaster. Such systems would include corporate budget and planning, and full personnel systems; such records might be still useful reports that were the products of expensive studies.
- *Legal records/systems* — those which are necessary for the organization to operate legally, to protect itself or individuals, or which, if lost, would leave the organization open to crippling litigation. Such systems would include data protection monitoring and safety controls; such records might be the articles of incorporation, a constitution, contracts, insurance policies, union agreements, trade marks, deeds.
- *Emergency records/systems* — those which are not vital except in the case of an emergency. Such systems would include all automatic building, door, safe, sprinkler, alarm systems; such records would include personnel lists, building plans, security clearances.
- *Vital objects* — those which satisfy any of the above criteria and which are necessary for the use of those records, but are not considered hardware. Such objects would be building keys and government seals.

Identifying vital records is a judgemental process and is best accomplished by relying on the originators' or users' understanding of the function of the record. The classification must be realistic. The 'two to six per cent' rule of thumb applies to the organization as a whole. A specific department may have no vital records at all, or it may find that as many as 50 per cent of its records holdings are vital. It is essential to capture only those records which fit the vital records definition, or the protection programme will become unwieldly, diluted and will not be taken seriously.

PROTECTION METHODS

Several methods are suitable for protecting vital records. The most important selection factor is the ratio of protection from hazards to the cost of that protection. Since relative security is all that can possibly be attained, the best choice is that which brings the cost of security most closely in line with the degree of risk. Beyond the evaluation of actual risks of loss for vital records, three other factors influence the selection of protection methods:

1 *Need for accessibility* In the event of an emergency, vital records would be needed

immediately. Paper records are preferable to avoid reliance on special equipment, but if it is necessary for the information to be on another medium, both the required equipment and its power source must be dependable under emergency conditions. Vital records which must be readily available for reference may require different methods of protection from those records infrequently used.

2 *Length of retention* Vital records of a short-term nature may require different methods of protection from long-term or permanent records.

3 *Physical qualities of records* Vital records are susceptible to destruction from heat, water, chemicals, and ageing depending upon the record medium and the duration of retention. Magnetic tape or microfilm require different protection from that needed for paper documents, and paper itself varies greatly in its ability to withstand ageing.

One or more of the following methods can be used to protect a vital record series.

Dispersal

The least expensive protection method is built-in or routine dispersal of vital records, wherein the information is routinely distributed to other departments, individuals or organizations located elsewhere. The assumption is that the same disaster is unlikely to strike two different locations, although to ensure protection of the dispersed copies, they should be located at least 50 miles apart.

Branch offices, subsidiaries, government agencies, and the like are apt to receive the dispersed records. If the organization is depending upon dispersed copies in the event of the disaster, the copyholders should be informed of this and of any retention and protection requirements. In the event of a disaster, this information must be retrievable promptly and with no restrictions.

Improvised or planned dispersal modifies a routine dispersal procedure by creating an additional copy specifically for protection purposes. The copy is then sent to the vital records repository or some other location. This is a fairly economical and easy approach, since copies are already being created and the cost and effort of making and distributing another is minimal.

Dispersal is equally effective for long- and short-term retention, durable or fragile records, and high- or low-reference requirements.

Duplication

Duplication is an effective protection method where the conditions for dispersal do not exist. While dispersal automatically creates a current vital record copy, duplication involves reproducing the record specifically for its protection. Protection by duplication is as effective in all ways as is dispersal.

The reproduction may be on the same medium, as in microfilm to microfilm or paper to paper. This approach is often less costly and complicated than changing the medium. However, such duplication methods as microfilming source documents, putting computer data directly onto microfiche (COM), or storing data off magnetic disc on to tape or optical disc, is justifiable under certain circumstances.

If a vital record is stored on any medium other than paper, there must be equipment readily available to retrieve, read, and reproduce the information. This means a reader/printer for microfilm or microfiche, data processing equipment for magnetic tapes or discs, and optical disc equipment for optical discs. In addition, the proper storage environment is more critical for these media than for paper. Machine-readable media require that the correct hardware, software, and operating system be available. Procedures should be established to ensure that the duplicate is actually made, whether this takes place when the record is created or at some other stage in its life cycle.

The frequency of required updates dictates the frequency of duplication. Some records have an annual cycle, such as annual reports or shareholders' meeting minutes. Others are updated monthly or more often, such as various accounting records. Still others, such as engineering drawings or contracts and agreements, are updated at irregular intervals.

The duplication of an original record raises the question of its acceptability as a legal document should the original be destroyed. A copy may be better than nothing, but if its legal value is nil, an alternative protection method should be considered.

Selection criteria

In analysing whether to rely on dispersal or duplication for vital records protection, the following selection criteria should be considered:

1 What is the cost and effectiveness of the following?
   - Using existing duplicates located elsewhere.
   - Creating a duplicate at the same time as the original for storage at another location.
   - Reproducing existing records either on the same or different media for storage at another location.
   - Removing inactive original records to an off-site location.

2 In determining the duplication medium, what considerations have been given to the following?
   - The availability of equipment needed to retrieve, read, and reproduce micro-images or machine-readable data.
   - The environmental controls of the storage facility (temperature, humidity, air filtration).

3 Can the dispersed or duplicated record be used for vital records purposes rather than the original? If not, is it because the copy does not have the same legal value as the original?

Three other methods offer some degree of protection, although should a major disaster occur in the building, or devastate the immediate geographic area, such methods would be of little or no use.

Special storage equipment

Original and unique records can be protected from most hazards through the use of special storage equipment such as vaults, fire resistant cabinets, or safes. The relative effectiveness of this method is less than dispersal or duplication, particularly if this does not physically remove the records from the organization. This method is usually the most costly and should be considered only when other methods are physically not feasible.

Removal of hazardous conditions

The effectiveness of this and the next method is low and should be considered only when other methods are not economically feasible. By removing unnecessary hazards, such as combustible materials and steam or water pipes, from the storage area, and by eliminating undesirable conditions, such as air-borne chemicals and extremes of heat or humidity, a relative improvement in the protection of vital records can be achieved.

Relocation of records

The effectiveness of relocating vital records to a less hazardous area within the organization is the same as, or slightly better than, removing the hazards, while the cost is as low or slightly lower. However, the feasibility of this protection method is further affected by the accessibility requirements for the records.

SELECTING A STORAGE FACILITY

An adjunct to selecting the best protection methods is the selection of the appropriate storage equipment or facility. Storage can either be off-site, that is, remote from its home location, or on-site, usually within the building or plant perimeter of the organization. Optimum protection comes from remote storage of the information; on-site storage of vital records compromises the programme, but may be the only feasible alternative, economically or physically.

Off-site storage

Off-site storage facilities can provide extra security and protection to original vital records and economical storage for those that have very little reference. Off-site facilities are usually located in low-rent areas, and some are underground in caves, mines (abandoned or active), former railroad tunnels, missile sites, and the like. Underground storage of certain vital records may be advisable if the risks associated with the destruction of the information are high.

Whether the off-site facility is owned and operated independently, by the organization itself, or by a group of organizations, certain factors influence the choice of storing the vital records in a remote location. The facility should be located away from high-risk areas, such as rivers, geological faults, coasts, and volcanoes or away from man-made structures that might pose a threat. It must be accessible to the organization's officials both in emergency and in non-emergency situations.

As with the selection criteria for off-site records centres, fire safety, atmospheric conditions, pest control, security, and technical services of the vital records facility must be carefully evaluated. The communication link between the organization and the storage facility must be reliable in the event of an emergency.

On-site storage

Vaults, file rooms, safes, and fire-resistant cabinets and containers provide some degree of protection for vital records.

Underwriters' Laboratories in the US have produced standards that rate the temperature and humidity levels records can undergo before deterioration. Paper can withstand 50°C while magnetic and photographic media can only withstand 15°C and 85 per cent relative humidity, and discettes 10°C and 80 per cent relative humidity.

Vaults are very expensive to construct, but can be justified if the volume of records is high or the needs of the organization dictate this type of protection. In buildings with a high fire risk, a vault may be the only recourse to protect records against this hazard. Vaults should be constructed of fireproof materials not only to resist a severe fire, but also to insulate against high temperatures. Vault doors come with 2-, 4-, or 6-hour ratings.

Although the likelihood of a fire starting within a vault is low, this has been known to happen, and a decision must be made regarding the installation of interior automatic fire protection. Certainly, precautions must be taken to ensure that no flammable or combustible materials are stored within, no smoking is allowed, wiring and electrical equipment is in accordance with the code, and no other conditions exist that could start a fire.

Vaults resist fire. However, they are not immune to water damage. Underground or basement vaults are susceptible to water leakage from faulty pipes or from flooding, and water used to extinguish a fire can get inside a vault and damage the records.

While fireproof safes do not provide as high a degree of fire protection as that of vaults, they will resist fire for up to four hours. Safes are useful for smaller volumes of records and for locating the records close to the point of use. It should also be remembered that safes are built to resist fire, not theft.

File rooms and fire-resistant cabinets and containers naturally provide less protection than the heavily insulated walls and doors of vaults and safes. They are also less expensive. The risk associated with the loss of the information being stored must be evaluated before investing in any of these on-site storage facilities or containers.

OPERATING PROCEDURES

Once the protection methods and storage facilities have been selected, procedures for operating and auditing the vital records protection programme must be established. These procedures should cover the following.

Vital records survey

Much information about vital records and information would have been revealed in the original survey. The survey forms, or the data base compiled from them, will yield a preliminary list of vital records, what storage media they are on, where they originate and are sent, what systems process them, etc. This provides an excellent starting point from which to begin questioning people in departments.

This questioning must be in greater detail than that of the original survey, and will involve more immediate evaluation to determine which steps in a series of procedures are vital or where, should a system break down completely, old manual procedures could be resurrected and used. Trying to protect and prepare plans for the emergency use of information will be costly and, eventually, detrimental to the programme. In a true emergency, people will have neither the time nor the inclination to maintain secondary records and systems.

Vital records information can be collected using a Vital Records Survey form, as shown in Figure 10.1. Once the survey is taken, the list of vital records and systems should be divided into two groups:

1   those which will be needed immediately; and
2   those which will be needed when the disaster has ended and recovery can begin.

Within these two groups, records and systems should be listed by department, then by function. For example:

> Immediate records and systems
> > Treasury:
> > > Nominal ledger system
> > > Invoices
> > > Printed cheques
> > Production:
> > > Robotic assembly system
> > > Backup procedures and tools for manual assembly
> > > Inventory records
> Recovery records and systems
> > Treasury:
> > > Expenditure analysis system

This information is collected during the analysis process and can be documented manually

VITAL RECORDS SURVEY

Originating department		Section	Dept no.	Schedule no.	Page of	

Record series no. *	Item no.	Record title	Storage location			Protection method and special instructions	Frequency	Retention
			A	B	C			

* or vital records code

Approved by:

_____
Department Manager

_____
Records manager

Figure 10.1   Vital records survey

145

```
┌─────────────────────────────────────────────────────────────────────┐
│                                                                       │
│              VITAL  RECORDS  TRANSMITTAL                              │
│                                                                       │
├──────────────────────────────────────────────┬──────────────────────┤
│  To (repository)                              │  Date sent           │
│      ┌────┐        ┌────┐      ┌────┐          │                      │
│      │    │  A     │    │  B   │    │  C       │                      │
│      └────┘        └────┘      └────┘          │                      │
├────────────────────────┬─────────────────────┴──────────────────────┤
│  Record series no.*     │  Record title                              │
│                         │                                            │
├────────────────────────┴───────────┬──────────────────────────────┤
│  Record date                        │  Frequency                   │
│                                     │                              │
├─────────────────────────────────────┴──────────────────────────────┤
│  Originating department (name or number)                            │
│                                                                     │
├─────────────────────────────────────────────────────────────────────┤
│  Special instructions                                               │
│                                                                     │
│                                                                     │
└─────────────────────────────────────────────────────────────────────┘
```

```
* or vital records code
```

Figure 10.2   Vital records transmittal label

on the form or keyed into a computer data base. The data base can be programmed to print the resulting inventory list directly on to the form or as a report. A number of commercially-available data base management software packages are suitable for creating a vital records data base on a microcomputer. If a data base has already been established for retention scheduling, the vital records data can easily be linked to it through one or more elements, for example records series, department name or number, or the retention schedule item.

The inventory list should be reviewed regularly, based on the volume of records and frequency of change in the organization. Usually the records identified as vital remain fairly constant, but the departmental responsibility or protection method may fluctuate, requiring more frequent updating of the list. The records manager and repository operating personnel should maintain a complete and up-to-date set of inventory lists, and each department should have a copy of its own.

Transfer instructions

Instructions for transferring vital records to storage are essential procedures. A transmittal label, as shown in Figure 10.2, should be placed on each box, tape, or container being transferred.

Receiving instructions

When records are received, the date of receipt, location of the material in the repository,

VITAL RECORDS CONTROL FORM			
Record series no.	Record title		Originating department
Date of receipt	Location	Date of disposition	Disposition instructions:
			Remarks:

Figure 10.3   Vital records control form

date of disposition of previously stored records in that series, disposition instructions, and other remarks are noted on a vital records control form, (see Figure 10.3), or in the data base. A link or cross reference is made to the inventory by way of any of the data elements in the form's header so that the frequency of transfer and the retention of the record can be monitored.

Instructions regarding the disposition of superseded records must be clear. For instance, once new records are received, the superseded ones may be destroyed, returned to the department, or transferred to inactive storage because their usefulness as a *vital* record has ended.

11 Disaster Planning and Recovery

Contrary to popular belief, a disaster is *not* something that always happens to someone else. Disaster can strike anywhere, at any time. Nature deals its blows with no respect for person, place, or thing; accidents, by definition, are unpredictable; sabotage or terrorism is not necessarily 'somebody else's problem'.

An organization has a responsibility to protect against and respond to disaster. To this end, it should establish a disaster recovery programme which is designed to:

- minimize disruption of normal business operations
- prevent further escalation of this disruption
- minimize the economic impact of the disaster
- establish alternative operating procedures
- train personnel with emergency procedures
- recover/salvage organizational assets
- provide for rapid and smooth restoration of service.

A disaster recovery programme should consist of three parts: prevention, preparation, and recovery. Establishment of a programme begins with the formation of a disaster team which is responsible for:

- ensuring that efforts are made to prevent against potential disasters;
- providing documentation of the organization's readiness to respond to a disaster; and
- possessing knowledge of salvage procedures, costs, and results to the extent necessary to ensure competent, timely response.

Members of the disaster team should represent the records management, accommodation, security, data processing, library, and archives departments. If the size of the organization warrants, the team may be divided into two committees: a pre-disaster committee, responsible for the prevention and preparation stages of the programme, and a post-disaster committee, responsible for the actual salvage operations. Since recovery operations demand quick response and emergency expenditures of money, one member of the team should have overall responsibility for the programme and complete authority to make decisions in the event of a disaster.

The basis of a disaster recovery programme is the disaster recovery plan. Because a disaster team should be concerned with all aspects of the organization, from damaged buildings to damaged information, the disaster plan should be comprehensive. This chapter concentrates on that portion of the plan dealing with the organization's records.

148

DISASTER PREVENTION

Disaster prevention has been discussed in Chapter 10. Common sense dictates taking steps to protect against fire in the records centre, hacking in the computer centre, and vermin in the vital records vault. As part of a disaster recovery programme, all the various prevention techniques are spelled out in one plan, wherein the protection of the organization's records are cast in the same light as the protection of its other assets and of its employees.

It would be unrealistic to suggest that all disasters can be prevented from ever happening. However, their threat can be minimized to some extent. One method of minimizing the problems that might occur is to identify potential hazards by regularly conducting a facility and security inspection of records storage areas, including off-site inactive and vital records facilities. The records manager should co-ordinate this inspection with the accommodation and security departments, which should already be including records storage areas in their regular inspection procedures.

The facility inspection should document:

- The general construction and condition of the records storage site or sites.
- The area in which the facility is located, specifically its susceptibility to disasters (flooding, high winds, etc.).
- The location and condition of the plumbing, electrical wiring, heating and air conditioning, drainpipes, steam and water pipes, roof, and mechanical equipment.
- Any past problems with leaks, seepage, faulty wiring, broken pipes, or similar problems.

The security inspection should cover active files areas, inactive and vital records storage, vaults and buildings, magnetic tape libraries and computer operations areas, and should identify:

- who has authorization to access the records
- how this access is controlled
- what security devices are in place to prevent or detect unauthorized access.

Basic precautions to consider fall into three categories: accommodation protection, security, and staff awareness.

Accommodation Protection

This requires that all parts of all buildings have the best possible protection against fires, floods, collapse, etc. While some areas, such as basements or storerooms, may not seem worth the expense of full fire protection, they must not be neglected to the point that they become hazardous.

There should be full compliance with local fire and safety codes and with the environmental requirements for information technology and equipment.

Accommodation and storage equipment requirements should include the following:

- The use of strong, non-inflammable, structurally sound filing shelves and cabinets (buckled shelves, broken drawers, and rusted equipment should be replaced).
- Floors strong enough to take the weight of equipment and hardware.
- Roofs strong enough to take the weight of support equipment, particularly air conditioners and generators.
- Bottom shelves on the ground floor should be 6 inches above the floor, in case of flooding.

Fire protection should begin with a discussion with the local fire prevention officers as to the most appropriate fire prevention and fire fighting precautions and equipment to have, and as to the problems that the water used in fighting fires can cause. Many records that survive a fire do not survive the fire hose. Fire precautions should include:

- the discouragement of smoking within any buildings and the complete ban on smoking in filing areas
- general tidiness and removal of hazardous clutter such as piles of files, papers, boxes, rubbish
- the timely destruction of all useless records and the transferral of all semi-current or inactive records to storage
- the removal of all inflammable liquids
- a clearly marked, and regularly tested, fire alarm system with triggers in every room
- fire extinguishers in all rooms which are checked regularly
- regular safety checks of all electrical wiring and rodent traps
- clearly posted fire escapes, exits, and procedures, with regular fire drills on their use.

Water damage and flood prevention is more important than many realize, especially in tropical climates where rainstorms regularly carry off whole buildings and towns. Water destroys tapes and discs, washes ink from paper, turns microfilm to jelly. Even a little water for a short time will cause sufficient humidity to allow mould to grow on paper and microfilm. Water damage and flood precautions should include the following:

The records and systems are placed far from water mains and drainage pipes.
Roofs should not be flat or leaking.
All possible sources of water leaks are checked and repaired regularly (for example, air conditioners, lavatories, water tanks, windows, down pipes, gutters).

Animals and insects cause major disasters particularly by chewing through wiring, but also by shedding fur into computers, nesting in or eating paper, swarming into computer rooms, even bringing diseases that wipe out the records staff. Precautions against animal and insect invasion should include the following:

- A full building inspection to discover and block all points of animal or bird entry.
- Strong, fine mesh screening over all necessary openings, such as windows, skylights, ventilators, chimneys; and screened doors for all external doorways.
- A total ban on all eating and food storage in records and systems areas.
- Regular fumigation.
- Regular and thorough cleaning of ceilings, walls, floors, underfloors, and of all furniture.
- The humidity level kept as stable, if not as near the ideal, as possible.

It should be noted that, too often, where ideals of structure, equipment, protection, and environment cannot be obtained, records managers despair. While it is true that some buildings seem too ghastly ever to be made safe, an attitude of ingenious common sense must prevail. Where screening is not available, what is there that will serve as well? Where fumigants are out of supply, what is available that might keep insects and moulds away? However it is possible to create a safe environment for records, systems, and their users, it should be done.

Security

Theft and sabotage are not 'natural' disasters as are fires and floods, but they are disastrous acts to the organization that has had its records purloined or destroyed. While no one would deny that security is important, some organizations tend to consider it as the sole function of records management. This is a slightly unhinged and obsessive approach which must be tempered by common sense. Security violations are of two types, intentional or negligent, and both are generally easy to prevent. (It is often argued that the best security is complete lack of records management, on the assumption that no intruder could sift through the disorder. The authors do not share this view.) Negligence can be combated with a strong awareness programme (see below) coupled with a certain amount of vetting.

Intentional security violations can be combated with vetting of staff and with the standard forms of protection devices. However, it must be accepted that truly valuable and sensitive information will always be at risk and will require a permanent war of wits between the security and the thieving experts.

One of the most important aspects of any security plan is the clear identification of what is most at risk, and of what truly merits full protection. Far too many innocuous records and systems are labelled secret or even confidential, putting a strain on the whole security team to protect the oversized mass. This is a consequence of the obsession with security taking precedence over common sense. If the confidential and secret classifications were used more wisely, the result would be greater security for the information that truly merits it. A full review and, if necessary, restructuring of classification criteria may be necessary before implementing any new security procedures.

Electronic records and systems, especially those on personal computers, are much more vulnerable to negligence and crime, and the consequences much more severe than with paper records. It takes time and hard work to break into a system, but it takes only moments for a user to leave a screen or printout visible to the wrong person, or to mistakenly enter data, or to leave a disc in an unsafe place, such as a car. In the UK, the requirements of the Data Protection Act 1984 have increased the need for security of electronic records by strictly limiting the people who may view personal data. This increasing concern over the security of electronic records and systems has often been distorted into a concern for the safety of the computer, when it is much more often the software, the records, and the information that are at risk. Thus, security measures must seek to protect the most important records and systems; and, while it is true that electronic systems are more vulnerable than paper, it must be remembered that it is the systems and the records that are to be protected, and not just the machine that houses them.

Security precautions for buildings, equipment, and personnel, should include the following:

* Staff responsibility for locking windows and doors at closing time.
* Automatic security alarms.
* Locks on all doors and windows.
* Strict control of all building keys, with locks changed when keys are lost.
* Strict supervision of non-staff who enter the building, especially of cleaners and maintenance workers.
* Bars or toughened glass on ground floor windows (but ensuring bars or grills can be opened in case of a fire).
* Nightly locking of all rooms which contain mainframe or personal computers.
* Limited access to systems, either by the use of passwords or, with personal computers, power locks.
* Confidential destruction of classified records, such as by shredding or burning.
* Data encryption.
* Auxiliary generators and surge protectors for computers.
* Control of static electricity near computers.
* Extreme care should be taken when handling any floppy or hard discs, or magnetic tapes.

Staff awareness

The best disaster prevention will always come from the staff. If they are trained to look for trouble spots, irregularities, and to report them, then, because of their daily familiarity with their records, systems and environment, they will be the first to notice anything problematic or suspicious. In preliminary discussions and interviews to identify vital records and systems, staff should also be encouraged to contribute opinions about risks and how to prevent them. In prevention plans, staff should be given responsibilities for specific areas, records, and systems, and encouraged to work together as a team to protect them. They should be fully trained in all disaster plan phases and drilled at regular intervals in them. At least annually, there should be a staff meeting to discuss any changes in the plans, any new risks or problems, or any new training in protection required. This kind of teamwork will enhance the vital records protection programme by boosting staff understanding and support of it and by reducing the tacit tolerance of internal theft.

Staff awareness programmes should include the following:

- The formation of department or area teams, with appointed team leaders.
- Visits and talks from police and fire prevention officers, and from those who design the vital records protection plan.
- Training and drills in following the plan, using fire extinguishers, testing auxiliary equipment, etc.
- The placement of copies of the vital records protection plan manual with each team.
- A certain amount of internal publicity to keep awareness high, for example, posters, articles in internal publications, refresher training programmes, etc.

Common sense must prevail in disaster prevention. Thoughtful planning by architects and by those responsible for records can avoid some problems before new construction or space utilization plans become final. For example, the floor on which a mobile shelving unit is placed must meet certain stress requirements so as not to end up on the floor below. An archives collection should not be housed directly below the air conditioning equipment, which is a potential water hazard. In fact, no records collections should be stored in areas which are especially vulnerable to water. That includes lavatories, water pipes, and even fish tanks!

Basements are another area of potential hazards that should be avoided if at all possible. If a basement must be used, however, the records should be stored several inches off the floor. A water sensing alarm that is wired to an outside monitor should be installed to detect any flooding when the area is unattended.

Basements also tend to be 'catch alls' for miscellaneous equipment or supplies. If the supplies happen to be chemicals, they should be stored as far away from the records as possible. A liquid chemical spill could not only damage any records it contacts, but also make the area inaccessible, so that by the time the records can be retrieved they may be beyond recovery. Fire prevention is virtually achievable, as described in Chapter 13. The installation and testing of modern fire detection and extinguishing equipment, correction of defective heating systems, installation of heavy-duty wiring to prevent electrical overloading, storage of flammable liquids in proper containers and cabinets, and good housekeeping and maintenance are effective prevention measures.

Protecting against loss of data or damage to data processing equipment or the operations site is another element of disaster prevention. Usually this falls under the auspices of the data processing manager, but the records manager should be knowledgeable of the type of disasters that can occur in a computer operation and be ready to co-operate with the data processing manager in all stages of the disaster recovery programme.

PREPARATION

Because an organization must respond very quickly to a disaster, recovery operation procedures must be spelled out clearly. A written plan developed by the disaster team is the key to preparing for such an emergency. It should define the scope of authority of the person in charge of recovery operations, list emergency personnel, equipment, sources, and supplies, and outline specific salvaging procedures. The plan should be in the hands of each member of the team and of those who will be instrumental in recovery efforts.

Authority

Usually, one member of the disaster team, designated as the disaster recovery director, is assigned complete authority to direct everyone when disaster strikes. This individual consults with other members of the team or with outside experts and is the final decision maker during recovery operations. He/she may delegate some authority to the various team members, such as designating the records manager to handle the records salvaging process. In any event, the records manager should provide whatever guidelines are needed to ensure that the director will respond quickly and properly to the disaster.

Equipment, sources, and supplies

Equipment and supplies for salvaging records are relatively easy to stock. Although some supplies may be quickly purchased in an emergency, one cannot count on stores being open at 3 o'clock in the morning! The telephone directory can supply sources of equipment and supplies that will not be kept on hand and for lists of companies that will provide refrigerated trucks and freezer facilities, freeze, vacuum, or air drying space and services, and conservation services. Agreements for provision of services in times of emergency should be established with these companies. This is especially important, since there may be certain times of the year that facilities may not be available. For example, freezer space during the Christmas holidays may be quite limited.

A telephone listing of all disaster team members to be contacted should be arranged in call priority order. This list should also include police, fire, other emergency numbers, and individuals having particular skills or expertise, such as electricians, plumbers, chemists, pest controllers, building maintenance service, etc. Both this list and the list of necessary equipment and supplies must be kept current and distributed to all team members.

Reproduction equipment must be available for recovery of vital records and information on magnetic and microfilm media. Service bureaux and vendors can be lined up in advance to provide equipment on short notice. Reciprocal backup agreements may be made with other nearby companies that have compatible data processing or micrographics equipment.

Preparation also includes providing system support in case of loss of data processing programs and procedures, as well as the data itself. Backup tapes and discs of program and data and the necessary application documentation should be stored off-site. The primary problems in maintaining backup information are ensuring that changes made to the master programme files are also made to the backup copy and ensuring that the tapes do not deteriorate.

Insurance coverage

Sometimes overlooked is the adequacy of insurance coverage for disaster situations. The insurance policy may specifically provide for salvage and restoration of records and information after any disaster, or this type of provision may be assumed under a general contents policy for equipment and materials. If the latter is the case, there must be adequate coverage, or alternatively, additional contracts with insurance companies specializing in recovery of damaged records after fire or flood should be considered.

RECOVERY

When writing recovery procedures, a list should be developed of records which should be salvaged first following a disaster. Keep in mind the following considerations when setting priorities:

- Can the information be replaced? At what cost?
- How important is the record? Is it a vital record?
- Is the record itself of intrinsic value? If so, can it be replaced, and at what cost?
- Would the cost of replacement be less or more than the cost of restoring the record?
- Is the information available elsewhere?

Once priorities are established, the specific steps for responding to the various types of disasters and for salvaging the various types of media are outlined as follows.

Damage assessment

The first step immediately following a disaster is, to assess the type and extent of the damage. Once an accurate assessment has been made, salvaging operations may proceed based on the priorities and procedures already outlined in the disaster plan. A word of caution — despite this careful planning, salvage estimates and final decisions must be made at the time the extent of the damage has been determined. The basic objectives of any salvage operation are:

1 to stabilize the condition of the records before and after removing them from the disaster area by creating the necessary environment to prevent further damage; and
2 to salvage the maximum amount of damaged records in a manner that will minimize restoration requirements and costs.

Water and fire are the most likely disasters to affect records, and there are specific salvaging techniques for water and fire damage. Other disasters, such as bombing, earthquakes, chemical contamination, and severe storms, can wreak havoc in a records area, but the actual damage to the records may be no more than tears and disarray and may allow for a deliberate recovery pace. This is not to minimize the effect of these disasters, since buildings and lives may be affected, only to concentrate on the more common water- and fire-related disasters, since their recovery procedures are precise and demand swift action.

Weather will greatly influence what course to take after any flood or fire in which records are damaged. When it is hot and humid, salvaging operations must begin with minimum delay to prevent or control the growth of mould. Cold weather allows for more time to be taken to plan salvage operations and experiment with various drying procedures. In addition, the selection of the proper salvaging technique for damaged records is influenced by the record media as well as the type of disaster.

Enter into a disaster area with caution. Because water-damaged records demand the quickest response, you will need a timely decision from fire and safety officials as to when the area is safe to enter. The building may be structurally damaged; the water may be concealing hazards such as sharp objects or broken live wires; a fire-ravaged area may require a number of days to cool off before being safe to enter. These types of problems require contingency planning for salvaging procedures.

Salvage Procedures

Paper

Fire   If paper records are charred or damaged by soot and smoke, there is no need to take care of them immediately. Fire-damaged paper is stable and can be successfully treated after many years have passed. About 70 years went by before conservators began treating documents damaged during the great New York State Library fire of 1911. Documents may only need trimming around the edges to be usable once again, or they can be photocopied and then destroyed if the duplicate is an acceptable substitute for the original. What frequently happens is that fire damage to records is usually compounded by water damage resulting from extinguishing the fire.

Water Water damage is likely to occur during most disasters, not just during a fire. Flooding is a problem in many locations. Pipes can easily burst during a bad freeze, a storm, or an earthquake. In fact, air conditioning systems and water pipes have been known to leak under the most benign climates, causing severe damage to the records.

Speedy reaction to water damage can happen only if the disaster plan has comprehensive steps for handling this situation. Supplementary publications on salvaging water-damaged materials can be a useful adjunct to the plan.

The age, condition and composition of paper determines the rate at which it will absorb water. Where large volumes of paper records are at stake, the approximate amount of water which will have to be extracted in the drying process must be calculated in advance, and there must be some understanding of the length of time each type of paper can be submerged in water before serious deterioration begins.

Paper manufactured later than 1840 absorbs water to an average of 60 per cent of its original weight. Thus, by estimating the original weight of a records storage box at 25 lb, drying techniques must be set up to remove 15 lb of water. That is approximately 75 000 lb of water to be removed if 5000 boxes of papers are affected.

Paper that is dated earlier than 1840 will absorb water to an average of 80 per cent. Older papers are especially vulnerable to mould because of their receptivity to water and because of the highly proteinaceous nature of the leather or vellum with which they are frequently bound. However, they are able to withstand longer periods of time submerged in water than can modern papers and books.

Bound volumes incur their greatest damage due to swelling during the first eight hours after they have been soaked. The paper in the text block and the cardboard cores of book covers have a greater capacity for swelling than the covering materials used for the bindings, resulting in the expansion of the text block such that the spine becomes concave and the fore-edge convex. These very wet volumes will need to be rebound after they have been thoroughly dried. Those that have absorbed less water may retain their normal shape and dry without distortion.

In the event of water damage the environment of flooded areas should be stabilized and controlled both before and during the removal of the damaged records. During the winter, all heat in the building should be turned off. During the summer, every effort should be made to reduce the heat and humidity as rapidly as possible and circulate the air. Mould growth may appear within 48 hours if the weather is hot and humid or in an unventilated area made warm and humid from a nearby fire. The object is to avoid pockets of stagnant, moist air.

The temperature should not be raised in an attempt to lower humidity, as this will only hasten the growth of mould. Hygrometers, hygroscopes, thermohygrometers, and the like can be used to measure and record temperature and humidity, and the results should be monitored regularly. Open doors and windows to create maximum air flow. Dehumidifiers and fans may be needed. If there is no electricity, portable generators should be brought in. If electricity is available, all electrical lines should be waterproofed and grounded.

Before and during removal and packing operations, a constant watch should be kept for signs of mould development. If access has not been permitted for several days, it may be necessary to use fungicidal fogging, a procedure that should be attempted only under supervision of a competent chemist or conservator.

Prior to removing water-soaked records, it should be determined whether freeze drying, vacuum drying, or air drying will be the recovery method. If the materials are to be frozen, arrangements should be made immediately to ship the packed materials to the freezing facilities within a few hours of being removed from the site. This may mean a number of trips to the facility, but packed material allowed to remain on or near the site for too long is subject to mould development.

When beginning the removal operations, it is best to cover all work surfaces with polyethylene sheeting. All unnecessary equipment and furniture should be removed from the area. Lighting, fans, dehumidifiers, and all possible venting should be operational.

The aisles and passageways in the records storage area will probably be strewn with sodden materials. These materials should be removed first in the exact condition in which they are found. By dividing the salvage team into two groups for removal and packing operations, with the removal team forming a human conveyor chain to move the material along to the packing team, it is possible to avoid bottlenecks and the need to stack records on the floor to await packing.

If records have been scattered about the area, an indication of the approximate location in which they are found during the salvage operation may be very helpful at a later date. Do not remove these items in large batches or leave them piled on top of each other, since excessive weight is very damaging.

Starting from the nearest point of access, pack the wettest records first. This will bring down the humidity level in the area. Then follow with removal of the very damp or partially wet records. Only then should the balance of the material be inspected. Records that are damaged beyond salvaging or not worth saving should be discarded and a record kept of this disposition. Time wasted salvaging records which can be replaced easily or for less money than they could be restored might result in the loss of other valuable records and information.

The contents of records storage boxes probably will not be saturated with water if they were previously positioned close together. Boxes with a corrugated inside layer may be very wet, however, even though the major portion of the contents is only damp. In such cases, it is best to repack the contents in new boxes or in plastic milk crates. This will help the drying in addition to making the box lighter to lift and preventing the collapse of a wet box. Be sure to identify the contents of the new boxes properly when repacking.

Even though closely packed materials are unlikely to develop mould internally, since they have been in a very humid atmosphere for several days, their external parts may have been exposed to a far greater quantity of mould spores than is usual under ordinary circumstances. These drier records should not be left in place but moved to a controlled environment during clean up of the area. They should be stacked with sufficient space between them to allow for good circulation of air.

After all materials have been removed from the area, it may be necessary to sterilize the shelves, walls, floors, and ceilings to prevent further mould growth, and to take care of any maintenance work to return the site to its former condition.

Freezing Freezing and storing records at low temperature is the most generally accepted and proven method of stabilizing water-damaged paper records. This technique buys time for determining the best drying method and for carefully co-ordinating and controlling the drying operation. It makes it possible to assess the value of the damaged material, determine which items can or cannot be replaced, estimate recovery costs, prepare adequate environmental storage conditions, and restore the affected buildings. Cold storage facilities provide accessible and inexpensive space in which large volumes of records can be stabilized in the condition in which they were found to prevent further deterioration.

Freezing will not dry the records nor will it kill mould spores, although it controls mould growth by causing the spores to become dormant. It will stabilize water-soluble materials, such as inks, dyes, watercolours, tempera, and the like, which may diffuse during conventional drying.

Before freezing, wash off accumulated mud and filth only if there is time within the 48 hours to do so without delaying the freezing of the bulk of the material. Washing should be done by a trained person so as to prevent further damage. Washing records containing water-soluble components should not be attempted in any circumstances.

Wet, coated papers should be frozen immediately. If permitted to dry, they will bond together. In fact, it may be desirable to leave them under water until a few hours before they are to be frozen, since the period between pumping out the water and beginning the salvage operation is critical. Freeze or vacuum drying is the only successful method for salvaging this type of paper.

Loose, single-sheet materials with no soluble components may be washed under clean, cold running water by trained personnel prior to freezing. If the single sheets are in masses, it is best not to try to separate them, but to freeze them as they are. They will easily separate during the freeze or vacuum drying process.

Groups of loose records may be wrapped in freezer paper, wax paper, or silicone paper to prevent their sticking together during the freezing process. Each package should be no more than two inches thick and marked to indicate the type of material, its previous location, and its priority. If it is known that the damaged material will be vacuum or freeze dried after freezing, the wrapping step may be avoided and the materials packed in plastic cartons or cardboard boxes to about three-quarters capacity. Never pack or wrap the records tightly.

Boxes and their contents should be frozen as found. Try not to turn boxes of records upside down. The wet contents may stick to the bottom and be torn if upended.

Records should be moved directly from the storage area to the freezing facility, preferably in refrigerated trucks. Small volumes of records can be packed in dry ice and transported in unrefrigerated trucks to the facility. If freezing space is limited, priority should be given to items which have already developed mould, important original documents that are irreplaceable or expensive to replace, art on paper, materials on coated stock, and artefacts with water-soluble components.

Freeze drying Once the records have been transferred to freezing facilities, the drying method must be selected. The least expensive and most successful method for drying large collections is vacuum and/or freeze drying. Freeze drying involves removing the water, which is now in solid form, from the records through the process of sublimation. The ice transforms directly to vapour without passing through an intermediary liquid stage. The result is that individual documents will not stick together as they would if heat-dried.

The costs of freeze drying will be a factor to consider when determining the volume of records to be dried. In some instances, the cost is for the freeze drying chamber, not for the number of records going into it, and it is more economical to fill the chamber as near to capacity as possible. Other companies charge by the volume of records.

Two elements combine to aid in the freeze drying process: low pressure and extreme cold. Typically, records are placed in a chamber designed to keep them frozen during processing. A vacuum system reduces the air pressure in the chamber to a near-absolute vacuum. This permits ice to vaporize without becoming liquid. A condenser, positioned in the direct path of the migrating vapours, collects and holds ice molecules removed from the material. Efficient rates of sublimation are obtained by maintaining a vapour pressure differential between the material and the condenser.

Freeze drying reduces stains and reduces or eliminates odour caused by smoke. It also virtually prevents the feathering of inks.

Vacuum drying Vacuum drying offers many advantages when large quantities of material are involved. Records may be put in plastic milk carton containers and placed in the drying chamber. At this time, the material is at room temperature. Air is evacuated from the chamber until the temperature reaches freezing point. The chamber is then filled with hot dry air and purged with this air until the wet material is warmed to 10°C. The number of cycles required depends on the initial wetness of the material. The effectiveness of this process is illustrated by the fact that a typical loading of one chamber with approximately 2000 milk container cases can result in the removal of approximately eight pounds of water per case or eight tons per chamber load.

Air drying Air drying is ideally suited for emergencies involving a small volume of records, when temperature and humidity are relatively low and conducive to drying (between 10° and 17°C and 25 to 35 per cent relative humidity). If weather conditions are not suitable, or if a large volume of records is involved, freezing followed by freeze or vacuum drying is the safer way to proceed.

Under proper environmental conditions, wet paper can be air dried. Damp paper can easily be dried if spread about in a space with cool and dry air and good air circulation. Very wet papers can be treated similarly but interleaved with absorbent paper such as unprinted newsprint or a good grade of paper towelling. The towelling is more effective than newsprint but significantly more expensive, especially if used with a large collection. The interleaving material should be frequently removed from the working area so that humidity will not increase or mould set in.

Some conservators recommend interleaving sheets, impregnated with a fungicide such as thymol dissolved in alcohol, between the documents so as to reduce the possibility of mould damage. However, working with large amounts of these chemicals is hazardous — the solution gives off toxic and flammable vapours — and such operations should be directed by trained personnel.

Bound volumes can be similarly air dried by interleaving the absorbent sheets at intervals of 50 pages (25 leaves). Care should be taken not to interleave too much, else the spine will become concave and the volume distorted. As with loose documents, frequent changing of the interleaving material is much more effective than allowing large numbers of sheets to remain in place for extended periods, and it should not be left in the volumes after the drying is complete. If the humidity is high, it might be necessary to interleave every 10 pages (5 leaves) and to change the sheets every two to three hours to hasten the drying and discourage mould growth.

Bound volumes weighing less than 6 lb, that have distorted spines as a result of the interleaving process can be hung, when partially dry, on thin, monofilament nylon lines to help return the spine to its original shape as it dries. The lines should be about 6 ft long and spaced approximately a $\frac{1}{2}$ in apart. Volumes of up to $1\frac{1}{2}$ in thickness can be hung on three lines; thicker volumes will require more lines. Bound volumes should never be hung when saturated with water. Not only can this damage the spines, it can also cause spine adhesives, particularly those made of gelatin, to migrate through the volume, staining the leaves and even gluing them together.

It may be necessary to separate a wet mass of single items for immediate hand drying. The safest method is one which takes advantage of the special properties of polyester non-woven fabric and film. A damp sheet of polyester film is laid on top of the wet pile. The surface energy of water makes it possible to ease away several sheets at the corner of the pile and roll or peel these back with the polyester. Transfer this material and the attached sheets, polyester side down, to a work surface covered with a polyethylene sheet.

Place another polyester film on top of the transferred batch of papers. Repeat the process until you are able to roll the film back with a single wet sheet attached. As each single sheet is removed and placed, polyester side down, on the work surface, a dry polyester web is placed on top of the wet sheet. Then the sandwich is turned over, the polyester film removed, and a second piece of dry polyester web is placed on top. (The final interleaving should be done only with web.) This process is repeated for each sheet. The items may be safely frozen or air dried at this stage.

If the volume is small enough, place each 'sandwich' separately on tables or closely spaced on nylon lines to dry. After 100 or so have been processed, the first sheets will be dry. Fans may be used but should not blow directly on the material. Gentle, warm air and good ventilation will remove excess moisture. Air-conditioners or dehumidifiers may also help the drying process.

Microfilm, negatives, and photographs

Water If microfilm has been soaked, it should be kept wet at all times. Large, clean containers filled with fresh water can be used to submerge the film and transfer it to a nearby microfilm processing centre for reprocessing. If possible, the film should be kept in its original package for future identification.

Freezing may damage the images on any film media. Photographic materials should not be frozen unless professional help is delayed longer than 48 hours, since the formation of ice crystals may rupture the emulsion layer and leave marks on the film. Wet, muddy black-and-white negative film and prints can be sealed, for emergency stabilization, in polyethylene bags and placed in plastic (not metal) rubbish bins under clean, cold running water and left under these conditions for no longer than three days before the emulsion will separate from the film backing.

The coloured layers of colour slides and colour negatives and positive film will separate, and the dyes will become weak or completely lost unless professionally treated within 48 hours. After this time, freezing the collection is the best way to save it until special arrangements can be made.

Diazo or vesicular films should be salvaged last since they are almost impervious to water damage and can be easily washed with liquid detergent, rinsed, and laid out to dry on absorbent paper.

Magnetic media

Fire Fire is most destructive to computer magnetic tapes. A live cigarette ash which lands on a tape surface can cause instant tape damage and data loss. Direct contact with open flames or an extremely hot environment reduces the chances of recovering data to virtually nothing. The damaging effects of heat are primarily in the form of physical and chemical media changes rather than magnetic data loss. Excessive heat affects the mechanical integrity of the tapes and the reels through warping, distortion, layer-to-layer adhesion (blocking), loss of durability, and binder breakdown and softening. Also, the chemistry of the binder (the compound used to bind the oxide particles to the base material) will be altered due to the volatile losses of its components.

Magnetic tape is a poor heat conductor. A properly wound reel with a very smooth pack offers more resistance to fire and water damage than a loose or uneven pack. The latter will allow more water to seep between windings and cause tape cupping and other distortions.

Tapes that have been subjected to extremely low temperatures for long periods of time should be relaxed and dried, if necessary, for a number of days at gradually increasing temperatures in order to relieve the stresses which may have developed with time. Tape shrinkage due to exposure to extreme cold can produce layer-to-layer adhesion, which can cause tape tearing and surface coating damage in portions of the reel.

Carbon dioxide, halon, and water can be used for direct fire fighting in a computer tape installation. Carbon dioxide and halon are clean and do not leave a residue. Tapes which have become wet during the fire-fighting effort can be salvaged.

If recorded computer tapes have been subjected to fire and heat, separate out those reels which appear to have sustained the least amount of physical damage as soon as possible and try to recover these first. All fire debris, ash, and smoke residue should be cleaned from the canisters, wrap-arounds, and flange surfaces before opening the canisters or wrap-arounds. Using the slowest speed transport available, perform at least two wind/rewind passes, inspecting the tapes as they are being wound. If they are badly warped or display layer-to-layer adhesion which is damaging the coating, or are shedding large amounts of coating debris, the chances for data recovery are poor. The transport should be cleaned after each tape is run. Then give the tapes two full cleaning passes on a tape cleaner/winder, preferably constant tension type, and rewind them on to clean or new reels and make new labels.

Relax these tapes for 24 to 48 hours in the normal operating environment. Then perform a read and recopying pass. If the tapes will not load on to the transport at this time, store them in a low humidity environment and retry at intervals. This process should be repeated for the next least damaged group of tapes until all tapes have been examined.

Water Magnetic tapes that have been inundated by or immersed in water are likely to have data recovery as long as high temperatures did not exist at the time to produce steam or very high humidity in the tape pack. Temperature and humidity in excess of 60°C and 85 per cent relative humidity can lead to significant tape damage. The hygroscopic effects of the extreme humidity can also produce binder breakdown.

Inundated tapes should be quickly separated into wet and dry groups; also vital records should be separated from less important ones. This organizes the salvage operation and permits a more rapid media recovery.

Move all tapes quickly out of standing water areas. If possible, move the smallest group (either the wet or the dry tapes) out of the storage area. Check all wet tape labels to be sure they are legible. Replace or make existing labels legible, but do not paste new labels over the wet original.

Begin a general drying of the entire storage area, including shelves, floors, canisters, safes, and vaults. Quickly open, check, and drain any water which may have entered the tape canisters. Since tape reel hubs are often capable of trapping and holding water, check for this, and shake and rotate the reel to empty the water. A wet-dry vacuum cleaner may be used to absorb any standing water that is accessible.

The air drying process should begin immediately. Wet tapes should not be replaced into their canisters. Hand dry all external wet surfaces. Do not force dry the wet tape pack with a heated airflow. This can cause high internal humidity which can lead to binder damage and layer-to-layer adhesion. Gently separate the reel flanges with spacers such as rubber grommets to allow airflow through the tape pack-flange interface. This reduces the probability of tape-to-flange sticking damage when the tapes are first run. It will also permit additional water run-off from the vertically standing tapes. If possible, maintain a forced, room temperature airflow through this tape-to-reel configuration.

The drying process begins most effectively when the individual tapes are run reel-to-reel on a device such as tape cleaner or winder. Wet tapes should never be run on a regular tape drive. They will not perform correctly in the vacuum columns, and they are likely to adhere to the column walls or on to the capstan, resulting in tape tearing or other damage. The tapes should be run over cleaning tissues only, not over the blades.

Recorded tapes have been successfully reactivated after being totally submerged for a period of time in unclean river water and in salt water. First, all accessible surfaces were hand dried as described above. Then the tapes stored in the normally recommended temperature and humidity environment for 48 hours.

Next the tapes were run for six or seven passes on a tape dry cleaner unit over tissue cleaners only. When they were reasonably dry, two cleaning passes were performed over tissues and cleaning blades. The tapes were then immediately read and recopied on to new reels. Recopying was important because of the potential for binder degradation to occur due to the water absorption.

This recovery process can also be applied to tapes which have been subjected to clean water inundation. In this case, it would probably be sufficient to recopy only the key tapes. Also, the two blade cleaning passes may be omitted.

Equipment and supplies checklist

Plastic milk crates

Plastic trash bags

Plastic sheeting

Garbage cans

Records storage boxes

Unprinted newsprint

Paper towels

Freezer wrap

Neoprene gloves (1 pair per worker)

Protective clothing

Portable fans

Dehumidifiers

Hygrothermograph or thermohygrometer

Flashlights

Floodlights

Portable generators

Portable electric pumps

Heavy duty extension cords (3-wire grounded, 50-foot cords)

Walkie-talkies

Pallets

Hand tools

Flatbed carts

Hand trucks

Forklift

Sources/services checklist

Drying space
Refrigerator trucks
Frozen food lockers
Freeze drying facilities
Document conservation services
Emergency telephone numbers
   Fire
   Police
   Ambulance
   Electrician
   Plumber
   Pest Control

Disaster Prevention Checklist

Building or Location:

Inspected by: Date:

Check each item to indicate that it has been inspected. Describe any problems.

Fire or smoke alarms — functional?

Sprinkler systems — functional?

Fire extinguishers — inspection date in accordance with local or state code?

Flashlights — at designated locations? Fresh batteries?

Hazards?

Emergency packets — complete? At designated locations?

Staff familiar with locations of last three items?

Part IV
Appraisal, Scheduling and Storage

INTRODUCTION

Records appraisal is probably the most difficult element of any records management programme since it involves the application of values to the records. There are, however, a number of relatively straightforward approaches that can be adopted when conducting appraisal and these are examined in some detail. Following appraisal is retention scheduling, the basis for all records management programmes. Chapter 12 provides guidance for both appraising and scheduling and explains how the two functions interrelate. When records are no longer required for the conduct of current business, they should be removed to records centres to provide better access to more current records and reduce storage costs.

The records centres must provide storage facilities for different media (paper, film, computer tape and disc) and must take account of security of confidential material. In addition an adequate level of service to departments and organizations depositing the records must be provided. Chapter 13 examines these aspects and considers the case for either in-house or commercial storage. It also discusses the use of computerized records management programmes in records centres.

12 Appraisal and Retention Scheduling

Records *appraisal* is often thought of as something that archivists do near the end of the records life cycle to determine which records contain information of enduring value and should therefore be placed in archives. While this is the situation one finds in far too many instances, it is not the best method imaginable for adequately documenting history, and additionally reflects a complete ignorance of the importance of 'managing' recorded information.

The practice of determining that a record has value at the end of its life cycle is uneconomical and inefficient. It inevitably results in records with significant value being destroyed and records with little value being retained.

The time to appraise a record is at its creation. By so doing, you are able to accomplish two very important functions:

- You can notify the record users of its value and thereby ensure that it is handled and maintained appropriately.
- You can, when necessary, ensure that the record is created on a lasting medium or provide for future media conversion so that information degradation does not occur.

Records scheduling is the process of documenting a record's value in terms of the length of time it is to be retained. By establishing a records schedule, an organization ensures that recordkeeping laws are adhered to and demonstrates that a systematic programme is in place to determine records values prior to destruction of the information. *Appraisal is the basis for scheduling*.

Records appraisal is not a subject that can be presented in the same way as other records management elements. Since appraisal involves fixing a value on something, it is bound to be immersed in some degree of subjectivity. Nevertheless, there are a number of key points to be appreciated before embarking on a programme of records appraisal:

- Functional association
- Procedural association
- Historical association
- Research association

The *functional association* involves a close examination of the organization that creates the records. Why are they created and in what specific function are they an informational source? The question of whether this function overlaps with others within or outside the organization should also be answered — it may avoid duplicating material. In addition, if

167

records covering the particular function make little sense without those from another part of the organization, the entire 'system' should be considered.

The *procedural association* requires the appraiser to look at how the records are used. It may be vital to know what level of importance they play in the administration or execution of the organization's policies and procedures.

The *historical association* can be established by a thorough grounding in the origins of the organization — for a government department this may be obtained from existing public records (acts, reports, policy papers, etc.); for a private business from annual reports, board minutes, and some public records, particularly those from the commercial area. This knowledge should include information on the general administrative history of the country and the importance of the subject matter of the records within that broader perspective. It is generally historians who would like a lapse of time before assessing the historical value of a record.

The *research association* means that the appraiser must be aware of research trends and, just as important, research methodology. Regular contact with researchers, scholars, and students plays a vital role in the appraiser's ability to formulate valid judgements on the value of records. While historians and their colleagues are generally keen to keep everything (which is, of course impossible), an awareness of their research projects and methods will be of great help.

Records appraisal is appraisal of the information in the records and as such the method adopted would be the same for different kinds of informational material. Appraisal of records should not be based on intuition or arbitrary suppositions of value. It should be based instead on thorough analyses of documentation bearing on the matter to which the records pertain. Analysis is the essence of records appraisal.

LEGAL CONSIDERATIONS

Laws affecting the use and retention of records and information vary greatly from country to country. The Canadian and US governments have powerful Privacy and Access to Information Acts, while in the UK the Data Protection Act 1984 covers the same subject. Rules of evidence in most countries state what kind of record is acceptable as evidence in court. Public record or archives acts state what government documentation must be retained permanently.

Numerous laws from many sources specify how long pertinent business records and documentation must be retained. In the preparation of schedules, records managers must work closely with their organization's legal advisors and must do their own research into the legal retention or privacy requirements affecting their organization's records.

RECORDS SCHEDULES

In simple terms a records schedule is a list of records for which predetermined destruction dates have been established. Such schedules are often referred to as retention schedules, disposition schedules, and even retention and disposition schedules. All the terms are interchangable.

Records scheduling has three broad objectives:

- Prompt disposal of records whose retention period has ended.
- Storage of records which must be temporarily retained after they are no longer needed in current business.
- Preservation of records which are of long-term value.

Large accumulations of all types of records reflect inadequate management not only on the part of the records manager but also on the part of the organization's overall administration. Some types of records require only one reading or action before disposal; others should be retained for short periods of time; a small number might warrant retention for longer periods; a selected few will be permanently preserved.

While an efficient active filing system is an essential element for the effective and economical management of active records, an equally essential element is an active scheduling programme. Retaining too many records will prove expensive in staff, time, space and equipment, and could have adverse legal consequences. The inclusion of as many records as possible on a disposition schedule will help to:

- save time by reducing the volume of records which must be searched for information;
- avoid legal problems
- promote efficiency by focusing managerial efforts on those records which are most important;
- save space by removing from the office records no longer required or no longer in current use;
- identify the valuable records for archival preservation.

The results of disposition schedules are therefore:

- fewer records
- better records
- more effective records
- more economical records.

The style of the schedule might vary according to individual taste, but certain types of information should be shown:

- the part of the organization responsible for maintaining the record;
- a schedule reference number (for example, a serial number followd by the year);
- file/paper reference(s), if any;
- description of series or collection;
- prescribed period of retention;
- signatures of section representative and the records manager;
- date of the schedule.

There are three main categories of records that might appear on the disposition schedule:

1 Those with specific retention periods (that is 'destroy after x years').
2 Those which are to be retained and examined again at a later date (that is, 'indefinite').
3 Those which are to be selected for permanent preservation.

There can be two types of schedule — general and specific.

General records schedule

The general records schedule is used by large government or corporate organizations and is compiled and maintained by a central organization (such as the National Archives or corporate headquarters) and covers records common to all departments or agencies, usually called 'housekeeping' records. These will largely comprise commonly-used forms, but will also include such material as accounting records (ledgers, journals, cash books, accounts, etc.), attendance books, accident books, circulars, notices, etc.

Departmental disposition schedule

Individual departments and organizations will vary in the style of schedule that they adopt, but the objective must be the same — the prompt disposition of records which do not warrant longer retention.

The type of records to appear on departmental disposition schedules will vary between different organizations. It would be impossible to produce a definitive list of such types, but the contents of those earmarked for destruction after a relatively short period are likely to have a number of common characteristics.

- Non-policy making
- Low level administration
- Low frequency of reference
- Clearly of no historical value whatsoever.

Monitoring and implementation

Once a schedule has been developed it must be monitored regularly to see that:

- retention periods are still realistic in the light of experience;
- records no longer in existence are removed from the schedule;
- new records created are added to the schedule.

The monitoring should be carried out by the records manager and any amendments or additions discussed with a representative of the appropriate department or section.

It is important that all who need to know about the schedule are given a copy and are supplied with amendments. Records managers should keep a complete set of schedules of the organization(s) for which they are responsible and they must ensure that action in accordance with the schedules is carried out.

The production of disposition schedules is one of the most important elements of any records management programme. Schedules can lead to wide-ranging benefits, not only in the efficient management of an organization as a whole but also in saving expenditure. It is worthwhile, therefore, to take special trouble over their compilation, monitoring, and execution.

Authority to destroy

If a disposition schedule is appropriately developed and carefully monitored, and if the schedule users receive regular communication from the records manager, then documents that have been included on the schedule can be destroyed in accordance with the terms of the schedule without additional formal authority. The schedule itself is authority enough. Often destruction can be carried out by the departmental representative; there is not always a need for records managers to become involved in the actual process of destruction. They should, however, make periodical checks to ensure that the work is being carried out in the prescribed manner commensurate with the sensitivity (confidentiality) of the material. Some records may be simply put in the wastepaper bin whereas others might require shredding, burning or other type of high security disposal.

APPRAISAL

How the appraisal of records is carried out is largely a matter of organizational preference. There are however, two basic steps that are usually taken;

1   Step one — individual assessment   One person is assigned to do an initial evaluation of what the records retention periods should be. This person may be the records manager or analyst in the organization itself.
2   Step 2 — Committee decision   After the initial assessment is made, a more formal appraisal is undertaken by a committee. Records that have been appraised will be

reviewed by key officials within an organization. The suggested membership of such a senior level records management committee was discussed in Chapter 3.

In the UK, a third possibility is sometimes considered which, because of its vagueness and informality, the authors do *not* recommend.

3 Group assessment A group of people may undertake the appraisal in an informal way.

Primary values

Records are created or received by organizations during the course of their normal business operations. Their values, in this regard, fall into three categories: administrative, fiscal, and legal.

- *Administrative value* refers to the value a record has to the original creating or receiving office. Its use by the office and its importance relative to performing the organization's assigned functions will determine its administrative value.
- *Fiscal value* refers to the value a record has with regard to documenting the receipt or use of funds.
- *Legal value* refers to the value a record has in documenting business transactions and in providing proof of compliance with regulatory requirements.

Often, a fourth category is included in the above list — historical value. It is not included here because records are not created for historical purposes. They may be historically significant, but they were not created for that reason. A treaty to end a war, for example, is drafted and signed to end a war, not to provide an interesting archival document for future historians. That the document has archival value can be determined by appraisal, but it is a secondary value, as will be discussed below, not a primary value.

The term secondary does not imply that the value is less or that the record is unimportant. It is simply a different value category, and one that deals with future record use as opposed to use in an active business environment. It should also be understood that value categories are not mutually exclusive and that a record may be valuable for more than one reason.

Secondary values

Records are preserved in archival institutions because they have historical values which will exist long after they cease to be of current use and these secondary values can be ascertained most easily if they are considered in relation to two kinds of value — evidential and informational.

Evidential value

Evidential characteristics cover the organization and functioning of the body that produced the records and are determined by an analysis of the administrative structure of that body and of the functions, activities, and transactions that resulted in the production of the records. There are three things that the appraiser should know:

- the position of an office in the administrative hierarchy of the organization;
- the functions performed by an office;
- the activities carried out under a given function.

In addition, all this assumes a knowledge of the general administrative history surrounding the organization's role at the time of the creation of the records. Armed with this, a valid judgement may be made.

The appraiser therefore seeks to explain the activities of the creating organization by preserving records of policy decisions, records which reflect the functions of the organizations, and records which are representative of a significant range of institutional or individual activities. Such records might include:

- directives
- organization charts
- annual reports
- official histories
- correspondence
- audit and inspection reports
- statistical summaries
- legal opinions and decisions
- handbooks and manuals
- minutes of meetings.

Evidential value in records is something that cannot easily be gauged until the material is quite old. For public records, the precise age will depend to a large extent on a country's statutory requirements to release material to the public, but a minimum age for a valid judgement of evidential value in the UK is 20 years.

Informational value

Informational characteristics are derived from the factual data that the records contain about persons, corporate bodies, events, problems, conditions, etc. They can be evaluated on the basis of:

- administrative needs;
- the uniqueness of the record;
- the information it contains:
- the importance of the content.

The informational needs of genealogists, historians, economists, sociologists, demographers, etc. have to be taken into account by the records appraiser. Current research interest in quantification analysis requires a concern for informational content. Because the informational content of particular instance papers or casefiles requires specialized appraisal considerations, guidance for such appraisal is provided in the following pages.

PARTICULAR INSTANCE PAPERS

Records having informational value are generally known as casefiles or particular instance papers and their appraisal and level of preservation have been the subject of much debate in the recent past. They are generally large collections of documents, each series being on the same subject but each individual file or paper in a series relates to a different person, organization, event, or whatever. The dilemma for the appraiser is to reconcile the demand for preservation from researchers with the capacity for storage of such large collections.

Examples of these records include census of population returns, ships passenger lists, unemployment returns, criminal case files, schools files, pension records, personal files and clinical case files.

In some instances these series shed light on the activity of the organization (that is, evidential value), but this is so small in proportion to their bulk that this is not an important factor in their selection for preservation.

The same holds true for particular instance papers as for general subject files, in that the appraiser must know the background to the organization, how the file/papers fit into the overall functions, the filing system, and the potential for research interest. In the case of particular instance papers, the latter requirement takes on added importance. Interest in these types of documents is increasing and shows no signs of slowing down. The shift from the study of administrative history to the study of social history continues.

Administrative needs

Before examining the appraisal of these collections, there is one major difficulty that must be recognized immediately. On many occasions the records are of long-term administrative use, usually far beyond the normal access period given by governments. For example, in the UK many of the war pensions awards files, although over 40 years old, are still active. As long as individual ex-servicemen are alive, their papers are required by the body administering their pension.

Personal files of civil servants are also required long after people retire, usually because there are questions of superannuation to be resolved. This category of records presents special problems in that the information on the file that is required for long-term use forms such a small proportion of the file itself, and yet the whole file is generally kept. This means that a disproportionate amount of storage space is being provided for the information. A simple way to reduce this drastically would be to use a system of personal record cards. This card, whose size would be dictated by the amount of information that needs to be preserved but would generally be standard A4 size (297mm × 210mm), is completed with details of service, qualifications, superannuation, performance, etc. when the person resigns or retires. The card is kept permanently while the file may be destroyed as soon as is convenient. (See Figure 12.1.)

Uniqueness

The term uniqueness means that the information contained in particular records is not to be found in other documentary sources in as complete and as usable form. Information is obviously unique if it cannot be found elsewhere. But information in public records is seldom completely unique, for generally such records relate to matters that are also dealt with in other documentary sources, and the information they contain may be similar or approximately similar to that contained in other sources.

In applying the test of uniqueness, an appraiser must bring into review all other sources of information on the matter under consideration. These sources should encompass materials produced outside as well as within the organization. The material produced outside may be published or unpublished; it may consist of private manuscripts, newspapers, or books.

Uniqueness also includes the matter of duplication. Records can be duplicated from one administrative level to another, and within an organization several copies of a particular record might exist. It is therefore essential to carefully compare records containing information on any particular matter to avoid retaining more than one copy.

Content

The degree to which the information is concentrated in the records may be in one of three ways:

1 *Extensive*   Few facts are presented about many persons, events, etc.
2 *Intensive*   Many facts are presented about a few persons, events, etc.
3 *Diverse*   Many facts are presented about various matters — persons, events, etc.

For example, census schedules and passenger lists may be said to provide extensive

PERSONAL RECORD

Surname: Title:

First name(s):

Last address:

Date of leaving:

Reason for leaving:

Date of birth: Nationality:

Date of entry: Previous employment:

Grade at entry

Record of service:

Date   Section   Grade

Record of performance:

Date   Markings

Qualifications:

Superannuation:

Remarks:

Figure 12.1   Personal record card

information in that each schedule or list pertains to many people. Pension files may be said to provide intensive information in that each file covers one person and gives a great deal of detail. Reports of consular or diplomatic agents would contain information on diverse matters. Content might also include the physical condition of the records as well as the information within them. Physical condition is important, for if the records are to be preserved in an archival institution, they should be in a form that will enable people, other than those who created them, to use them without difficulty and without resort to expensive mechanical or electronic equipment.

Importance

In applying the test of importance, the appraiser is in the realm of the imponderable. Who can say definitely if a given body of records is important, and for what purpose, and for whom?

There is no question that the informational value of particular instance papers is high, but the needs of the researcher has to be balanced against the economic necessities of governments and other organizations.

The appraiser should take into account the actual research methods of various groups of people and the likelihood that they would under ordinary circumstances make effective use of archival materials. By and large the scholar can usually rely on the overwhelming mass of published material on recent day-to-day social and economic matters, but, while records appraisers might normally give priority to the needs of the historian and social scientists, they must also preserve records of vital interest to the genealogist and the student of local history. They should not, however, preserve records for very unlikely users, such as persons in highly-specialized technical and scientific fields who do not use records extensively in the normal exercise of their professions and are not likely to use archival materials relating to them.

Research values are normally derived from the importance of information in aggregates of records, not from information in single records. Documents are collectively significant if the information they contain is useful for studies of social, economic and political matters, as distinct from matters relating to individual persons or things.

Records relating to persons or things may, of course, have an individual research value. Normally the more important a person is, the more important is the record relating to him/her. Such records might also have sentimental value because of their association with heroes, dramatic episodes, or places where significant events took place.

Appraisal criteria

Before applying these tests for the appraisal of the informational value in particular instance papers, as much background information as possible must be known. One way of doing this is to conduct a survey of these records (see Chapter 5) and compile a separate register of particular instance papers. The register should contain an information sheet for each collection which would show dates covered, creating section/branch, content, references, number of units, whether any formal reports have been produced on the subject matter, related material, and statutory background. Room should be left on the sheet for appraisal and review comments and the register should be made available for academic consultation.

When actually applying the tests of informational value, the records can be categorized into three types:

1 Records relating to persons
2 Records relating to things
3 Records relating to events.

Records relating to persons

These records are produced in great quantities by modern governments and other organizations. Certain types of records, like census schedules, are intended to cover all individuals in the country; others, relating to specific classes, often represent large segments of the population (such as labourers, farmers, soldiers, or recipients of welfare services); still others relate to even more specialized classes, such as a group of students taking a particular course at a particular university. As the controls of government over its individual citizens are extended, more records are created in relation to them.

Besides being very great in quantity, the records are duplicative in content. If considered singly and solely with reference to the personal information they contain, most records pertaining to persons have little research value. From the point of view of their significance for demographic, sociological or economic studies, they are usually important only in the aggregate. For such studies they have value only if used collectively — because of their information on phenomena that concern a number of persons and not because of their information on single persons.

In addition summarizations of the data they contain are usually available in statistical enumerations and tabulations, either in published or unpublished form.

Records relating to things

When selecting records relating to places, buildings and other material objects, the values to be considered are those that derive from the information they contain on the things themselves, not necessarily from the information on what happens to things.

Among the most fundamental things with which people are concerned is the land on which they live. The kind of material that is likely to be preserved are records on ownership of land, on survey and exploration, on mineral resources, and various other topographical or geological features.

Records on buildings need not be kept to any extensive degree. They need not even be kept for their architectural or structural details, for printed information is usually available on such matters. Records on buildings are archivally important only if the buildings themselves are important, and buildings acquire an importance because they are identified with important historical persons, with important historical events, or because they are outstanding examples of period buildings.

Records relating to events

The selection of records relating to events or phenomena is largely self-productive. Subjectivity on the part of the appraiser is difficult to avoid. A knowledge of the historical background of the organization and of administrative policy are essential elements in the appraisal process.

Appraisal method

In selecting records for their informational value, two alternative courses are available:

1 To select complete those series of records that represent concentrations of information, such as census schedules, where single documents provide extensive information in a concentrated form.
2 To select a limited number of documents that are representative of the whole.

Because of the bulk of these records, there are few that will be selected as a complete collection. Census records are an obvious exception, because experience has shown that they are extremely popular and useful to a particular, fairly large, group of researchers.

When it comes to selecting a limited number of documents from a collection — or sampling, as it is usually called — there are three methods which can be followed:

1 Special selection
2 Random sampling
3 Systematic sampling.

Special selection

This is a method that has little true archival merit and may also be of uncertain value for research purposes. Nevertheless, there are occasions when it can be adopted with some justice. The method simply means the selection from a relatively ephemeral series of papers of one or more specimens to illustrate administrative practice at a particular date. The resultant sample represents a very limited historical or other use since it can only be cited as an indicator and in no way be used for comparative or statistical study.

Special selection is often applied to personal files, where those of eminent persons may be selected for their intrinsic value only.

Random sampling

This method implies that every unit in a series has an equal chance of representing that series, and in this context it is necessary to use a random number table — a list of numbers normally generated by computer and checked in a number of different ways to ensure that they are as random as possible. The table is applied to file reference numbers and documents are selected accordingly.

Systematic sampling

This is the usual method for selection of particular instance papers and it is carried out at various degrees of complexity.

The most simple way is to decide on the size of the sample required and to select every 5th, 10th, 50th, 100th or whatever file from the series, starting from the beginning of the run on the shelves and continuing until the end is reached. In a collection of regional papers, the system might be to select records for one particular year from region A, for the following year from region B, and so on, in a continuous cycle. In a series with annual cycles, the files from every 10th year might be selected as the sample. In an alphabetical series, all the files with a particular initial letter might be selected for particular years.

Whatever selection system is used will depend very much on the characteristics of the whole collection, and, to a certain extent, on the size of the sample required.

For researchers, the problem with systematic sampling is that it depends on a subjective decision of the criteria to be used. Although academic historians are being increasingly consulted before these decisions are made, this sampling method remains the least liked by them.

Problems

Although the scholar can very often rely on the mass of published literature for information on social and economic developments, it can be argued that the existence of published conclusions drawn from a collection of particular instance papers is not in itself a valid reason for destroying the raw data. Such data can be used for further research purposes, other than those for which it was originally compiled. In addition, published abstracts often give rise to false, or at least contentious, conclusions which are not supported by original data.

These large collections of papers take up an inordinate amount of space and the general feeling is that as many of them as possible must be destroyed. On the other hand, however, the needs of the researchers are being deprived of valuable sources of study. A number of solutions to these problems has been suggested, including:

- The collections be microfilmed, the film preserved and the original documents destroyed. The main argument against this is one of cost.
- Collections not selected be kept in an intermediate repository and made available to researchers for a specified period, say between 5 and 10 years, so that they can carry out any research on them. After that period they would be destroyed.
- Collections not considered worthy of permanent preservation in the National Archives may be offered to other historical institutions and associations, including those privately owned.

DEVELOPING RETENTION SCHEDULES

Records cannot be haphazardly scheduled for disposition. They must be grouped into records series and, preferably, further organized according to file plan. This is because appraisal to determine the retention requirements involves an analysis of the entire information system (and, indeed, the entire organization) in which the record is used.

Once the determination has been made as to the value of each record series, a retention period can be established. This retention period may be based on the records manager's or analyst's experience with similar records, knowledge relating to other organization's retention of similar records, original research of government statutes and regulations, or from other sources such as published retention information, as long as such information can be deemed reliable.

Additional factors also influence the determination of retention periods. These factors are organizational, governmental, or archival, and relate to the administrative, fiscal, legal, and historical record values previously described. They should be dealt with by the individual most knowledgable about the specific area involved. That is, administrative factors should be considered by someone in the originating office, fiscal factors should be considered by the organization's comptroller or accountant, legal factors should be considered by the solicitor or general counsel, and historical factors should be considered by the archivist, historian, or records manager.

When the records manager or analyst has received the best possible information from all of the individuals concerned, a records retention schedule can be finalized and submitted to the senior level records management committee for approval.

The information on a retention schedule might include the length of time the records are to remain in the originating office, the length of time they are to be retained in a storage facility, and the date of scheduled destruction or transfer to an archives. As a general rule, records should be retained in the originating office as long as they are active (referred to once per file drawer per month). When records become inactive they should be transferred to a storage facility. For those records which will have no archival value, disposition should occur at the earliest possible time after retention requirements have been met.

A sample retention schedule is shown in Figure 12.2.

MACHINE-READABLE RECORDS

The main elements involved in the appraisal and scheduling of machine-readable records

RECORD SERIES NO	RECORD SERIES TITLE & DESCRIPTION	RETENTION PERIOD	NOTES/LEGAL CITATIONS
00231	DISTRIBUTION - CASH RECEIPTS DISTRIBUTION REPORT OF BANK DEPOSITS BY PAYER AND ACCOUNT.	TDC	DESTROY RECORDS FY79 AND EARLIER TAX REQUIREMENTS TAX FUNCTION = F 5/86
004	**COST ACCOUNTING**		
00400	INVENTORY AND NON-INVENTORY WORK ORDERS COST SUMMARIES OF INVENTORY WORK ORDERS AND PRODUCTION RUNS. INCLUDES SPECIAL HANDLING SHOP ORDERS. ALSO INCLUDES NON-INVENTORY WORK ORDERS. COST SUMMARIES OF WORK ORDERS FOR CAPITAL GOODS. PRODUCT DEVELOPMENT OR OTHER INTERNAL USE (INCLUDING OVERHEAD)	TDC	DESTROY RECORDS FY79 AND EARLIER TAX AND LEGAL REQUIREMENTS TAX FUNCTION = P.F.S SU 5/86 FAR 48 CFR 4.705-1(b) 4 YRS
00401	STANDARD COST RECORDS & REVISIONS DOCUMENTATION STANDARD OPERATION AND PARTS COSTS FOR ALL ITEMS HAVING STANDARD COSTS. INCLUDES DOCUMENTATION SUPPORTING THE CALCULATION OF THE EFFECT ON THE INVENTORY VALUATION OF A CHANGE IN THE STANDARD COST (INCLUDING OVERHEAD RATE CHANGES).	TDC	DESTROY RECORDS FY79 & EARLIER TAX REQUIREMENTS TAX FUNCTION = P.F.S. SU 5/86 COMBINES 00401 AND 00401 FY 88
00414	ROYALTY REPORTS REPORT OF SALES ON WHICH TRADE AND INTRACORPORATE ROYALTIES MUST BE PAID. LICENSEE IS RESPONSIBLE.	TDC	DESTROY RECORDS FY79 & EARLIER TAX REQUIREMENTS SUPPORT OF LICENSE AGREEMENTS. TAX FUNCTION = F. S. SU 5/86
00416	MATERIAL ISSUE & RETURN RECORDS RECORD OF MATERIAL ISSUED FROM OR RETURNED TO STORES. INCLUDES MRT. MATERIAL REQUEST SHEET. BACK ORDER TAG. RTS TAG. SCRAP REPORTS. REWORK REPORTS. MATERIAL ACCUMULATION SYSTEM ERROR REPORTS. FIELD EXCESS STOCK DETAIL REPORTS. ORDER FORMS. AND PART RETURN TAGS.	C+1	LEGAL REQUIREMENTS FAR 48 CFR 4.705-3(a) 2 YRS
00421	VARIANCE REPORTS MONTHLY DETAIL. ANALYSIS AND SUMMARIES OF VARIANCES.	TDC	DESTROY RECORDS FY79 AND EARLIER TAX REQUIREMENTS TAX FUNCTION = F. S 5/86
00427	LABOUR VOUCHERS RECORD OF THE AMOUNT OF AN EMPLOYEE'S TIME CHARGED TO ONE OR MORE PROJECTS OR WORK ORDERS. INCLUDES JOB VOUCHERS. USE 00906 FOR EMPLOYEE'S PAYROLL TIME CARD.	C+2	LEGAL REQUIREMENTS FAR 48 CFR 4.705-1(f) 2 YRS

RETENTION PERIOD CODES: C=CURRENT FISCAL YEAR CY=ONE YEAR OR LESS F=FINAL N=SEE NOTES IN GENERAL RETENTION SCHEDULE
P=PERMANENT S/O=SUPERSEDED/OBSOLETE TDC=TAX DEPARTMENT CLEARANCE

Figure 12.2 Sample Disposition Schedule

are essentially no different from those involved in dealing with paper records. But because of the format in which they are held and because of the technical problems involved in handling them, certain considerations have to be taken into account.

Because of the extreme compactness with which data can be stored in machine-readable form, large collections of information can be considered for long-term or permanent preservation in their entirety. Before such a decision is made, however, there should be absolute certainty that the records pose no possible threat to the organization should litigation arise.

Despite the savings in costs of physical storage, there is a high technical cost and a high cost in skilled manpower involved in the maintenance and preservation of such records. These include the necessity to convert the several different types of systems etc. to a common archival medium or to ensure that the equipment necessary for 'reading' the information is available, functional, and, if need be, fixable.

The main criteria to be borne in mind when appraising machine-readable records are:

- The informational content of the records should be high.
- The information available in the records should not also be available from conventional records in an acceptable form.
- The records should constitute a main data set and not a compilation from various other sources, available in this or another medium elsewhere.
- The information should not be aggregated to any significant degree.
- The information should be susceptible to analysis for purposes beyond that for which it was originally collected.
- Small data sets ought not to be taken unless there are positive advantages in taking the data in machine-readable form in preference to the conventional records from which they were compiled.
- Accompanying documentation must be sufficient for full and proper understanding of the data.

The authors are aware of the differences in appraisal traditions between and within countries. While in Canada and the US both business and government appraise at the point of records creation, only some businesses in the UK do. The UK government, and most government-linked organizations and businesses, still appraise at the end of the records' life cycles. While recognizing these differences, the authors firmly believe that the right time to appraise is at the point of creation; and that it is our duty in this book to tell people the correct way of doing things, rather than merely to reiterate the wrong way currently being done.

13   Records Storage

Records 'storage' refers to the housing of records when they are semi-active or inactive, but must still be retained. Those records that are rarely used but that must be retained for occasional reference, for auditing, or for legal or archival reasons are less expensively stored outside the office area. For this simple economy alone, records centres were created. They exist solely to keep the records which are too old and voluminous to remain in offices, but which are impermanent or still used too often for the archives to take. The objectives in creating and operating a records centre are to:

- achieve economy and efficiency in the storage, retrieval and disposition of semi-active and inactive records;
- secure against both unauthorized access to and destruction of these records in keeping with its obligations to its customers;
- protect stored records against the risk of natural disaster such as fire, flood, earthquake, etc.

The economic advantages of storing semi-active and inactive records somewhere other than the office is clear. While floor space costs per foot vary (offices in large cities undoubtedly command a higher occupancy rate than those in small villages), they are still greater than warehouse space. Add to that the volume space savings from storing records to near-ceiling height in the centre as against in active filing equipment, and the records centre storage costs drop dramatically.

Records centres are of great importance in the management of records because they enable significant savings in space and equipment costs:

- Records centre space is better utilized — five times as many records can be stored per square foot as in equivalent office space through the use of compact high-density equipment.
- Records centre storage space away from city centres costs less — on average there is a saving of between 750 and 1500 per cent.
- Staff costs are less away from city centre locations.
- Records centre storage equipment costs less — high-density equipment can cost on average 25 per cent of traditional office storage equipment.

It should be noted that while cost saving has been traditionally the primary reason for, and function of, records storage, there is a growing trend toward requiring more reference services from records centres.

181

Whether on a minimal or full basis, the records centre is a service operation. While, initially, senior management in an organization may agree to the establishment of a records storage programme because it will save costs, the only points that will interest the users of the records are security and reference. If there is no guarantee that the records they surrender will be protected from damage or loss, people will not surrender them. If there is no guarantee that they can quickly get back the record or information they need, they will not release it. Thus, a records storage facility may be established to save money, but it will survive only if it provides a faultless service.

Though the records storage programme manages records during the latter part of their life cycle, it is usually one of the first programmes the records manager must establish after doing the initial survey. The survey will have revealed numerous problems, for example, confused filing systems, inappropriate software, lack of backup or protection procedures, antiquated or inefficient filing equipment. While all of these problems need to be addressed and improvements made, it would be a great waste of time and money to make any improvements on semi-active or even dead records. Before writing new filing systems or software, ordering new equipment or folders, and transferring anything to computers, the mess of old records must be cleared out and put into records storage.

Ideally, a records storage programme would be able to handle all records of all media, to provide the appropriate environment for all media, to ensure complete security, and to provide a full reference service. However, limitations of funds, space, personnel, equipment, or expertise often require that a less than ideal records storage programme be established. Even so, as with all records management endeavours, it is always better to start with the less than ideal and to work to improve it, than to wait for the highly unlikely event of all necessary conditions for the perfect programme being satisfied.

In establishing a records storage programme, four things must be determined:

1 What is to be stored:
   - what media of records?
   - what levels of secrecy or confidentiality?
   - what is the volume?
2 How it must be stored:
   - special environment, humidity, temperature?
   - extra security?
3 What level of service will be provided.
4 Where it will be stored:
   - purpose-built records centre?
   - the archives?
   - commercial storage?
   - the basement?

What is to be stored

The records survey will have revealed those records that are semi-active. Those papers, files and discs that are referred to or used less than once a month are semi-active. A decision must be taken as to what records or collection of information elements will be accepted into records storage. Paper but not books? Engineering drawings but not photographs? Tapes but not floppy discs? Each requires special containers, environments, or equipment for maintenance. Can all of these be obtained, maintained, and operated? Can full confidentiality and secrecy be assured? Will the budget permit the higher salaries of vetted, or security-cleared, staff?

The records survey will have revealed an approximation of the volume of semi-active or inactive records. To estimate the volume of records expected to become semi-active in future years, take one-third of the total from the survey, per year. Thus, if there were 12 000 linear filing feet of semi-active and inactive records in the survey, then an estimated 4000 more will become semi-active each year. (However, where major changes in systems or equipment are planned, the media and volume of records can change dramatically. To estimate the rate or production of semi-active records here, the records manager must work closely with the planners.)

How it must be stored

Most non-paper records require a strictly controlled environment for long-term storage. While many records in storage may be destroyed after a very short time, others may be transferred to the archives, so the archival conditions must prevail in the records storage area. However, according to the medium of the records, these environmental requirements vary widely and are, at times, incompatible:

- *Paper* should be stored in a steady temperature between 13°C and 18°C, with the relative humidity between 55 and 65 per cent.
- *Microfilm* must be stored in a temperature between 15°C and 20°C, with a relative humidity between 20 and 40 per cent. It must also be free of dust and exposure to the gases exuded from most filing cabinets and from diazo and vesicular duplicate films. (See BS 1153.)
- *Colour slides* require complete dark, a steady temperature of 18°C and a relative humidity between 30 and 35 per cent.
- *Magnetic tapes and discs* require a steady temperature of 20°C with a relative humidity of 50 per cent, and a dust-free atmosphere.

Thus, separate rooms or storage facilities must have different environment for different media. It is not advisable to try to store all media together in a sort of 'average environment'.

Security is another issue to be considered. Whether or not confidential or secret records are in the storage area, all users will expect their records and information to be fully protected against damage, destruction, or loss. Security against theft of information from a magnetic tape is much easier to guarantee than that of files, because a thief would have to know the precise software and hardware with which to run the tape, whereas files are easily read. Yet the destruction of the same tape would be a much greater loss than that of a single file.

What level of service will be provided

The storage facility can be as simple or as elaborate as needs require and costs allow. It is here, in the differences in service to users of stored, semi-active records, that the difference between records warehousing and information management can most clearly be seen. Of the two extremes described below, the simplest storage service treats only the objects, the records, on which information is stored. A box of files, a file, a tape, a floppy disc, are all so many objects. The information they may contain is of no interest to the managed records centre, the centre being little more than a warehouse. The much more elaborate service that provides a full reference service is less concerned with the object than with the information stored on it. Information on 1986 capital gains taxes may be on many objects, a file and a floppy disc for example. The reference service would not simply return the objects, but would extract and compile the information for the user.

A storage facility can be simply a secure and environmentally controlled building, in which departments or organizations are allotted a certain amount of space. This space is divided, and each department holds the key to its own area. The department sends its own personnel to deposit, retrieve, and maintain all of its records. The records manager does nothing more than to maintain the building's environment and security. The advantage of this is that it is very inexpensive, requiring almost no staff or administration. The disadvantage is that while providing physical storage, it is an inefficient use of the space, and the records manager is not, in any way, providing assistance with the management of records. However, it does provide slightly more control than if the departments had no storage, or contracted individually with commercial storage facilities.

The most elaborate records centre will provide a full information reference and storage service. In this, the entire facility is secure and is operated wholly by records management staff. The delivery, accessioning, storage, protection, retrieval, destruction, and transferring are all done by the records management staff. A full reference department will retrieve files, documents, or tapes on request; or will search information on tape or disc, or run reports. The advantages of this are greater security for the information and, in managing it as a resource, a much greater exploitation of it, to the benefit of the organization. The disadvantage is that, in requiring large numbers of qualified staff, vehicles, computer hardware and software, it is expensive.

Most organizations are forced to settle for something between the two extremes. The criteria on which to base the decision as to the level of service are those that reflect the needs and abilities of the organization:

- *The users' information needs* Do the users need to access their semi-active information regularly? Is their information retained simply for legal requirements, as with most accounts records, or because its information is still useful and is used, though not daily, as with studies? Where the information has a consistent and long-term value, a full reference service would be of real benefit to the users. Where the records and information are simply retained but rarely referenced, a supervised storage with a simple reference service may be adequate.

  The survey will have revealed most of the answers to these questions, but it will be necessary to discuss them further with those departments most likely to benefit from such a service. This will heighten their awareness of new possibilities for exploitation of their information, and will gain their support.

- *The benefits of information sharing* From the survey, the records manager will have discovered which sections or departments are duplicating one another's efforts in obtaining and producing information. If there is a large amount of duplication, work in these departments could be greatly reduced through controlled sharing of semi-active information services. A full reference service could ensure the security of all information, while facilitating the work-saving sharing of some of it.

  The security, when sharing is discussed with users, must be stressed. They must be assured that sharing will be limited to only the information that may legally be shared and that no sharing will be without the creating department head's consent.

- *Cost* While cost is always a consideration in every programme, it is particularly so with reference services. A full reference service, whether done by the records management or commercial storage staff, is extremely expensive. The service must clearly benefit users if the cost is to be justified.

- *Availability of qualified people* While a simple service will require staff who are literate, do not transpose numbers or letters, and have an understanding of the importance of security, a full service will require a number of highly-qualified people. A computer systems staff and trained archivists and/or reference librarians will be needed to access, understand, and analyse the information. If such people are not available in an area (and it is unlikely that they will all be in the commercial storage companies), then a full reference service cannot be considered.

The choice of the level of service to be provided by records storage is not a final but an open-ended decision. The best service that the organization truly needs and can afford will, naturally, be selected; and it can and should always be improved.

Where it will be stored

Where the records can be stored is a deceptively simple decision. 'They must be stored wherever there is space', it is usually said — that is entirely possible, if that space is brought up to the very stringent archival standards necessary. In the United States, a number of records storage facilities, both commercial and private, is in caves and what were abandoned salt mines. In London, they can be found in disused underground tunnels and dockyard warehouses. The history of records centres must be one of the great stories of industrial reclamation.

Most records managers are not, however, in the business of commercial storage, and most have to decide not where to build a records centre, but if to build one. After it has been determined what records and how much of them must be stored, what their requirements are, and what services are to be offered, the question then is: Is this to be done by the organization itself or is it to be contracted out to a commercial storage company? In some areas or countries there are no commercial storage companies. On the other hand, for some organizations it would be out of the question to purchase land, construct a building, and staff a records centre. Restraints such as these, of availability, of cost, of policy, may make a records manager's decision for him. Indeed, most records managers use existing space as best they can.

Yet, all things being possible, the choice still requires much consideration. The results of the earlier questions must be ranked according to importance.

- Media — must the facility be able to accept all kinds of records?
- Volume — is the most important thing simply to find a place big enough to take all the records?
- Security — is security more important than anything?
- Environment — or is the proper environment, to ensure the survival of the records, more important?
- Service — finally, is the quality and amount of reference service the primary consideration?

There is no rule as to how the above criteria should be ordered in importance. Each situation is different. Each organization has its own structure, policy, finances, plans, opportunities, records, and information. While records managers will want to work towards providing the best protection and service; in the beginning they will have to weigh all of the circumstances and influences in order to choose the best solution possible. Once this is done, they can then compare the facilities available with those they might create to see which would best satisfy their requirements.

Commercial storage centres

An organization may wish to use the services of a commercial records centre if:

- it has too few inactive records to justify operating its own facility.
- it is important to store records more than 50 miles away (for vital records, disaster planning, or other reasons).
- it has no available low-cost space for records storage.
- it has exceeded the capacity of its own records centre.
- it is simply not inclined to run its own operation.

Perhaps the biggest concern for an organization considering a commercial facility is the security of its information. The management of the records centre must take the utmost precautions to ensure the integrity and protection of its customers' records. Many centres require that their staff be bonded. Strict procedures should be in effect at all times to ensure that only authorized records centre personnel have access to the storage area and to any information (inventory, billing, circulation) that the records centre maintains on its customers' records, and that only authorized customer personnel are permitted to retrieve their organization's records.

Commercial storage centres are a big business and many people have set up storage centres of extremely poor quality in order to make quick money. There is currently no inspectorate for, or certification of, commercial storage facilities and there is no single standard to cover all aspects of such facilities and their services. This means that records managers must educate themselves about the relevant standards, demand their own certification, and make their own inspections. The checklist provided at the end of this chapter should help with this effort.

The steps for the selection and contracting of a service are given and explained in Appendix A. They should be followed when choosing a commercial storage facility. Standards that are applicable to records storage centres are BS 5454: Guidance to the storage of archives and BS 4783: Recommendations for care of magnetic tape. Points to look for in a good commercial storage facility are:

1 *Sound construction* The storage centre should be in a sound, modern (or well modernized) building that fully complies with all local building codes and specifications. There should be proper drainage to prevent a build up of water, and there should be no exposed pipes. Temperature and humidity controls should be working at all times. There should be a room where clients can work with their records in privacy.

2 *Full fire protection facilities* These include sprinkler systems, heat and smoke detectors, fire extinguishers, and a halon gas fire system where tapes and discs are stored. All of these should have labels showing that they are checked and tested regularly. There should be no exposed wires; and no smoking within the building.

3 *Cleanliness* The appearance should be neat, orderly, and dust free. There should be no evidence of insects or rodents; and no piles of files on the floor that 'will be destroyed this afternoon'.

4 *Security* Where electrical security systems are unreliable, the building must have round-the-clock security guards on duty. There should be no windows, and access limited to employees only. All personnel, including drivers, must be fully bonded.

5 *Convenience* The facility should be near enough to allow for regular deliveries within two hours, and accessible to the records manager for occasional inspections.

6 *Deliveries* There should be at least one fully operational and insured vehicle; and a guarantee that, if it breaks down, deliveries will still be made, on time, at no extra charge to the client. Delivery service should be regular and reliable. There should be a round-the-clock service for emergency deliveries. Ask:

- How quickly does the centre respond to requests, that is get the information to the customer?
- How are 'rush' requests handled, or those which are placed outside normal working hours?
- Can specific files from boxes or information from within files be requested, or must entire boxes be returned to the organization?
- Can the customer's staff access the records at the facility at any time?

7 *Insurance* This should cover the full value of the information, not the object on which it is stored, and the cost of re-creation. It should cover the records from the moment they are picked up and signed for by the delivery person to the moment they are returned to the owning organization. Such comprehensive coverage would be expensive and the cost would, of course, have to be weighed against the risks.

8 *Destruction* There should be an established programme for notification when records are due for destruction, and an adequate facility for the destruction of both confidential and non-confidential records.

9 *Containers* Many storage centres will provide, at a cost, boxes or cartons as well as tape canisters. Ensure that these are made according to standards, and that using this service will truly be less costly than purchasing the containers from another source.

10 *Knowledge and attitude* Finally, the management and supervisory staff should have a thorough knowledge of all applicable standards, and of the principles of records

storage, retention, and destruction. They should show a general willingness to provide the best possible service, and to constantly improve on that service.

Cost, of course, influences an organization's decision to use or not use a commercial facility. Not only is there a charge for storage (usually based on one cubic foot per year), there are various charges for the services — accessioning new boxes, generating customer-specific reports, etc. These charges may be built into one overall charge per box or calculated individually.

The more adaptable the commercial facility is to the needs of the customer, the better. As a prospective customer, an organization should learn first-hand from the centre's other customers of the quality of service.

In the final analysis, a number of factors should be considered which encompass security, retrievability, and cost:

1 Does the facility have sufficient space to store the customers' records, including room for growth?
2 What type of security procedures and systems are in place, and how well are they followed?
3 What reputation does this facility have among the business community?
4 What type of contract or agreement is required? What is built into the standard charge? What additional charges are to be expected?
5 What inventory and circulation systems do the centre have?
6 Is the staff well trained, courteous, accommodating?
7 Are proper environmental controls in effect?
8 What record media can be stored?
9 What destruction procedures and methods are used?
10 Is there proper fire protection?
11 How far is it located from the organization?
12 How accessible are the records to the organization?
13 Is the facility clean and neat?

14 Insurance:

   • What type of insurance cover does the centre have?
   • Is it necessary for the organization to obtain additional cover?

15 Security:

   • Are there adequate physical security controls inside and outside the facility?
   • Are there adequate controls for limiting access to your records?
   • Are there special areas for storing classified or sensitive information?

16 Communications:

   • Is the communication link between your organization and the storage facility reliable?

17 Technical services:

   • What is the level of records management expertise among operating personnel?
   • Does the facility offer inventory control?
   • Does it provide microfilming, duplication, reproduction, reference and other services?

Records managers must take the time to visit each facility, to discuss services and standards with the manager, and to interview other clients. During contract negotiations, they should insist on a certificate of compliance, stable prices for a reasonable period of time, and full insurance coverage. Any commercial storage company that will not include these as part of its contract has an obvious reason for not doing so and should not be considered. After the contract is signed and the records stored, the service should be monitored closely as to:

- the prompt notification when records are due for destruction
- the reliability of the delivery/pick-up service
- the clarity of labelling
- the appearance and order of records or information retrieved
- the timeliness and correctness of invoices
- the general attitude and willingness to provide a service to all personnel who come in contact with the organization.

At least once a year, a surprise visit to the facility should be made. A schedule should be established for periodic review of the service. If it is unsatisfactory, a warning should be given to the company, with a three-month probation period. If the service is not substantially improved in that time, the contract should be terminated and the records transferred to a better facility.

In-house storage centres

Two key reasons for maintaining an in-house records centre are security and cost. Many organizations simply prefer their records to be controlled by their own employees. This does not preclude the need for security procedures, however. Cost, of course, is a major determinant in choosing in-house over commercial storage. Another factor that may require an organization to operate its own records centre is its distance from a commercial facility, although some commercial storage centres are able to serve distant customers.

Planning an in-house facility requires the same evaluation effort as that made when selecting a commercial facility, in addition to evaluating staffing, equipment, systems, and layout requirements.

Facility   The records centre building should be within easy access of the users, either in the same building as the users (if economically practical) or in a nearby building. The farther the facility, the more difficult to service the users quickly. The building should also be located in an area that is not subject to flooding or other hazards.

The centre should preferably be the sole occupant of the building, and if possible, a stand-alone facility. This adds to the protection against fire and external hazards. The building must have adequate space for office, reference, and processing areas as well as for the stacks.

For the stack area, the ceiling height has a direct relationship to the cubic foot capacity of the centre. Fourteen feet high ceilings generally provide a 5 to 1 square foot to cubic foot ratio. This height is easily accessible by safety ladders. Higher shelving may require scissor-lift type picking equipment, special ladders, or mezzanines. Aisles must be wide enough to allow easy movement of ladders and other equipment, taking into consideration that boxes hang over the edge of the shelves by a few inches.

Floor strength requirements are based on the ceiling heights. A standard records centre carton (12 × 15 × 10 in) can weigh 25 to 30 lb. If the centre is on the ground floor with no basement, floor strength is probably not of concern. The records manager should work with the facilities engineer to determine the requirements for the building based on current and future storage requirements.

Protection   The protection of the records is of utmost importance. Precautions must be taken to guard against fire, water, pests, and vandals and to ensure that proper environmental controls are in place and functioning.

The building itself should be fire resistive, and fire prevention procedures should be established in addition to the installation of fire control systems. Local fire standards and controls should be followed.

Most older buildings and many new ones have sprinkler systems, but such deterrents can pose a problem for records since water can inflict more damage than fire. Nevertheless, an automatic wet-pipe sprinkler system is the most effective fire protection element and the most economical automatic fire control system for the protection of records.

Alternative fire control systems are high-expansion foam, halon gas, and carbon dioxide. High expansion foam inundates the entire volume of the storage space, quickly extinguishing a fire. However, the foam contains a small amount of water, and records exposed to foam would need to be put through a drying process.

Halon 1301 is a liquified gas under pressure which inhibits the flames while exhibiting low toxic and corrosive properties that will not affect information stored on magnetic or other media. It is relatively safe to use in an enclosed area, although an alarm system is important to avoid personnel breathing halon or halon decomposition products. It is also an expensive alternative to water or other chemical systems.

A fire can also be extinguished by flooding the area with carbon dioxide followed by a soaking period. The danger is that carbon dioxide is fatal, and the design and proper installation of such a system is critical.

In addition to fire protection systems, the roof and drains of the facility should be periodically inspected and repaired, replaced, or cleaned as needed. Some older buildings have roofs that drain through iron pipes within the building walls. These pipes are susceptible to deterioration and can expose records to water damage. Bad plumbing and defective heating and air-conditioning systems are also avoidable potential hazards.

PHYSICAL ARRANGEMENT

Floor plan

The floor plan of the records centre should include office, reference, shipping and receiving space, as well as the stack area. Each non-stack area should be designed to serve the volume of records flowing in and out of the centre, the number and responsibilities of the records centre staff, and the number and frequency of customers visiting the centre. Ceiling height, fire and building codes, floor strength, and existing wiring and pipes will influence the specific layout of the shelves in the stack area.

Shelving

The most common shelving units are open shelf arrangement with 42 inches wide by 30 to 32 inches deep shelves. This allows for six boxes — three abreast and two deep — to be stored on a single level or twelve boxes when stacked two-high. In the former case, the shelves are placed 12 inches apart; in the latter, 23 inches apart. The 32-inch depth is preferable to 30 inches to avoid having the boxes hang over the edge and obstruct the aisle. Shelving is also available in 69-inch wide by 30 to 32 inches deep dimensions. Shelving material usually consists of steel frame, posts, and shelves, although wood shelves are sometimes used.

Shelving units can be set up in single banks with aisles on each side. Boxes are easily accessible from either aisle, but this arrangement does not provide maximum use of floor space. Placing the units back-to-back results in a more efficient layout, which more than compensates for the increased effort in handling the boxes. Triple units can also be set up if space requirements warrant, but access to the boxes in the centre unit is awkward, making this arrangement difficult to justify. A better alternative, if space is a critical factor, may be mobile shelving, if floor loading requirements allow. Single units, of course, are the logical choice for placement along a wall.

From a practical standpoint, it is best to provide a break in any row of shelving that exceeds 50 feet in length for employees to pass through to the next aisle. Long rows should also end no closer than 36 inches to the wall to allow for faster access to other aisles.

Aisles

Aisle space is determined by the height of the shelving, the wheelbase clearance requirements of material handling equipment, the needs of the employees, as well as any local fire or building code specifications. A shelf height of 8 feet or less can easily be accessed with small platform ladders, so aisle space of 30 to 34 inches is adequate. Anything less than 30 inches is difficult for the operator to pull out boxes. Some platform ladders and mechanical material handling equipment that are needed to access higher shelving will fit within 36 inch aisles.

Main aisles, such as would be found in larger records centres, should be at least 48 inches wide to allow for movement of bulk shipments and for employees and standard equipment to pass freely.

Lighting

A critical part of the layout of any records centre is the placement and method of lighting. Lights should be centred lengthwise over the aisles and over the shelves. Most areas have local fire codes that fix the minimum distance between the lights and the highest cartons. Lights should also be high enough so as not to interfere with handling the highest cartons. Fluorescent lighting is preferred to incandescent because it minimizes glare and shadows. However, fluorescent light is harmful to paper over the long term, so archival documents should not be stored where they will be exposed to this kind of light.

Wiring and Piping

In addition to lighting, wiring and pipes of any sort should not be installed over the shelving but over the aisles and other workspace.

Bracing

Bracing the shelving units is a good safety practice, and in some areas it is a building code requirement. Anchoring the units to the floor provides stability. Structurally tying the shelving at the top across the aisle is advised when the height to the top of the highest load exceeds six times the depth of the shelving. For example, a standard 42-inch wide by 32-inch deep unit may warrant tying if the height to the top of the highest carton approaches or exceeds 15 feet.

SPACE NUMBERING SYSTEMS

Once the shelving has been installed, a system for identifying the location or address of each container must be established. Rows, units or sections, shelves, and spaces, or any combination of these can be numbered and used for the address. This allows for many variations to what is essentially one basic system: row-space.

Row-space

This basic method simply assigns a number to each row and a number to each container space in that row. For example, a box stored in row 5, space 47 could be numbered 0547 (or 5-47, or 05-47, or 05/47, etc.). The advantage to this system is its simplicity; there are only two elements within the code to interpret. The disadvantage lies in learning the order in which the space numbers are assigned from unit to unit and on each shelf. The longer the row and higher the unit, the more spaces available, and the more space numbers to keep track of. For instance, a row made up of 25 units with 7 shelves each containing 12 boxes, would require spaces numbered 1 through 2100.

Row-unit-space

An improvement on the simple row-space system is to add a third element to the address: the unit or section. Within each row, the units are assigned sequential numbers, and within each unit the space numbers are assigned. Using the example of a 7-shelf unit storing 12 containers per shelf, the space number would run 1 through 84. Thus, a container on row 5, unit 12, space 47 could be written 051247 (or 5-12-47, or 05/12/47, or 5/12/47, etc.). Although this third element lengthens the address, it does allow for faster locating of the containers, and therefore faster retrieval. On the other hand, there is still the problem of remembering where each space is.

Row-unit-shelf-space

By adding a fourth element to the address, the shelf number, the process of identifying the location of the container becomes more exact. Thus, a container on row 5, unit 12, shelf 4, would have a space number of only 1 through 12 and could be written something like this: 05120407 (or 5-12-4-7, or 05/12/04/07, or 5/12/4/7, etc.). An advantage of naming the shelf number is that the records centre operator can know whether or not special equipment is necessary to retrieve or shelve the container. The disadvantage of this identifier is the length of the number and the possible difficulty of remembering the order and meaning of each element.

Row-unit-shelf

It is possible to ignore the particular space in which the container is placed on the shelf and limit the address to the three elements: row, unit, and shelf. Thus, a container with the address, 051204 (or whatever variation is used), is one of up to twelve containers found on row 5, unit 12, shelf 4, (if they are stored twelve to a shelf). The greatest advantage to this method is not having to worry about exact placement of the container on the shelf; it can go in any of twelve spaces. A three-element address is easier to read than a four-element one. The disadvantage is that the operator may handle the containers more with this method because the exact space is not known. However, this loss of time may be no greater than that spent remembering a space number.

EQUIPMENT

Ladders

Since records centre shelving takes advantage of height to gain maximum storage, equipment is needed to handle the containers that are out of reach when standing on the floor. Ladders of various heights are the most common equipment used, and platform ladders offer the most utility. The number required depends upon the number of operators and level of activity.

Any ladder should meet safety standards, regardless of height. The platform should measure the width of the ladder, be at least 10 to 12 inches deep, and securely fastened to the top of the ladder to carry the weight of the operator and a few containers. At least one side of the ladder, and preferably both, should be equipped with a safety hand rail. The platform should also be surrounded by a safety hand rail.

The width and depth of the steps must allow ease of ascent and descent while handling containers; the standard step size is 8 inches deep. Waffle, ribbed plate, rubber-covered, and open grid treads are available. Open grid is preferable since it is anti-skid and self-cleaning; rubber treads tend to loosen about the edges and deteriorate with use. The number of steps depends upon the height to be reached and the height of the persons using the ladder. Five steps is generally adequate to service shelving nine feet high, while ladders with seven or nine steps can be used with shelving that exceeds nine feet. A two- or three-step platform ladder is useful for servicing lower shelves.

The ladder should be equipped with rubber-tipped legs or casters that lock into place when weight is placed on the steps. Rolling casters will allow ease of movement. Steel construction is recommended being durable, light weight, and manoeuvrable.

Carts

Rolling, tabletop carts with one or two shelves are useful for handling containers, folders, and individual documents. The height should be approximately 32 inches high for ease of use and to prevent back strain. A small platform ladder can serve a dual role as cart and ladder.

Catwalks

Catwalks are used in some very large records centres where the ceiling height allows for tall shelving. Either for safety or practical purposes, access to the highest shelves is easier by catwalk than by ladder or lift. The catwalks should meet safety standards and should be open grid construction so as to allow maximum lighting to reach the lower shelves.

Other equipment

Hydraulic lifts can be used instead of, or in addition to, ladders. These usually have larger platform space, can accommodate more weight than ladders, and eliminate climbing up and down; however, they are quite expensive. As with ladders, health and safety standards will provide safety guidance when purchasing a lift.

A forklift is necessary if pallets are used for moving large quantities of containers. Records centre operators should be properly trained in forklift operation.

Conveyors can be used to move containers a short distance, such as inside a truck, or over a long or elevated distance, such as to a second level of shelving.

Floor guides or rails, post protectors, and other aids and buffers can be installed to prevent any of the equipment from hitting the shelving or containers.

CONTAINERS

The most common type of records centre container is the standard carton measuring 10 inches high by 12 inches wide by 15 inches deep. This carton, approximately one cubic foot in volume, easily stores letter size ($8\frac{1}{2} \times 11$ inch), legal size ($8\frac{1}{2} \times 14$ inch), and computer printout ($8\frac{1}{2} \times 12$ inch or 11×14 inch) documents.

Containers should be constructed of at least 200 lb test corrugated fibreboard. This is standard for most manufacturers. Containers may be either single- or double-wall construction. For short-term storage single-wall containers may be satisfactory, although they do not hold up as well as double-wall containers under the stress of stacking and frequent handling. Some organizations offset the higher cost of double-wall containers by reusing them after the contents have been destroyed.

Useful features of a records centre container include handholes on the ends, a shoebox-type lid, and custom printing or markings on the side. Handholes are placed below the lip of the lid on the 12-inch wide ends. Their placement is critical to hand fatigue. If placed too far (more than 3 inches) down from the top, an operator with small hands could find this puts too much strain on the thumbs. Placing the handholes too close to the top, however, could cause the cardboard to weaken and tear. Lid lips are usually $1\frac{1}{2}$ to 3 inches. The shorter the lip, the more likely it is to pop off the top of the container.

'Acid-free', that is, alkaline-buffered, containers are available for storing archival documents. These come in standard size or a smaller manuscript size.

Containers are available in other ready-made sizes to fit various needs. Invoices, cheques, microfilm and microfiche are accommodated by smaller boxes. Large (approximately two cubic feet) cartons, also referred to as transfer cases, are available, but are very heavy when filled and may require special handling. Long, narrow tubes or containers hold various sizes of rolled documents, such as engineering drawings. In addition, custom-size containers may be ordered from most corrugated box manufacturers.

RECORDS CENTRE OPERATIONS

The primary goal of all records centre operations is 100 per cent accuracy in maintaining control over the records entrusted to the records centre. The procedures for achieving this goal are critical to the success of the operation. These procedures, outlined below, should be followed with the utmost care.

Responsibilities

In most organizations, the customer (department, office, or individual) who transfers records to inactive storage retains ownership responsibility. That is, the customer has the authority to designate the time of transfer to storage and the destruction of the records at the appropriate time. The customer also has the authority to withdraw its records from the centre either on a permanent or a temporary basis at any time and to rearrange the contents of the container.

Under these circumstances, the records centre is simply the custodian of the records, responsible for protecting them, tracking their movement within and without the centre, and ensuring their proper destruction. (This holds true for both in-house and commercial facilities.)

In a few cases, the records centre becomes the owner of the records upon transfer from the user. In these instances, it may be responsible for maintaining the integrity of the container contents and for authorizing the destruction of the records.

Clarity of responsibility is important from both a legal and a customer satisfaction standpoint. A well-run operation in which the customer receives timely, accurate, and co-operative service will do more to instill trust and encourage the use of the centre than one or two instances of negligence. Negligence can haunt both the customer and the records centre. The absence of records because of their premature destruction, loss, or misplacement (essentially lost), regardless of the offending party, is not acceptable during a tax audit, lawsuit, or other required review of the information. Missing records could result in monetary damage to the organization and, perhaps, in the dismissal of those responsible for the protection of the records. A commercial records centre may have certain liabilities, depending upon the terms of the contract with the customer.

Accessioning

Records centre operations begin with the transfer of semi-active or inactive records from the office to the centre. Records should be transferred on a regular basis to avoid overloading the records centre staff with incoming shipments. Ideally, the transfer of records from the office area to the records centre should be designated on the retention schedule. During the records inventory and retention scheduling process, customers may indicate the length of time records are to be stored in the office, based on reference activity, and their subsequent transfer to the records centre. With this indication, the retention schedule can act as a control point for notifying departments to review records for transfer and for ensuring that all stored records are listed on the schedule.

It is essential for there to be evidence of what has been transferred to the records centre, however that may be described. All consignments, therefore, must be accompanied by a transmittal list. (See Figures 13.1, 13.2 and 13.3.)

The form should have a unique identifier which links it with its box and with no other. This identifier could be a sequential number or a combination of codes such as retention schedule number/date/department box number, department code/record series number/ date, etc. The sequential number is advantageous in that it is simple to understand and incorporate into an automated control system, it provides an easy way to file the forms, and it can serve as the actual box number. The other types of identifier are just as capable of providing control, but can be cumbersome if used as access points to an automated data base.

The transmittal list should be completed by the transferring section/department. It need not be of archival standard; it is, after all, merely an inventory and will only be used internally. The form of the list should, however, be uniform.

Information on the transmittal may include record series number, record title, transfer date, record date, destruction date, media type, department code, department name, retention schedule number, and box contents description. The organization should determine which information is relevant and will ensure the highest control for the protection, retrieval, and disposition of the records.

The transmittal should be at least a two-part form. A three-part form in which one part is the box label itself is useful. One part is the original, one part is the copy. The original should be retained by the customer as owner of the records. The copy is submitted with the box to the records centre. If an intermediary prepares the forms and transfers the records on behalf of the customer, that person may also keep a copy.

As an example, the accounting department (the customer) fills out a transmittal, keeps one copy, sends one copy to the records management department, and sends one copy with the box to the records centre. Accounting uses its copy to request the records and keeps it until the records are destroyed. Records management uses its copy to update the inventory data base and then disposes of it. The records centre uses its copy as part of the inventory control process.

The transmittal must contain clear and concise instructions for filling it out and dispersing the multiple copies. The customer is responsible for filling out the form with accuracy and describing the box contents to the extent necessary to retrieve the information at a much later date. Common errors in filling out these forms are mis-stating the record date and inadequately describing the contents. The records manager or designated person should educate customers as to the importance of the various fields on the forms.

Procedures for packing storage containers should be clearly communicated to customers. Records should first be removed from binders or hanging folders and placed loose or in file folders in the boxes. This avoids injury from the metal edges to those handling the boxes and the high cost of replacing these supplies in the department. Boxes should be packed loosely to allow for additions, interfiling, and easy retrieval of the records.

It is advisable to pack records with identical retention periods in one box. This avoids the premature destruction of some records or the elongated retention of others. Some

BOX STORAGE LOCATION
RECORDS CENTER USE ONLY

SITE/BLDG	ROW	SECTION	SHELF	DATE

RECORDS TRANSFER LIST

435746

NAME		TODAYS DATE	MEDIA CODE	LOCATION CODE				
				ENTITY	SUB ENT	DEPARTMENT	W.F.	P.T
		MO YR						

RECORD DATE	ORIGINATING DEPARTMENT NAME	RECORD SERIES NO.	RECORD SERIES TITLE
MO YR			

BOX CONTENTS

RANGE
FROM   TO

1. _____ _____

2. _____ _____

3. _____ _____

4. _____ _____

5. _____ _____

6. _____ _____

7. _____ _____

8. _____ _____

9. _____ _____

10. _____ _____

11. _____ _____

12. _____ _____

13. _____ _____

14. _____ _____

15. _____ _____

16. _____ _____

17. _____ _____

BOX NO. 435746

9320-3899 (8/86)   **RECORDS CENTER COPY**   **BOX ACTIVITY LOG ON REVERSE**

Figure 13.1   Records transfer list (*courtesy of Hewlett-Packard Company*)

RECORDS TRANSFER LIST

HEWLETT PACKARD

1. FILL OUT LABEL TO THE RIGHT
2. SEPARATE TOP SHEET AND CARBON AT STUB
3. AFFIX LABEL TO BOX
4. FILL OUT REMAINDER OF FORM PER IN-STRUCTION SHEET

RECORDS CENTER USE ONLY
ROW _____ SECTION _____ SHELF _____

MOISTEN LABEL - PLACE ON NARROW END OF BOX

435746

TODAYS DATE	MEDIA CODE	LOCATION CODE				
		ENTITY	SUB ENT	DEPARTMENT	W.F.	P.T
MO YR						

INSTRUCTIONS

STORE ONLY **ONE RECORD SERIES** IN THIS BOX

DO NOT STORE HANGING FOLDERS OR 3-RING BINDERS IN THIS BOX

RECORDS TRANSFER LIST

370243

BOX CONTENTS

① PLACE LABEL ON NARROW END OF BOX

② NAME OF PERSON FILLING OUT FORM

③ DATE THIS FORM IS FILLED OUT

④ MEDIA CODES: 10 = PAPER 20 = DISC 30 = MAGNETIC TAPE 40 = MICROFORM 90 = OTHER

⑤ ENTITY AND DEPARTMENT CODES ARE REQUIRED. SUB-ENTITY, WORK-FORCE AND PRODUCT TYPE ARE OPTIONAL.

⑥ MONTH AND YEAR OF MOST RECENT RECORD IN BOX.

⑦ NAME SHOULD COINCIDE WITH LOCA-TION CODE

⑧ 5-DIGIT NUMBER OBTAINED FROM CURRENT DEPARTMENT RETENTION SCHEDULE.

⑨ TITLE OF RECORD DESIGNATED BY DEPARTMENT OR TITLE OF RECORD SERIES GIVEN ON DEPARTMENT RETENTION SCHEDULE.

⑩ IDENTIFIES SPECIFIC CONTENTS OF BOX. ITEMIZE INDIVIDUAL FILE FOLD-ERS BATCHES, UNIQUE AND MULTIPLE RECORD TITLES IN THIS RECORD SERIES. INCLUDE DATE, NUMERIC OR ALPHABETIC RANGE.

BOX NO. 435746

ORIGINATOR COPY

THIS IS THE OFFICIAL RECORD RETAIN IN OFFICE 10 YEARS AFTER DESTRUCTION OF RECORDS

9320-3899 (8/86)

Figure 13.2   Records transfer list (*courtesy of Hewlett-Packard Company*)

		TRANSMITTAL FORM		
Originator:			Contact:	
Address:			Telephone no:	
			Date:	

Box number	Reference	Title	Date	
			Review	Destroy

Figure 13.3   Transmittal form

organizations require packing only one record series in a box, even if multiple records series have the same retention period. This ensures that retention changes to any record series will not result in needing to remove records from a box. One records series per box and one record date (which translates into one destruction date) per box is the best procedure when using a computer data base.

When a record is no longer required for immediate administrative use, it may be removed from the active records office (registry) and placed in a suitable records centre. Experience shows that the need to consult a closed file or other document that is no longer required for the conduct of current business evaporates rapidly after the first 18 months. Removal should therefore be carried out two years after closure of the document.

Documents stored in records centres can be kept in simple boxes or cartons and must be marked clearly with the container number, the name of the organization, additional useful information, and, above all, a date when the records are to be reviewed or destroyed. Without that date material languishes on the shelves indefinitely and thereby defeats the whole object of why it was put there in the first place. Records managers will check these dates annually in order to identify those records which are due for review or destruction in the current year and will arrange for the appropriate action to be carried out. This exercise is made simpler by ensuring that documents with a common review or destruction date are packed in the same box. The contents should *not* be described on the outside of the box, but on the transmittal form. This provides another level of security as does using a code, rather than the name of the department. The record date, indicated either on the box or in the computer data base, is essential.

RECORDS CENTRE SERVICES

Records centres should provide the maximum service given the available resources. Services may include accessioning new containers, loaning out containers and later picking them up, looking up information in containers, pulling files to be loaned out, refiling returned files, interfiling new files into existing containers, providing specific turnaround time, disposing of containers, providing management reports, and charging back costs to the customer.

There are three levels of records storage service:

1 Minimal storage
2 Standard inventory control storage
3 Full reference storage

Minimal storage

This type of centre, also known as an intermediate repository, is used simply for the storage of material that is awaiting review or destruction. Little or no servicing is carried out on the records, other than to produce files and papers required for consultation. There is usually no lists or index of the material, other than those originally produced when the records were active. Boxes are normally marked only with the references of the contents and the date of destruction/review.

Some intermediate repositories are large enough to hold material from a number of organizations. These will usually be administered by a central staff, but the records themselves will be serviced by staff from the organizations to which the records belong.

Minimal storage records centres which remain an integral part of the creating organization will be under the control of the departmental records section.

Standard inventory control storage

Standard inventory control is the traditional form of records centre management. Its sole objective is to account for the whereabouts of each container at all times. Inventory control procedures may be manual, automated, or a combination of the two. There is no best way; the procedures simply must meet the objective.

Once the records are accessioned they are placed in a staging or processing area. If they have not already been checked against the transmittal at the pick-up point, this should be done. The containers are now ready to be placed on the shelves. The procedures may call for assigning the space number/location either prior to or at the time of actual placement on the shelf. If containers are given a permanent location, so that they are always returned to the same place after being on loan, the space number assignment should be marked on the front-facing end. If the containers are randomly shelved and reshelved, the number may be omitted. The records centre should be solely responsible for assigning space numbers and maintaining this information. Reliance on the customer for this information is risky.

The space number assignment, along with the date of receipt and the initials of the records centre operator handling the box, should be indicated on control card or form, such as the actual transmittal if it is designed to include this information. Control data may also be recorded online, if operations are automated. The control card or data-base fields may also be used to note the movement of containers in and out of the records centre.

Full reference storage

Many centres of this type are run by private commercial organizations, supplying a comprehensive storage and referencing service to their clients. A number of countries, notably Canada and the United States, operate their government centres by providing this high level of service.

Detailed requirements have to be met before the centre will accept records for storage. These include the completion of a transmittal and receipt form, a document information schedule (to enable lists and indexes to be compiled), the use of standard containers, and reference to a records control schedule.

The centres provide a full reference service, including loan or return of records to the agency of origin, preparation of authenticated reproductions of documents, and furnishing of information from records.

These centres will have a high degree of computerization and will provide facilities for the storage of records in various media — microfilm, microfiche, computer tape and disc, photographs, etc.

Procedures for requisition services are established to ensure consistency in responding to each request and in documenting the movement of requested material. Procedures may require that all requests be in writing, sent via inter-office or electronic mail; or they may allow for telephone requests. The latter can prove unproductive if records centre personnel are frequently interrupted by telephone calls for services. However, the use of a telephone answering machine on which customers identify themselves and state the nature of their request allows the staff to respond to the calls at their own convenience. A drawback to verbal requests of any sort is the speaker's difficulty in enunciating clearly, resulting in time wasted by the staff in tracking down accurate request information.

All requests should be recorded on a service or work order form. If customers are required to submit all requests in writing, a preprinted form should be available to them. This ensures consistent information is provided by all requestors. If customers submit verbal requests, the records centre staff should record the information on the form. If this information is to go into the data-base, the data should be arranged on the form in the order that it is to be keyed in. The service order form should indicate the following:

- requestor
- requesting department
- telephone number
- requestor's location
- type of service requested
- container number(s) involved
- billing and other information, as appropriate.

Accessions

Accession procedures have already been covered. As a service, new containers should be picked up in the office. Transmittals should be readily available for the customers. It is preferable that only one or two persons in a department be responsible for preparing containers for transfer to ensure consistency and competence in this step, otherwise the records centre personnel may spend unnecessary time advising others of the proper procedures. All containers in a department should be collected from a central point in the office, again, to save time and effort. If it is not practical to pick up from individual departments, pick-up points may be strategically located throughout the organization. Access to any pick-up point should be unrestricted, enabling the necessary material-handling equipment to be moved throughout the building.

Some records centres require the use of outside personnel for the transportation of containers. Procedures for using in-house or commercial carriers should be established with the organization's traffic management operation.

Retrieval

Only authorized personnel should have access to material in the records centre. Retrieval of containers or files should be done by the records centre staff so as to control the documentation of the movement of the records in and out of the centre. Requestors should be verified as authorized to call for and receive the records. Records should be given only to the organizing department unless that department has given written permission to another to receive the records. Some records, such as employee-related information, may be sensitive enough to require only authorized individuals within the department to request and receive them.

In some instances it may be expedient for customers to visit the records centre in order to review material or search for specific records within containers. A service area should be provided for this, away from the incoming and outgoing staging area, so that customers can have uninterrupted, private access to records, and their material will not inadvertently be mixed with others. All visitors should be required to sign a visitors' log to document the presence of non-records centre personnel on the premises.

Records centre staff should be prepared to respond to after-hours or emergency requests. Supervisory personnel are usually 'on-call' at all hours, but it may be necessary to schedule one or more staff members on 'stand-by' on a rotating basis.

Delivery of containers and files should be directly to the requestor or to a central point in the requesting department. From a cost standpoint, centralized delivery points servicing more than one department may be more advantageous, but the personal touch does more to enhance the image of the records centre from a customer satisfaction standpoint.

Turnaround time for responding to requests depends on available resources, including personnel and transportation. A 24-hour response, with exceptions allowed for emergency requests, is adequate for most operations.

If records are delivered by non-records centre personnel, verification of receipt should be obtained from the requestor and returned to the records centre. Containers should be handled in such a manner as to ensure the contents remain intact. Files should be placed in an envelope to ensure that the contents do not spill out. Inter-office mail may be used for files instead of personal delivery, assuming the turnaround time is met. Confidential records should be placed in a sealed envelope, marked 'To be opened by addressee only'.

Records that are on loan should be noted in such a way as to allow for follow-up, for example on the data-base, in a tickler card file. Notices should be sent to customers on a regular basis, reminding them to return the records to storage. All too often, without notifying the records centre, a container is dismantled, and the records destroyed by the customer or reboxed and shipped to the records centre as a 'new' item. Customers should be given the option of returning the records, extending the loan period, or permanently withdrawing the material from the records centre, but these actions should always be communicated to the records centre.

Storage arrangement

There are three main ways in which the records can be stored at a records centre:

1 In box number order
2 In review/destruction date order
3 In file/document reference order.

Box number order

When files and papers are ready to be sent to the records centre, they are boxed up and the boxes labelled simply with a box number and other information, as needed. A master list of box numbers may be kept by the records manager who issues the numbers. It is important to keep files and papers with the same destruction/review date (year) in the same box. The transmittal form is then completed, as previously described. The records manager keeps the master set of forms, and copies of their own deposits will go to the originating sections (see Figure 13.3).

If a file is required for consultation, the person requesting it has to quote the box number. It is then a simple operation to locate the box and extract the file.

With this arrangement, the review/destruction exercise is normally carried out annually (towards the end of a year). It is straightforward to remove all boxes marked with the year in question in order to carry out the necessary action. However, while this means that gaps in the run of boxes on the shelves will appear each year, there are a number of ways to identify space availability to ensure optimum use of the shelving (see section on Space Allocation, p. 202).

Review/destruction date order

All files, papers, etc. are kept on the shelves in strict chronological order (month/year) of the date of review or destruction. Within this arrangement, files may, as far as possible, be kept in reference number order although there are bound to be large gaps in the sequence, since all files in a series are not likely to have the same review/destruction date. It will be seen that series of records will be dissipated among a number of boxes and that an efficient index is necessary in order to locate particular files/papers. As an aid to finding requisitioned documents, boxes need to be numbered.

With this arrangement, however, it is a straightforward operation to carry out review and destruction and, because sections of the shelving are emptied in one exercise, optimum use is made of the storage facilities.

File/document reference order

All files, papers etc. are kept on the shelves in strict numerical order within their series, that is in the same order as that in the active records office (see p.122). This arrangement makes it very straightforward to locate files and documents that may be required for consultation, without the need for a special list or index.

It will be seen, however, that dates of destruction and review will be spread quite randomly round the series, making it necessary to examine each box when carrying out the monthly or annual exercise of destruction or review. This can be made a little simpler by marking the index of files with the destruction/review date, and, if the index is in a suitable form (for example, docket sheets), by keeping a duplicate set of index slips in chronological order of destruction/review date.

Space allocation

Space availability is handled in a number of ways. A chart may be created of all spaces, with each occupied space marked with an 'x' and each available space left blank. While this may be practical for a small centre, the disadvantage is readily apparent when hundreds, or even thousands, of boxes are being stored. The size of the chart alone, not to mention the erasures when hundreds of containers are destroyed, points to the need of a more efficient method.

Another procedure is to maintain a card file of vacant spaces, arranged in space number order. As each space is filled, the card is attached to the container. When the container is destroyed or returned to the customer, the card is returned to the file. This file represents vacant spaces only.

Coloured magnets may be used on the shelves to designate empty spaces. A plastic-coated magnet placed on each shelf has written on it the number of available spaces. This number can easily be erased and rewritten as the spaces are filled. Another colour may be used, in addition, to note the number of empty spaces caused by boxes on loan. An alternative to writing on the magnets is to use one magnet for each empty space.

If the inventory information is maintained in a computer data-base, the space number assignment should be part of that information. Computerization of the inventory control process should allow for the reporting of available spaces for new boxes in addition to the unavailable, empty spaces of boxes on loan.

Once a box has been assigned a location, it should not be moved to another. From a practical standpoint, the more active boxes (that is, the ones that are recalled most frequently by the departments) should be stored on the most accessible shelves, usually those between knee and eye level of the operator, while the more inactive ones should be placed on the upper shelves, the very bottom shelf, or in rear positions. When a box is returned to the records centre after being borrowed by the department, it should be placed in the same space from which it was removed. Placing it in a new location would require changing the space number written on the box and on the control card or in the data-base.

It is a good practice to store boxes randomly on the shelves regardless of box identification number or originating department. Likewise, it is advisable to mark each box with the minimum amount of identifying information, such as box number and space number only. The resulting anonymity of box content and ownership contributes to the security of the records, and those two numbers are the only elements necessary to locate a box on the shelf because the properly filled-out transfer list or control card has pointed the way to it.

If the inventory control procedure is to assign a unique number to each box, it is best to avoid assigning blocks of numbers to each department. Rather, distribute the transfer lists randomly, in quantities needed by the customers. This proves useful when the forms are updated.

Physical inventory

A physical inventory of boxes should be taken periodically, preferably annually. This activity provides an audit trail of the inventory activity and assists in determining if any procedures need improvement.

The inventory process should identify four conditions:

- *Matched* Container on the shelf is in the correct/assigned location.
- *Away* Container is away from its assigned location, properly checked out.
- *Missing* Container should be in its assigned location but is not.
- *Found* Container is found in a location where not assigned.

The physical inventory is easier to accomplish when the inventory information is online. A report which sorts the containers in space number order can be divided among the operators who would be responsible for specific rows. Pairing off sometimes expedites the process, with one person handling the boxes while the other calls off the number.

Regardless of whether the physical inventory is a manual or an automated process and whether it is performed as an ongoing or an annual activity, the exceptions (points 3 and 4 above) must be reconciled immediately. Otherwise, the 'snapshot' of the collection at the completion of the inventory becomes less accurate with each passing day because of the constant movement of boxes in and out of the records centre.

Bar code

The use of bar coding in conjunction with a computerized data-base can be very useful in records centre inventory control. It provides for error-free data entry of box numbers, space assignments, and other data. Applications include circulation control and physical inventory support. Bar code applications require bar code labels using a standard format, bar code scanning equipment (wand), a portable or hand-held data collection device, and if necessary, a cable interface and software program to upload data to the records centre data-base. Bar code labels representing each box number are placed on each box. Certain computer printers are capable of generating bar code labels, or the bar code can be designed as part of the box label form and printed by the forms manufacturer. Bar code labels should also be created for space locations and if desired, for each customer, using a numeric code. If the row-section-shelf space numbering system is used, only one label is adhered to each shelf. If the specific space on each shelf is designated, a label must be created for every space.

When a container is received into the records centre, its number is scanned by the bar code wand which is connected to the data terminal. If customers have been assigned numeric codes, these can be listed on a large sheet of heavy paper stock with the corresponding bar code labels next to each one. The appropriate customer code is then scanned. Additional container information is then keyed into the data base. When the container is assigned its location or placed on the shelf, the space number label is scanned. This procedure avoids transposition and other data entry errors that affect the integrity of the data-base.

The circulation of containers loaned back to and returned from customers can be tracked using bar codes. Once again, the container, space, and customer codes are scanned by the bar code wand. The software has been programmed to interpret this data as charge out or return information rather than accession information.

Bar codes can speed the physical inventory process. Rather than checking off each container on the inventory report, writing down the exceptions, and then manually comparing the results against the data-base, the container and space numbers are quickly scanned, the data is uploaded into the computer and matched against the data-base.

Storage conditions

With increased diversity in the size and type of records, a corresponding diversity in storage equipment and conditions has evolved. The basic concept of any records centre, however, must be to provide as much storage capacity as possible in as little space as possible. By definition the records in the centre are not going to be used or requisitioned by the public and the call on them by the originating organizations and agencies is likely to be minimal. Access to the records, therefore, is less important than the conditions under which they are stored.

Although a minority of the records in a centre will eventually find their way into the archives, it is necessary to provide an environment that will guard against excessive deterioration. In this respect, air-conditioning is the best system. In its absence, heating and ventilation must be kept within tolerable limits. In addition, centres must be protected from fire by sprinklers or smoke-detectors or both, and must be secure against unauthorized intrusion. By their very nature, a great many of the records will be sensitive.

If the records centre staff themselves are deputed to carry out the destruction of material, there needs to be some kind of chronological 'trigger' to indicate which boxes are due to be destroyed in any particular month or year. Rather than examine large collections of transmittal lists, this can be achieved by a simple system of a standard box label (see Figure 13.4). All boxes transferred to the records centre will bear this label, two copies of which will be produced (either by the transferring department or by the records centre). One will be affixed to the box, the other will form a card index, kept in chronological order of destruction/review dates. It is then a simple matter to extract from this index each month, or each year, those labels for records due for destruction or review at that particular time and to locate the boxes accordingly. Such a system can be used however the boxes are stored and whether the documentation at the centre is computerized or not.

If a file is required for consultation and is removed from its box at the records centre, two essential pieces of documentation are required:

```
Dept/section:



Location/box number:                    Review/destruction date:



File ref:               Description



```

Figure 13.4   Box label

- A slip or note must be left in place of the file in the box to indicate its reference, to whom it was sent, and when it was sent. This will enable any further request for the file in the period before it is returned to be met (if only to explain that the file is in use), and will guard against files going astray.
- An indication must be made on the file of the box number or location reference at the records centre so that it can be replaced properly when it is returned. This indicator might be a label or it might be written on the file itself.

Specialized records centres

A number of countries have introduced records centres for special categories of records, particularly personal records of government employees, both military and civilian. Essentially, the operations of such centres need not be different from other records centres but it is inevitable that they will have to provide a very full reference service. Normally, this is the main reason why they have been set up in the first place, especially in countries (such as Canada and the USA) where there is freedom of information legislation.

PROMOTING USE OF RECORDS STORAGE

As any records manager knows, a large part of the job entails the publicity and promotion of records management services, especially the records storage services. Because the facility is out of sight it is out of the users' and the potential users' minds. They must constantly be reminded of the wonders of records storage, or they will forget to use it, and it is the records manager who must do the reminding. While some may find this sales aspect of records management distasteful, it is vital to the success of a records storage programme.

In promoting records storage services, it is necessary to make contact with potential users, explain the services to them, and to encourage them to try the services.

- *Contact* can be as simple as strolling into an office, noticing piles of records on the floor, and striking up a discussion with the manager about how best to remove them, or it can be as complex as a full user orientation programme. Publicity is a key to contact. Simple memos, printed leaflets, booklets, posters, or a full video can all be used to describe and encourage use of records storage services. Consider also a photographic display about the facility, articles in the internal press and tours of the facility.
- *Explain* in publicity, briefing sessions, or in conversation, the services offered through records storage, emphasizing security, cost savings, quick retrieval, time and space released in users' offices. When possible, arrange a meeting between those who use the storage and those who do not, to have a full discussion of the benefits.
- *Encourage* users to test the services, to ask for trial retrievals, to deposit records for trial periods of time. This not only gives them the chance to approve the services, but it keeps records storage staff in practice.

Promotion is a constant in records management, and a good storage promotion programme will increase use of the facility and thus, appreciation of records management.

AUTOMATED RECORDS MANAGEMENT SYSTEMS

As most of the software sold as 'records management systems' is designed for use in records centres, it is expedient to discuss the subject here.

There are a number of different, small software packages with the words 'records management' included in the title, and they have many different applications. The systems for the management of records centres, of registries, of files, etc. tend to focus on the dates of creation and expected destruction, and on tracking the location of the object. They do little or nothing to manage the information, and some, particularly the registry management systems, create more confusion and work than existed before they were implemented. There are few, and even fewer tested, systems that apply records management principles to the information that is created, used, exchanged, stored, and destroyed electronically.

Most of the records management systems available today suffer from two flaws at their point of origination:

- They are adaptations of systems designed for another, remotely related, application.
- They incorporate many procedures that are antiquated and, because of computerization, no longer necessary.

The first flaw comes from the fact that vendors of library cataloguing or stock control systems recognized similarities between library book lending and file movement, or between stock control and records centre management. With a very small amount of development, they turned their existing systems into 'records management systems' that are, indeed, adequate, but clumsy, unclear, quickly obsolete, and that show, in their structure, a lack of any real understanding of records management principles today.

The second flaw comes from the fact that those who developed the 'records management systems' did so not with records managers but with records centre or file supervisors, thus looking at procedures, not principles. This gave the systems an extremely narrow focus. Particularly disappointing is the fact that many do no more than automate, but certainly not improve, manual procedures. For example, the double numbering of boxes stored randomly in a records centre is necessary with a manual system but not with an automated system; or a registry will need a complex filing system on files controlled manually, but could have a much simpler one when computerized. This is not to say that all management software is useless. A records centre quite obviously is better run, more efficient, and provides a much better service if it is computerized. Even a registry will almost certainly be assisted (though hardly improved) by a system that will track the myriad movements of files and documents.

However, both systems in an organization will have to manage the same records as they move from active to semi-active, and any two systems are almost always incompatible. Some system developers claim that they can control 'boxes, files, even documents' all using the same access point to the same data base, but they usually have trouble indicating that, in a group of files and boxes treated identically by the system, some of the files may be put inside some of the boxes. Flaws such as this are numerous, but certainly not necessary. They exist simply because vendors sought to get a product on to the market quickly and cheaply, with little research or development into the real records management needs. Generally, the results are dismal.

More encouraging are the systems that have been designed within large organizations for their own needs, and then marketed externally. These tend to manage records (but not yet the information they hold) satisfactorily from the point of file creation and activity, through its semi-active phases, to its destruction. However, these tend to be large and expensive systems, requiring a mainframe computer, and are not within the budgets of smaller organizations.

The need for a system that will manage all information becomes increasingly urgent as more information is held electronically, and especially as more is held on personal computers (PCs). On PCs, whether or not they are networked, records and information can be created, routed, used, and deleted, entirely without any records management control. The effect of this is to remove all information on PCs from the supervision or even knowledge of the organization. It may own the PCs and discs but it has no knowledge of the information on them. What is needed is a system that will supervise networked PCs and automatically apply records management principles to records as they are created. Some systems, similar in concept, are beginning to appear for use on mainframe computers, and are being marketed by large systems or accountancy consulting corporations. The problems with these are that they, too, are large and expensive, they have not been tested for very long, and, reversing the narrow focus of small systems, they address only electronically held and not paper information.

Essentially, then, there is not yet a true records management system. Knowing this, a records manager can make a selection from the narrowly applied systems available, without unduly high expectations.

Selecting or creating software for records management

In most larger organizations there is a mainframe computer and a data processing department and the records manager has the choice of either purchasing software or of working with the DP manager to create one; and of either using the mainframe or of purchasing (or using existing) PCs. In either case, it will be necessary to investigate what is on the market in records management software, whether with a mind to buying or to getting ideas for in-house creation. Advantages of in-house creation and use of the mainframe are that the system will be designed for that specific organization's needs and that alterations and expansions will be done by those who wrote and work with it. Disadvantages are that even in-house programming time is very expensive and, if the records manager is ignorant of computers or the DP manager is ignorant of records management, or both, the in-house programme will be a disaster. A third option, of hiring a consultancy firm to come in and redesign the entirety of the organization's data bases and software and to incorporate records management into the redesigned system, can be considered only by very wealthy organizations.

In preparing to computerize any records management programmes, certain steps basic to all computerization projects should be followed.

1 *Analyse* current procedures of the programme. The computerization can rigidify bad practices as easily as it can solve problems. It is imperative to analyse closely the whole programme as it stands, keeping the purpose of it, the goals it is to achieve, in mind. Does it currently do what it is supposed to do? For example, are records stored and retrieved efficiently? Are they destroyed on time? Are the right ones destroyed, etc.

    It is the achievement of these goals that is to be automated, not the current procedures. If this is kept in mind, then unnecessary adherence to outdated or even pointless procedures will not be built into the software.

    Look also for specific problems in reaching those goals again, not in the procedures that automation can solve. Then, try to be creative and look for improvements and new uses of the information that automation might bring.

2 *List* exactly what the new system should accomplish, both immediately and in the future. Also list all of the reports it should produce. (Always include in this list the facility to query the system for unique reports.)

3 *Learn* as much as possible about software uses and abuses.

4 *Build a team* of internal personnel to help evaluate the products. Include someone from the DP department with knowledge of software and hardware, and the supervisors of the records management programmes to be computerized.

5 *Consider* with the team, what the project should entail in purchases and time: hardware, software, studies, trials, training, conversion, documenting new procedures, both within the records management department and with users.

6 *Budget* the money and time to be spent and the project.

7 *Evaluation* can now begin, following the steps in Appendix A.

Once the software is selected, it will be necessary to plan carefully the implementation and conversion. (If, however, the records manager is in the position of purchasing and implementing the software before the records programmes are begun, there will be, of course, no conversion from paper to electronic systems.) The plan should include:

- Where the new computer is to go. Does it need a room with a particular temperature and environment? Is there sufficient wiring for it? Is a special trolley needed for it?
- Who is to enter the data? If records management staff, do they have the time and training? If external or temporary staff, do they understand the data to be entered? Will their entries be checked?
- When will the conversion be done? During or outside of normal work hours? During holidays or slack times of year?
- How long should it take? Plan this very realistically! It takes time for people to learn the system to the point where they are entering data quickly; and it takes time to understand and work quickly with the reports produced. A rushed conversion will produce only mistakes and delays.
- How will users be educated? They will need explanations of new procedures and reports which they must follow and use. This should also be used as an opportunity to promote the use of the records management programmes. Both to keep staff morale high and to educate users, demonstrations of the new system (when it is fully working) should be given.

Any computerization project will take a great deal of time and effort, especially at the planning stage if the results are to be of any worth at all. There is no question that a well planned and implemented computerization project will bring major improvements in efficiency and services, and increased respect for the records management department.

Records centre selection criteria checklist

	Must	Avoid	Not an issue

Location

1 Proximity to offices

- same site
- no further than x miles/kilometres

2 Adjacent properties/tenants

- records centre is sole tenant of building
- building is shared with another department
- building is shared with another company
- building located away from fields or food storage (potential rodent problem)
- records are stored away from heat-generating equipment
- records are stored away from hazardous materials

Facility

1 Ownership

- company-owned
- leased

2 Fire safety

- fire-resistive
- meets NFPA (National Fire Protection Association) standards
- fire protection system
  — sprinkler
  — halon
- 'No smoking' signs posted
- no smoking policy strictly enforced
- regular fire inspections
- fire extinguishers strategically located and properly identified

	Must	**Avoid**	**Not an issue**

- staff trained in fire prevention

3   Water safety

- sprinkler system has manual shut-off safeguards
- no overhead pipes
- records are stored above ground (above flood level)

4   Environmental controls

- natural environment
- man-made environment
- temperature between 18 to 22°C
- relative humidity 50 to 60 per cent
- reliable power source
- back-up power source available
- controls monitored regularly

5   Lighting

- incandescent
- fluorescent

6   Shelving

- meets local building code(s)
- braced and/or reinforced for safety
- open-type units
- mobile units
- construction
  — steel only
  — steel and wood

7   Other

- building constructed to withstand
  high winds, storms, floods,
  earthquakes, etc.
- pest control procedures followed
- available space for growth
  ($\times$ per cent growth per year required)
- signs conspicuously posted (for example,
  'no eating', 'no drinking',
  'authorized personnel only', etc.)

Security

1   Access to records

- company personnel only
- one person per department only
- one person per company (when using a
  commercial facility)
- security clearance required

2   Confidential/classified records

- government classified records
  storage capability

	Must	**Avoid**	**Not an issue**

• separate area for company-confidential records

Vault

1 Location
   • same site
   • company-owned building
   • same criteria as for records centre

2 Construction
   • x-hour fire constructed vault
   • x-hour door

Services

1 Turn around time
   • x-hours for container pick-up
   • x-hours for container/file retrieval and delivery
   • 24-hour emergency retrieval available

2 Reports to customer
   • inventory listing
   • billing detail
     — by cost centre
     — by service type
     — other
   • frequency of report distribution
     — monthly
     — on demand
     — other

3 Destruction
   • methods used for *non*-sensitive records
     — recycle
     — skip (dumpster)
     — shred or render unreconstructable
   • methods used for *sensitive* records
     — shred
     — render unreconstructable

4 Transportation
   • provided by records centre staff
   • provided by company employees
   • provided by

5 Allocation of expenses
   • charge back to departments or cost centres
   • charge to overhead account
   • consolidate storage and service charges

Commercial storage facility (unique issues)

1 Contract provisions
   • future cost increases

	Must	Avoid	Not an issue

- cost of permanently removing records
- contract termination clause

2 Employees

- bonded
- labour union(s) involved
- access to customer offices
  — unlimited
  — limited to central drop-off point

3 Other

- procedures compatible with company policy
- comparisons with in-house facility
— storage and service rates
— remaining lease costs if company-owned building
  is being vacated
— available services

Part V
Ultimate Disposition

INTRODUCTION

When records have ended their useful (active or inactive) lives, they will either be destroyed or transferred to an archival institution. A great deal has been written on archival storage and archives operations and, while archives administration is essentially a part of records management, it has always been considered in a separate light. Although we see no reason to depart from this tradition, there are a number of aspects of archives without which a records managment programme would be incomplete. These include archives management, arrangement, classification, listing, and accessioning and they are the subject of Chapter 14.

14 Archiving

While file maintenance and appraisal are two of the basic functions of records management, the communication and description of records which are finally transferred to an archive for permanent preservation is an essential operation if the information in them is to be properly made available for research.

It is not our intention to describe in detail the functions and procedures of an archival institution — a great many works have been produced on that subject alone — but rather to outline those elements of archiving which follow naturally from the appraisal and scheduling processes, namely archives management, arrangement, classification, listing, accessioning, finding aids, access and security and storage and preservation techniques.

MANAGEMENT

Archives are established to preserve history for the benefit of those who would learn from it. An archives is a memory book. It may house collections on specific subjects or represent the life of its parent organization. It may contain artefacts and be a showplace. But its fundamental purpose is to preserve and make available for research, information of enduring value.

Archives traditionally refers to the agency or department responsible for preserving the records of its parent organization. The Public Record Office, for example, is the department which preserves the records of the central government of the UK, and the National Archives is the federal agency for preserving the records of the government of the US. In addition there may be archives for local public administrations, and some corporations and smaller companies have established their own business archives. The definition has evolved over time to include organizations such as documentation centres, universities and museums that collect the records and papers of others. Archives has also come to mean the collection itself.

Since the advent of formal records management, the administration of archives has generally been looked upon as a separate profession. Being the last phase of the information cycle, however, archives administration is really part of the overall records management function, albeit a specialized element. An archivist may not necessarily be a records manager or even a historian. The records manager, whose primary concern is with the controlled creation, maintenance and final disposition of records, may not have the training for pure archival work, although in some organizations he/she may have the responsibility. The archivist receives a large body of material into a collection and must identify and locate distinct items while not losing sight of generic relationships. The records manager similarly receives a large body of material but may not be concerned with describing the content of the records for future research, however historical they may be.

Public archives Official records created by federal, state, central or local governments fall into two categories:
- Records filed with or by a government agency as proof of private ownership of a commodity or privilege, or which establish citizenship or other rights (deeds, wills, licences, birth records, naturalization papers, etc.).
- Records of the administration of governmental functions (policies, methods, results, etc., affecting society).

A public archives is the repository of those records whose enduring value may be primarily legal, but which may become historical over time. Legislation frequently designates the officer and agency responsible for public records, as well as which records have permanent archival value. The integrity of these records must be protected in such a manner that their value to the individual and to the government will not be impaired.

Historical manuscript repositories Some organizations, particularly universities, maintain archives comprising records other than their own and not necessarily related to their own functions and activities. Collections in manuscript repositories are usually acquired by gift or purchase under a written collections policy. Donors of papers sometimes impose restrictions upon the use of all or parts of their gift.

Business archives Non-governmental records preserve the history of corporations, companies, and similar enterprises, bodies which create and own their records. There is usually no legislation to govern preservation and availability for research — such functions being mainly a matter of company policy.

Preserving the corporate memory

Managers generally are not as aware as they should be of the importance of company archives. Historical material is frequently viewed as a handy resource for celebrating a significant anniversary and for little else. The contents of the past are given more emphasis than the historical process of which the present is part. But corporate history should be a way of thinking about the company, a way of understanding why the present is what it is and what might be possible for the future.

Managers must recognize the potentially high value-added uses of the organization's history and need to consider how to preserve high-quality data for future use. Organizations have aptly mastered quantitative recording in the finance and accounting area, but are lagging in their understanding of the importance of maintaining good records on the processes of management and decision making. Because the electronic age has made the task of preserving the corporate memory more difficult, it is imperative that methods of recording and preserving important facts be developed.

The first consideration in establishing the business archives is the nature and purpose of the archival function. Before any action is taken, these questions must be resolved.

- What is the state of the corporate memory?
- What does the organization expect from the archives?
- What departments are or will be using the historical material most frequently?
- What records management policies pertain to the archives?
- Will it be part of the records management programme or, if not, how will the functions be integrated?

- Will only the organization's records be collected, or will materials documenting the role of the organization in the community be preserved as well?
- Will the archives collect the personal papers of the organization's officials?

The placement of the business archives in the organizational structure is critical. The directive authorizing its establishment should provide the archivist with the right to seek out, collect, and preserve inactive office files of enduring value.

The business archives should be part of the records management function with the archivist reporting directly to the records manager. Because of the complexity and specialized nature of archival organization and methodology and the difficulty of dealing with the past, it is important that a qualified professional be responsible for the business archives. Organizations too small to cost-justify an archivist should seek professional archival advice.

Programmes that use corporate history

An organization can develop programmes that use a well-researched history. Some useful questions managers can ask are:

- How does the organization communicate its history to new employees? What is the historical content of training programmes or on-going management seminars?
- Would it be useful for the organization to have ongoing public relations activities based on its history? Should it create a museum or open a library? Should it create ties to universities, museums, historical societies, or other community agencies that might have an interest in its history?
- When major policy changes are debated at the senior level, does the history of existing policy inform that debate? Should histories of policies be prepared for ready access?
- Should histories of organization strategies and other decisions be developed to assess the past performance of the organization in qualitative as well as quantitative terms?
- Should histories of the organization's experience with social and government pressures be prepared to aid responses to public policy debates?

General principles and techniques

Although archives are records, there are methodologies for managing them which differ from records management activities. Techniques relating to active files management, to the design and control of forms, and to the development of a directives or reporting system are very dissimilar from archival techniques. Even when they relate to activities that parallel those of archives, records management techniques have a different emphasis. For example, the activity of classifying and filing current records differs from the arrangement of archival material. Finding aids produced for current records are not the same as those developed for the archives collection.

Generally, archivists must give careful and analytical attention to records while arranging, describing and servicing them. They may be concerned with the management of current records, especially in a small archival programme, just as they may be concerned with the management of books and museum objects. But if they are engaged in both kinds, the techniques of one would not necessarily apply to the other.

ARRANGEMENT

There are two main objectives in the arrangement of records selected for permanent preservation:

1   To preserve their evidential/informational value.
2   To make them accessible for use.

Two basic principles of archival arrangement have been used:

1   *By provenance*   This means that the records are maintained in the order in which they were transferred to the archives, which is not necessarily the order in which they were created. With frequent changes in organizations, the principle has come to mean the order of the institution that transferred the records rather than that which created them. When large organizations are created by merger, for example, they often take over the records from smaller organizations. In addition records within an organization are often rearranged after they have served their current uses.

2   *Original order*   With this principle, records are maintained in the order in which they were kept when in current use in file reference order, case number sequence, committee paper number order, etc. When arranging by provenance more than one series may be grouped together, but when preserving by original order, records series are kept apart.

Original order may present difficulties where a series of records is the subject of a succession of separate but overlapping transfers. In such cases it is generally preferable to keep the records of each transfer in their own proper sequence and to draw the user's attention to the overlap by means of an introductory note or a contents list (see Listing, p. 220).

In general, records will have been created to serve some specific purpose in an organization and there is little point in rearranging them when they are selected for permanent preservation. The original order should, as far as possible, be maintained.

Arranging records in this way seems to run counter to the ways researchers and others would use the information, that is by subject. However, it serves to protect the evidential value of the records, in the context within which they were created. Since records are usually produced to accomplish some purpose rather than to elucidate some subject, their rearrangement by subject or some other classification would obscure or lose the evidence of the activities of their source.

The order in which records are kept during their current life reveals much about the office of origin. Original order sometimes indicates a sequence of actions, shows administrative processes, reveals organizational relationships, and generally reflects how things are done in that particular office. Strict adherence to this principle means that the archivist should preserve the records in the condition they were maintained during active use, whether that condition was orderly or disorderly. In practice, the records must be accessible and the archivist should have no qualms about rearranging them so that they are intelligible and serviceable.

CLASSIFICATION

It is essential that each item (volume, file, or other assembly of documents which can be produced to the researcher separately) in an archives bears a unique reference so that it can be called up for reference or research. It is impossible to use the original references of the files/volume for the archival classification because:

•   there will be gaps in the sequence, since an appraisal and selection will have been carried out;
•   there is a good chance that individual departments or sections of ministries, companies, etc. will have used similar or identical references (the reference 'GEN', for example, is very common).

Archives should be designated classes, which might be of three kinds:

1   Containing records of the organization which created them.

2 Containing records of the organization which transferred them to the archives.
3 Containing records from one original series, whether that was created by one organization and transferred by another or a combination of both.

Each class must be given a short descriptive title, which should be based as far as possible on an existing series title given to the records by the creating organization. Class titles may be amended at a later date to take account of changing circumstances.

Archival references are then allocated to classes and to pieces/units within classes so that each item has its unique reference. This allocation may be carried out in one of three ways:

1 Group/Class
2 Type/Class
3 Class only.

Group/Class

Classes may be grouped into the organizations that created or transferred them, and each of those organizations allocated a code number or letters. If this code comprises a letter, or letters, it may be an abbreviation of the organization's title or it may be completely artificial. For example:

- BT, for records created by, or transferred from the Board of Trade; FO, similarly for the Foreign Office.
- AB, for records created by, or transferred from the UK Atomic Energy Authority; DR, similarly for the Civil Aviation Authority.

If classes are to contain specific records series, regardless of creating/transferring organization, then an artificial coding would be necessary. For example:

- GB, might be allocated to a records series of the National Air Traffic Services, which might have been created by the Ministry of Civil Aviation but transferred by the successor body, the Civil Aviation Authority.

The structures of modern government adminstration and private companies are complex and changing. This latter type of classification might be preferred to avoid records from one series being assigned to different classes. It is common for a series to continue through a change in the structure of an organization and also for a new organization to inherit records from its predecessor prior to their appraisal, selection and transfer to the archives.

Within the groups, particular series of records, which should equate with the original registry arrangement, are allocated class numbers. For example:

BT 22 Railway Department: Correspondence and Papers
BT 31 Files of Dissolved Companies

Within each class, each file, volume, folder etc. is allocated a piece number. For example:

BT 22/4
BT 31/102

In this way the unique reference is built up. No two pieces in an archives will have the same archival reference number.

Type/Class

Classes of records may be grouped very broadly by type, rather than by creating or transferring organization. For example:

F may be allocated to federal records
S to state records
LG to local government records.

No other grouping would be used and a running number is allocated to each class of records as and when it is transferred to the archives. For example:

S 456   Central State: General Correspondence
S 1012   Central State: Financial Returns
S 1462   Northern State: General Correspondence

Within each class, piece numbers are allocated in the same way as in the group/class method.

Class only

The group concept may be abandoned altogether and running class numbers allocated to each series as and when it is transferred, regardless of its origin. For example:

56   Ministry of Finance: Annual Appropriation Accounts
57   Department of Transport: Issue of Driving Licences: Policy
58   Ministry of Public Service: Personal Files
59   Ministry of Finance: Auditing Policy

In this system a good index of classes would be required to guide the researcher to the records being sought.

Variations

1   Each of these three main systems might include variations. For example, sub-classes might be used to give a more deliberate breakdown of the file series:

  • Group:
    A   Agriculture department
    C   Customs department
    PRI   Prison department
  • Class:
    A/1   In letters
    A/2   Out letters
  • Sub-class:
    A/2/1   Out letters: General
    A/2/2   Out letters: Cotton Growers Association
    A/2/3   Out letters: Governor's Office
  • Piece numbers:
    A/2/1/1
    A/2/1/2
    A/2/1/3, etc.

2   Original file references might be used as the piece number, for example:
    S 456/64/10
    S 456/68/4
    S 456/GEN/21/1

Whatever system of archival classification is used, the archives must be consistent. Changes in systems only serve to confuse the users.

LISTING

When records are transferred to the archives, a list of the contents of the class must be completed by the transferring organization. This list will enable the archives, the researcher and the transferring organization to know what the class contains and to identify readily any individual record required for reference.

The list should reflect the arrangement that has been agreed upon by the archives and transferring staffs (see above). The choice of type of list for any particular class should be the outcome of evaluation of the specific nature of the records and of the uses to which they are likely to be put. There are a number of different types of lists:

- *Numerical* This would be the normal arrangement for registered files, numbered reports, etc. Each transfer of files are listed in file reference number order and this original reference is also shown in the list itself.
- *Chronological* This arrangement is applied especially to unregistered papers, chronologically-arranged volumes, periodical reports, etc.
- *Alphabetical* Personnel files and other case papers (see Chapter 12) are best filed alphabetically. Users will generally be looking for the names of particular persons, places, etc. and the original file reference order would therefore be unhelpful.
- *Hierarchical* This arrangement is particularly suitable for classes of records of an organization whose constituent parts have a definite hierarchical arrangement, such as committees and their sub-committees, military formations and units, etc.
- *Record type* This arrangement will only be used rarely since in most cases different types of records require separate classes. However, some collections, such as the records of a commission of inquiry, small research institution, etc., may be better arranged together in one class. Within this class the primary arrangement might be: minutes of meetings, papers considered at meetings, reports, correspondence, etc.

Descriptions

Files have a tendency to outgrow their original titles or contain abbreviations and technical phrases which may not be understood by the user. The list description, however, should not depart too far from the original title and should not be extended beyond a general statement of the subject of a file, volume, etc. The description should reflect as accurately as possible the contents of the piece without being too long or unwieldy.

The extent of the dates of each piece will depend upon the range of the records themselves, but generally it will be sufficient to give years only and not year/month or year/month/day.

The dates must be the actual dates when the documents were compiled, the date of the earliest paper in the piece and the date of the latest paper. If a piece consists of, or includes copies of or extracts from, documents of earlier dates, such dates should (if cited) be included in the description of the piece rather than the date.

Introductory notes

Each class list should be prefaced by a brief introductory note, which will complement the list itself and furnish the user with essential information not given in the body of the list. The introductory note should contain the following information, where appropriate:

- *Name, origin and history of the creating body* When a creating body is a ministry or a company it is usually sufficient just to name it, but for small departments, commissions, boards of inquiry, divisions or sections of organizations, etc., it will be necessary to give brief details of their origin, history and functions. For private collections an outline of the career of the person concerned should be given.
- *Legislative background to the records* This will be necessary if the records were kept or created as a result of a particular statute or other piece of legislation.
- *Nature and form of the records* This should be included where it is not obvious from

the title of the class, for example correspondence with local authorities, minutes of meetings, etc.

- *Series*   Where several series of files, reports, etc. are included in the class, it may be necessary to draw attention to and explain these.
- *Geographical scope*   It may sometimes be relevant to indicate whether the records relate to the whole of the country or to some part of it or to give some other indication of the geographical area covered by the records.
- *Preservation*   Any special circumstances affecting the preservation of the records, such as dispersal, accidental damage, or custody by a body which did not create them, are worth noting.
- *Selection*   If selection has been made in some special way, this should be stated. For example: specimens, sample, representative selection, collection of notable cases, etc.
- *Other means of reference*   Where there are registers, indexes, or other finding aids produced by the creating organization, whether within the class or elsewhere, mention should be made of them.
- *Publications*   If the class has been used as a source for official publications, this should be mentioned. Attention might also be drawn to any other publications which would assist in understanding the records.
- *Related records*   Where related records exist in other classes, they should be mentioned and the relationship explained.
- *Access*   A statement should be made of the period of access given to the records, especially if this differs from any general access rule.

Lists and introductory notes are best compiled by the organization that is transferring the records, since they will have a more detailed knowledge of their content, make-up, etc., but rules and guidelines for standard listing format should be formulated by the archives. The value of a standard form of list is great and conformity to the standard does not make the task of listing any more difficult.

ACCESSIONING

When the list has been compiled and agreed, and when the records have been numbered, packed in suitable archival boxes and labelled, formal arrangements for their physical transfer to the archives must be made.

A simple transfer/accession form may be used, part of which is completed by the transferring organization, while the rest is completed by the archives — see Figure 14.1.

The archives should also keep a record of accessions; this may be easily achieved by using a register showing date of transfer, transferring organization, class and pieces references, description of class, agreed access arrangements, and location of the records in the archives repository. Other supplementary information may be kept, such as an alphabetical list of groups and numerical list of classes within groups, showing the number of pieces within each class and the repository location.

FINDING AIDS

Finding aids is the key to making the holdings in an archival collection accessible for use. A descriptive programme to prepare appropriate finding aids should be designed with the following objectives.

- To provide information on all records in a repository. This can be in the form of summary finding aids such as guides and catalogues which concisely describe all groups and collections, or inventories describing records series within large or significant collections.

Departmental reference:	Archives file reference:		
Proposal for the transfer of a class of records *selected for permanent preservation* PART I – to be completed by the transferring department			
Department proposing the transfer			
Description of class (e.g. name of division, or branch formerly responsible; title of file series, etc.)			
Physical type of the documents (e.g. files, volumes, maps rolled or flat, etc.) If a mixed class, give number of each type			
Dates covered			
Number of pieces		Foot run occupied:	Is class accruing?
Dimensions of boxes, volumes, or bundles (as a guide to arrangement of shelving)			
Physical condition			
Indexes, registers or other means of reference available			
Access: does the 30-year rule apply? If not, what variation is proposed?			
May access be given to pages of the list containing both closed and open items?			
Any further remarks (e.g. as to origin of documents if not created by the department; whether other series of documents have been incorporated in the class; purpose or subject-matter of documents if not self-evident from title):			
Signature and date:			

Figure 14.1   Transfer/accession form

PART II: to be completed y the Archives			
Approval or acceptance of transfer		By RAD	By Repository
To be entered by Records Administration Division			
New Class/ Addition	nbatch abatch		
Group and class code	00		
First piece number	–		
Last piece number	02		
First date	03		
Last date	04		
Physical nature	05		
Class title	06		
Report on listing	–		
Report on packing and labelling	–		
Labels affixed according to agreed access	–		
Any further comments or remarks	–		
To be entered by Repository			
Documents received	–		
Accumulated foot run	09		
Location	10	Site Room First press Last press First piece no. – – – – – – – –	
Transfer register	–		
Fields 02 and 05 checked	–		
To be entered by Administrating Officer, Modern Records Section			
Form AA 6/1 completed	–		

Figure 14.1 (cont.)

- To provide special information that may be needed about the records. Since different groups of records have different values, and, consequently, different uses, different types of finding aids are needed by different types of researchers. The descriptive programme should be adapted to accommodate the special uses to which particular records series may be put.
- To provide specific information about particular records. While the second objective focuses on selecting the type of finding aid to be prepared, this emphasizes the degree of detail in the finding aid. The more intensive the description, the more likely it is that the quality of reference service is improved.
- To produce finding aids in a form that best facilitates use of the records and best reveals their significance and content. The card catalogue is particularly flexible in that subject entries as well as record titles or series can be included. An online data base of descriptive information can be searched and sorted in a variety of ways for the researcher.
- To make the finding aids readily accessible to the user. Depending on who may have access to the collection, these aids may be solely in-house reference service material, such as would be most appropriate in a business archives, or they may be published for external use, such as might be done by a university archives, or they may be a combination of both.

'Finding aid' is a term used generically to cover all types of archival descriptive documents. It may be comprehensive or limited in its coverage, general or detailed in its descriptive data, and may pertain to holdings of any size. The previously described class list is the primary finding aid used in the UK. A finding aid may also be a catalogue, guide, inventory, calendar, list, index, or similar document; it may be in paper, micro, or magnetic form.

The types of finding aids most suitable for the archives depend on how the archives will be put to use and the judgement of the archivist. For years a catalogue, usually in card form, has been a basic finding aid in archives. Cataloguing basically treats both single documents and extensive collections in such a way as a librarian would treat a single book or series of books. An adjunct to the catalogue is the index which allows the material to be described in great depth. Online indexing provides the most flexibility in meeting current and future needs.

Another useful tool is the accessions log. Because it records the type, amount and date of arrival of new materials to the archives, it constitutes the first record of new acquisitions and therefore is a fundamental means of control. Should the processing of a record collection and preparation of appropriate finding aids be delayed, the accessions log can be a preliminary descriptive tool.

An inventory of records series within an archival collection is the principle finding aid that reflects arrangement and, as such, is the most thorough single description of a collection since it combines the arrangement information with that of the content. Common elements in an inventory include:

1 Provenance, or the source of the records.
2 Biographical sketch of the major persons mentioned in the records or historical overview of the office or unit whose records are being described.
3 The scope and general content of the records.
4 A description of the files within the series, including their order, inclusive dates, and volume.
5 A container listing, including physical location.
6 A guide to related materials on the topic or unit.
7 Subject index to the content of the records if justified.

Some archives create a brief checklist or guide to their holdings in addition to the card catalogue. A calendar may be produced which provides a chronological list of record items with a brief summary of the contents of each.

Although machine-readable records are not usually arranged in the traditional manner of paper- or film-based collections, finding aids can be developed in the form of code books or indexes. These should provide a good general sense of the structure of a collection and as much specific information as possible. Essentially, this uses the same principles governing the preparation of finding aids for paper records.

ACCESS AND SECURITY

Archives have a dual responsibility: preservation and use. Preservation of records has little value in and of itself; the primary value is in their use. Access to the records by researchers and other users should be explicitly stated as policy.

The degree of access depends upon the type of repository. Public archives usually have generous access policies, which are usually mandated by statute, welcoming the general public as well as the serious researcher. College and university archives may also open their collections to those outside the institution. Private repositories vary in their access policies, often limiting access to a specific constituency.

The rationale for imposing restrictions on the use of a collection is based on privacy considerations. Such restrictions may be mandated by law or regulation as in certain public records or classes of information. Donors may impose restrictions to protect their own or others' privacy and interests. A repository may need to restrict access to protect itself from privacy suits should the information derived from confidential data be misused.

The two types of business archives present two possible access policies. A business archives housed within the company may feel under no obligation to open its archival information to those outside the company or office that deposited the material. However, if it is maintained as part of a research collection of an academic or historical archives, access is probably not as restrictive.

Limited access is also important from a security standpoint. Archives staff should serve the users rather than allowing them to serve themselves. The stack areas should always be locked to prevent unauthorized access. More often than not, the theft of archival materials takes place during normal working hours. The level of access and value of the collection determines the extent to which users must be registered and properly identified before gaining access to the material. At the very least, users of any archives should sign a visitor's log.

Even though break-ins do not commonly occur at archival repositories, they can happen. The archivist is responsible for the security of the archives after closing as well as during normal working hours. Security devices, such as locking systems, security alarms, and surveillance equipment, should be installed. (See also Chapter 13.)

STORAGE REQUIREMENTS AND PRESERVATION TECHNIQUES

Archival materials are best stored in acid-free (also referred to as 'alkaline buffered') containers to minimize deterioration of the records inside and on steel shelving with baked enamel finishing to minimize fire hazard. Boxes come in several sizes and shapes for different types of material. It is particularly important that they be acid-free because acidity causes destruction of the records. The acceptable range for archival storage containers and folders is a pH of 7.0 to 8.5 (neutral to basic). Acid-free containers are more expensive than standard records centre boxes. Acid-free folders are also available.

Since an archives preserves records permanently, it is important to create a proper environment for long-term storage. The temperature and humidity controls recommended for vital records (see Chapter 10) apply to archives as well. High humidity promotes mould growth and accelerates acid deterioration of paper; low humidity will cause paper to desiccate. Microfilm, ideally, should first be processed by archival standards to ensure a longer life expectancy for the image. All records in an archives, whether paper, film, magnetic media, or other, require a constant temperature and humidity, protective casing, and a clean environment, and should be protected against fire, water, and other hazards.

Preservation techniques are more specific than providing the proper equipment and environment, although this is the most important preservation measure. All loose materials should be stored in protective containers where dust contamination is kept to a minimum. Whenever possible, paper records should be stored lying flat to reduce strain on the paper edge. If paper must be stored on edge, the containers should be packed firmly to prevent bending. The best storage for maps and posters are map cases in which they lie flat. Magnetic tape should be stored on end in boxes in tape cabinets or on hanging tape racks.

Photographs may be stored the same way as paper records, or mounted. The mounting paper and process should be acceptable for long-term storage. Negatives should be kept separate from the photographs for back-up reasons and should be stored in darkness in transparent jackets (sleeves) of cellulose acetate or polyethylene.

Only safety film should be allowed in the archives. Nitrate-based film is highly flammable, self-combustible, and deteriorates rapidly. While it has not been used for years, some older films may become part of the archives. These films should be examined to determine if they are on nitrate base. If so, they should be removed from the archives and recopied on to safety film as quickly as possible.

Paper

Many materials received into the archives require preparation and cleaning. Letters should be removed from envelopes and unfolded, since folding breaks down the paper and results in deterioration. Loose surface dirt should be gently removed. Paper clips, rubber bands, and staples should be removed; rust-proof paper clips may be substituted. Pressure-sensitive tape should never be used to repair torn documents. Tape that is already on the records can be removed through a special process.

Paper deterioration is a serious problem for the archivist. Modern records, which are most prevalent in business archives, deteriorate quickly because of their acidic nature. Because acid can migrate from one piece of paper to another, even a small amount can contaminate a collection. Thus the importance of acid-free folders and containers and of proper environmental conditions.

Ultraviolet radiation from natural sunlight and fluorescent light contributes to paper deterioration. It causes a bleaching action that can fade certain inks and coloured paper, and it reacts with the wood fibres to turn paper yellow or brownish. This photo-oxidation process is further exacerbated by high temperatures and unfiltered air. It can be minimized by keeping paper records out of direct sunlight for any period of time, filtering fluorescent lighting with protective screens, maintaining light levels in record storage areas at 50 lux or lower and turning off lights when the areas are not being used, and using incandescent lighting, which emits no harmful light radiation, wherever possible.

Regardless of the storage conditions and containers, newspaper clippings deteriorate rapidly because of the especially high acid content of the wood from which newsprint is made. Clippings should be reproduced, preferably on acid-free paper, microfilm, or other enduring medium, and the copy substituted for the original.

If it is necessary to add identifying information to photographs or paper records, the archivist should use pencil to make the notations lightly and place a heavy glass under the document to avoid making impressions on the paper.

Records which are in very poor condition may be conserved either through encapsulation or lamination. Encapsulation involves sandwiching a document between sheets of polyester film without plasticizer and sealing the edges with 3M/415 double-faced, quarter-inch tape. This can be done in-house by the archivist. It increases the durability of the document without causing inherent changes to the paper itself, but it will not increase its permanence unless the acid content of the paper is first neutralized. Most importantly, it is completely reversible by carefully snipping the film edges to release the document.

Lamination, on the other hand, is generally an irreversible process requiring the services of a conservation specialist. Papers must be washed, deacidified, and dried before being laminated. The adhesive that binds the film to the document is extremely harmful to the record and eventually may leach through both the document and the plastic, causing the document to become almost transparent and the plastic to stick to any adjacent records. Commercially available plastic film laminating material should never be used.

Conservation laboratories are available to handle any difficult conservation measure such as tape removal, deacidification, fumigation, or lamination.

Microfilm

Microfilming documents is an acceptable preservation technique since silver halide film has a long life-expectancy. It also substantially reduces space requirements. Microfilm should be produced in accordance with American National Standards Institute (ANSI) 'Specifications for Photographic Film for Archival Records, Silver-Gelatin Type, on Cellulose Ester Base' (PH1.28), 'Specifications for Photographic Film for Archival Records, Silver-Gelatin Type, on Polyester Base' (PH1.41), and stored according to 'Practice for Storage of Processed Safety Photographic Film' (PH1.43). In non-US archives, the corresponding International Standards Organization (ISO) standards should be followed: 'Photography-Processed Photographic Film for Archival Records — Silver Gelatin Type on Cellulose Ester Base — Specifications' (ISO 4331) and 'Photography-Processed Photographic Film for Archival Records — Silver Gelatin Type on Poly (ethylene terephtholate) Base — Specifications' (ISO 4332).

By adhering to these standards and to those governing the formats and reduction ratios of microfilm and microfiche, information that is now readable on standard micro-image equipment will be so many years hence.

To date there are no standards covering the archival usage of diazo, vesicular, dry process silver, or updatable microfilms. Diazo film, which is ammonia processed, will fade upon exposure to light. There can also be image loss after prolonged storage in the dark. Under correct storage conditions, however, diazo is likely to last for 100 years or more, making it suitable for long term, although not archival, storage. Tests conducted on the stability of processed vesicular film indicate that it is suitable for medium to long-term storage. Thus diazo and vesicular film serve a useful function providing a cheap medium for duplicating original microfilm and will probably last for many years, but they should not be used for the archival storage of valuable original documents.

Dry process silver film is still a relatively unproven medium, primarily used in computer-output-microfilm (COM) recorders. It is suited to medium- to long-term storage. If archival data is transferred to COM using this process, it should be duplicated on to silver halide film. An alternative is to keep a wet process COM recorder on hand to output archival data directly to silver halide film.

Updatable microfilm, as with dry process film is designed primarily to widen the appeal of microfilm rather than to serve as an archival medium, but is suitable at least for medium-term storage.

Colour film, on the other hand, is specifically excluded from standards for archival microfilm and cannot be regarded as an archival medium. Colour film dyes are subject to change over time, and colour images will fade upon excessive exposure to light.

Magnetic media

Magnetic media is developed primarily as backup storage for computer data and not for archival preservation. Fixed and floppy magnetic discs provide adequate intermediate storage. Both are susceptible to physical damage from 'head crashes' or improper handling. They are hardware dependent, needing expensive disc drives to read and record data. They are also designed to be easily amended, erased, and updated, which can result in the alteration of valuable documents.

Magnetic tape is designed primarily for the short- to medium-term storage of the kind of data that regularly needs to be processed on a computer; for example, financial data, statistics, etc. International standards have been written to cover the general dimensional requirements (ISO 1859) and the physical properties and test methods of unrecorded tapes (ISO 2690), but there are no standards regarding the production, recording, and storage of archival magnetic tape.

The two major drawbacks to retaining archival information on magnetic tapes are obsolescence and quality. The storage and transportation of unrecorded tapes prior to arrival at the computer centre as well as of recorded tapes during usage can adversely affect the quality of the tape and therefore render the information unreadable. Obsolescence affects the ability to access the data. Packing density, for instance, has changed over the years from very low (100 bits per square inch (bpi)) to very high (6250 bpi). This and other software and hardware dependencies can obsolete that part of the collection within a few years.

The only way to guarantee the preservation of machine-readable records is to output them on to a more stable medium such as silver halide (wet processed) computer output microfiche. This is undeniably expensive for large amounts of information and may be utterly impractical. Until such time as standards are in place to ensure that magnetic tapes meet archival requirements, the archivist should use duplicate tapes for reference rather than the original (as with microfilm), refresh (recopy) the tapes at regular intervals to ensure that they remain in good condition, and maintain them under proper environmental conditions (maximum 65 to 70°F and 40 per cent relative humidity).

Optical disc

Optical data discs offer the high storage capacity and rapid retrieval of magnetic media without the danger of erasing valuable information. The key to their archival life is the stability of the material from which the discs are made. Possibly by the early 1990s optical discs will be sufficiently well established for archival tests to be carried out, standards laid down, and for meaningful predictions to be made about their storage potential.

If optical discs were ever to be proven archival, they would provide a very high storage capacity alternative to COM since computer data can be directly recorded on to them. As with magnetic tape, however, this would be a rather expensive alternative because of the hardware and software that is required to retrieve and read the information. To rival microfilm as an archival document storage medium, an optical disc system would probably need removable discs or disc packs so that the archivist would only need to purchase one recorder/player unit and could store hundreds of discs offline, as with magnetic tape.

Part VI
The Future

INTRODUCTION

Records managers and their staff all need to develop particular skills to meet the challenge of records management. In practice these are acquired by experience as well as by formal training. Chapter 15 examines the characteristics required of records management personnel and the subjects in which training should be pursued. The most important of these is considered to be an awareness of the opportunities and future trends of the profession.

15 Training and Changing

While other functions in an organization will have been clearly defined and described, records management often does not have that luxury. Records managers must create or discover their functions and the procedures to follow, then educate the rest of the organization about them, and convince people that they are necessary. A procedures manual rarely will have a section on records management; the records manager will have to write it, and then have it included in the manual. To work alone like this in creating records management policies and procedures requires a certain blind confidence, stamina, and some independence. It is also necessary to have the patience to explain, over and over again, the purpose and importance of records management.

The job of a records manager can be said to cover three roles. Initially, he/she is a problem solver, then a trouble-shooter, then a creative designer of new approaches to, and uses of, information and records.

In the first stages of records management, problems have to be discovered and analysed. The solutions proposed will have to be carefully planned and implemented. Where new procedures are implemented, it will take time for them to become so much a part of the routine that the original problems do not recur. The stage of discovery and analysis leads naturally to implementation.

Once the proposals are implemented, and there is a satisfactory records management programme in place, the second stage can begin. This can be either stagnation or innovation. After months of exhausting effort, explanations, and training, records managers will justifiably want to sit back and watch their programmes operate efficiently, and take pride in all of their accomplishments. However, if they do so, people will begin to forget about them and their programmes, and fail to see the purpose of their presence. This is the stage at which people, many of them professional records managers, have asked, 'What more is there for the records manager to do? Once the new procedures are accepted and followed, isn't the records manager superfluous? Couldn't the programmes be supervised by someone at a clerical level?' Some records managers deal with their being thus becalmed by having well publicized, yearly campaigns to clear out offices of old records. This raises the records management profile, and temporarily increases record centre usage statistics. It is hardly enough to justify a full-time employee with a manager's salary and responsibility.

Records managers must assume two new roles, that of the trouble shooter and that of the creative designer. In the former, they are constantly looking for new problems with records and information. This means that they have to visit offices, talk with people, look at

233

records and equipment, and always offer assistance. Sitting in an office and sending out reminding letters will only make the records manager an anonymous irritant. In order to be aware of new developments or changes in procedures or structures, all of which affect records and information, the records manager must go out and see what people in the organization are doing.

The role of the creative designer develops out of the knowledge gained from the original survey, and subsequently consolidated and built upon. Once all of the information that is created, held, and needed by the organization is known to records managers, they can then begin to see where combinations or separations would be a better use of the information. They also can begin to see completely new uses of the information. Instead of simply solving a problem or fulfilling a need, they can propose new ways to exploit a resource. Whether it be as basic as setting up a paper recycling plant for those mountains of shredded documents, or as complex as turning disparate groups of information into a single data base, there is much that a creative records manager can and should be doing long after the programme is 'established'.

CHARACTERISTICS OF A RECORDS MANAGER

Successful records managers will be those who can work independently, often in isolation, to achieve results. They must be self-motivated and must constantly seek out and work with all users of information within the organization. Although fairly well established in the United States and Canada, records management is in some respects still in its infancy in the UK and most other countries, and those who are establishing it within their organizations must be innovative. Records managers and the staff they select should have the following characteristics:

- The ability to consider new ideas, new possibilities, new ways of doing things. Never content with 'just muddling through', the innovative records manager is always looking for better ways to do things, at less expense, and with greater efficiency.
- The determination to achieve results. Refusing to be crippled by tradition or bureaucracy, they will try every avenue until they are successful. They will be able to imagine alternative possibilities, finding one that will work. They will never be stalled or aimlessly waiting for encouragement.
- The freedom from concerns about status. They may have to get their hands dirty moving boxes in a records centre. They may be improperly placed in the organization structure. These factors should not matter to the innovative records manager, who cares more about creating and establishing an important programme than about status.

Innovative records managers will be introducing change into their organization and, when they start hiring, need to surround themselves with a team of innovators. They must always be working not only toward efficiency, but toward improvement. The management analyst who can only streamline a form, instead of recognizing that it can be eliminated if certain simpler procedures are introduced, will continually cling to tradition and to what is familiar. This kind of conservatism will ensure the kind of records management department that does nothing to solve problems, and merely adds to the bureaucratic snags. A strong team of creative individuals can, on the other hand, transform an organization's information structure.

Selecting and training the team

Training in records management has traditionally been very limited. At the professional level within the UK there are a few archives diploma or MA programmes which offer one or two records management classes. Within the US there are a few degree programmes for the discipline, but not within the schools of 'management'. In continuing training programmes there are some one- or two-day seminars offered by the professional associations. Thus, most of those working as records managers have been trained for some other profession, and it is this situation that records managers must face when they hire their staff.

Equally important to consider is the kind of experience in information work applicants will have had. The more exposure to management techniques and analysis, the better qualified they will be to assist in the management, as opposed to the mere maintenance, of records and information. Lastly, even the records clerk or analyst must have some initiative and creativity if the team is to effect worthwhile changes. The techniques of training and staff development have been covered thoroughly in numerous publications and will not be repeated here. The areas in which training should be pursued are as follows:

1   The director of information

- Business administration
- Data processing
- Records management
- Archives
- Library services
- Information law

2   The records manager

- Management and management analysis
- Information studies (either via library or archives training)
- Micrographics
- Marketing
- The essentials of data processing.

3   The records management analyst

- Management analysis
- Forms and reports management
- Indexing and classification
- Stock control or warehouse management

4   File or registry supervisor

- Basic records management programme procedures
- Personnel supervision
- Supplies management

5   The records clerk

- Basic clerical skills
- Indexing and classification
- Registry/filing procedures, including rules for alphabetical filing
- Correspondence analysis

Because of the lack of a standard curriculum in which all of these subjects can be learned, staff will have to be sent to courses sponsored by a variety of schools and organizations. This can, however, be an advantage, for it allows the records manager to carefully select the training to be received, and to structure it according to each individual's, and also the organizations, needs.

What next

For established records managers to know in what subjects to train themselves, they need to know how the profession will grow and change, where they should expect and where they should create opportunities.

As we said at the beginning, concepts of information and consequently the information professions are in a state of flux. Information technology is moving and changing so rapidly that it is difficult to determine anything but the fact of constant change. This change goes deeper than the technology, the storage media, and the processes. The change is beginning to appear in the way we think about and use information.

Electronic technology has changed not only the office environment and jobs, it has changed the way information users and creators think. As more people become first familiar, then creative, with computers, they cease to think of information as synonymous with the medium on which it is stored. Books are no longer knowledge; a long, single, documentary film is no longer the factual truth; 'the file on Jones' no longer has any clear meaning at all. Information is obviously contained in all of these, but less rigidly, not absolutely, as it once seemed to be. Information is fluid. In offices, information can be divided, reassembled, transferred wholly or partly across files, data bases, national borders. Realizing this, we begin to see all information, that in books, audio or video cassettes, archived files, as equally fluid, and we expect to have it all, consolidated and indexed, available to us.

Once the foundations of a records management programme are in place, the initial streamlining and cost savings achieved, the real benefits can begin. Once the most awkward and amorphous area of information — records — is brought under control, it can be amalgamated with the other areas of the library, information technology, and communications, to provide a full information service to the organization. It is no longer practical to divide information according to its storage medium, formal, or traditional care. It must all be brought together, for only then can the information which flows through computers, telephones, periodicals, files, the mail room, the registry, be managed as a single resource.

The person who quite logically could fill the role of director of information services is the records manager. To prepare for this role, he/she will have to keep abreast of developments in all of the information professions as well as have a thorough grounding in the management and goals of the business or agency. However, if he/she chooses to do nothing more than maintain the basic records management programmes, the contented records manager will not be left alone to stagnate but will see the department swept up by the inevitable consolidation of information services, headed by someone else.

While only 1 per cent of British companies have hired someone to manage all of their information services, nearly 40 per cent of American companies have done so. In the British government, the role seems to be taken up only by certain dynamic national archivists. Within the US government, dynamic data processing managers are taking the information management lead.

It is this dynamism that is most valuable in records managers and in directors of information services. With that, one can move mountains (of records?) and be at the front of the information professions.

Appendices

Appendix A: Steps to the Selection and Contracting of services/products/consultants

The following steps are applicable to any contracted service, for example commercial storage; a microfilm bureau; the purchase, installation, and maintenance of any equipment; consulting services, data processing bureaux, etc.

1 *Education* Become thoroughly familiar with the product or type of service, with what it can and cannot be expected to accomplish.

- read books and articles on the subject
- purchase copies of the appropriate standards and codes
- attend seminars and lectures on the subject
- talk to any local experts on the subject, and to experienced users of such products or services.
- find the organization of professionals in that subject and ask if they have published advice for potential clients.

2 *Preparation of a brief* The brief should clearly outline what product or service is desired. It is as much for the client as for the vendor, for it will force the clarification of the whole purchasing situation long before any trouble can begin.

(a) Write a short but complete description of the service/product needed, including details of;

- the problem it is to solve (for example, boxes to be stored per year, tapes per day to be exchanged, office to be computerized, people to be trained, etc.)
- any other solutions already tried
- any limitations to new solutions
- an approximation of the amount of money to be spent on the product/service.

239

(b) Include with the brief:

- a copy of your organization's most recent annual report
- any of the legal or purchasing department's procedural rules or requirements for contracts or purchases.

3 *Submission of the brief* The brief should be sent to a number of vendors as a request for a quotation or proposal to supply the service/product. In the covering letter, also ask:

(a)
- that they respond within a given period of time
- that they send a copy of their most recent annual report
- that they submit the names, addresses, telephone numbers, and contact people of at least three client references, each of whom has purchased a product/service similar or identical to the one under consideration.

4 *Shortlisting the vendors* Take sufficient time and ask for any needed advice on the evaluation of the proposals. Keep the list to two to five vendors:
- ask for any further documentation, samples, brochures, explanations, demonstrations, etc. necessary to understand and evaluate fully
- visit the vendors' sites, if they will be providing a service, for example, storage facilities, microfilming bureaux, etc.
- visit each of the client references, view the products/services they received from the vendor, ask for their honest opinion of the vendor's service, maintenance, support, reliability
- ask for the vendor's bank and credit references and check financial viability.

5 *Negotiation of the contract* After selecting the vendor, let the legal department or advisor to the organization negotiate the contract (or ask them to review the one negotiated by the records manager). *Insist* that the contract include:

- a certificate or letter of compliance with the relevant standards, which must be cited by number and title
- a full maintenance agreement
- a guarantee, on large orders, that parts and supplies will be available, at a fixed price, for a certain number of years
- an insurance agreement that covers the value of the information, not just the tape or papers on which it is stored.

6 *Periodic review* All contracts and services should be reviewed at least annually. If the service or products are not satisfactory, either:

(a) cancel or decline to renew the contract; or
(b) meet with the vendor, tell them the products/services are unsatisfactory, and give them a limited period of time to try to make improvements. If they fail, cancel the contract and look for someone better.

Appendix B: Organizations Relating to or of Interest to Records Management

ARMA International Inc.
4200 Somerset, Suite 215
Prairie Village,
Kansas 66208
USA

ASLIB
Information House,
26/27Boswell Street,
London WC1N 3JZ
England

British Institute of Management,
Management House,
Parker Street,
London EC2
England

British Standards Institution,
2 Park Street,
London W1A 2BS
England

Business Archives Council,
185 Tower Bridge Road,
London SE1 2UF
England

Data Protection Registrar,
Springfield House,

Water Lane,
Wilmslow,
Cheshire SK9 5AX
England

Institute of Information Scientists,
44 Museum Street,
London WC1 1LY
England

International Image and Information
   Management Congress,
PO Box 34404,
Bethesda,
Maryland 20817
USA

International Records Management
   Council,
22243 Miston Drive,
Woodland Hills,
California 91364
USA

The Society of American Archivists,
330 S. Wells Street,
Suite 810,
Chicago,
Illinois 60606
USA

International Standards Organisation,
1 Rue de Varende,
Case Postale 56,
1211 Geneva 20,
Switzerland

Records & Archives Management
Programme,
General Information Programme,
UNESCO,
7 Place de Fontenoy,
75700 Paris,
France

Society of Archivists/Records Management
Group,
c/o Miss K M Thompson,
Honorary Assistant Secretary,
Leicestershire Record Office,
57 New Walk,
Leicester LE1 7JB
England

Centre for Information Media and
Technology (CIMTECH),
The Hatfield Polytechnic,
Bayfordbury,
Hertford,
Herts SG13 8LD
England

Association for Information and Image
Management (AIIM)
1100 Wayne Avenue,
Silver Spring,
Maryland 20910
USA

Nuclear Records Management Association,
PO Box 624,
Wading River,
New York,
NY 11792
USA

Records Management Society,
c/o Rooftop Secretarial Services,
6 Sheraton Drive,
High Wycombe,
Bucks HP13 6DE
England

Selected Readings

This is a highly subjective list and is meant to suggest works which might be considered complementary to this book. The periodicals referred to obviously contain many relevant and interesting articles, to such an extent that to make a list would more or less mean repeating the title of all articles published in them. This is clearly not a worthwhile exercise here, so only the basic details of the periodicals are given.

Books

Business Archives Administration, edited by Alison Turton, Business Archives Council, London, 1989.

Business Documents: their origins, sources and uses in historical research, John Armstrong and Stephanie Jones, Mansell, London, 1987.

The Business Forms Handbook, Schied, National Business Forms Association, 2nd edition.

File Management and Information Retrieval, by Suzanne L. Gill, Libraries Unlimited, 1981.

Productivity and Records Automation, by Kalthoff and Lee, Prentice-Hall, Englewood Cliffs, New Jersey, 1981.

Periodicals

Bulletin, Records Management Society, London.

Journal of Records Management, Aslib, London.

Records Management Quarterly, ARMA, Prairie Village, Kansas, USA.

Records and Retrieval Report, Greenwood Press, Westport, Connecticut, USA.

Index